VENTURING FORWARD

A PRACTICAL GUIDE TO RAISING EQUITY CAPITAL IN IRELAND

DIANE MULCAHY

www.oaktreepress.com

Published by
OAK TREE PRESS
19 Rutland Street, Cork, Ireland
www.oaktreepress.com

© 2005 Diane Mulcahy

A catalogue record of this book is
available from the British Library.

ISBN 1 904887 04 X

All rights reserved.
No part of this publication may be reproduced or transmitted in any form or by any means, including photocopying and recording, without written permission of the publisher. Such written permission must also be obtained before any part of this publication is stored in a retrieval system of any nature. Requests for permission should be directed to
Oak Tree Press, 19 Rutland Street, Cork, Ireland.

Printed in Ireland by ColourBooks.

CONTENTS

Figures	ix
Disclaimer	x
Acknowledgements	xi
Foreword	xiii
Preface	xv

1 Introduction — 1
   What is Equity Financing? — 2
   Overview of this Book — 6

PART I: PREPARING TO RAISE EQUITY CAPITAL

2 In the Beginning ... How to Get Started — 11
   Structuring Your Company to Raise Equity Capital — 12
   Corporate Recordkeeping — 17
   The Importance of Advisors — 21
   Conclusion — 24

3 Developing a Financing Strategy — 25
   What is a Financing Strategy? — 26
   When to Raise Capital — 28
   How Much Capital to Raise — 29
   Conclusion — 32

4	**Valuation**	**33**
	The Valuation Market	34
	Valuation Methodologies	35
	Getting the Best Valuation	38
	Pre- and Post-money Valuations	40
	Dilution	42
	Conclusion	46
5	**Should Employees Be Owners?**	**47**
	Should You Issue Equity to Employees?	47
	Types of Equity Awards	49
	The Share Option Agreement	55
	Conclusion	64

PART II: INFORMAL INVESTORS

6	**Friends & Family**	**67**
	Preparing to Raise Friends & Family Capital	67
	Finding Friends & Family Investors	69
	Valuing & Structuring a Friends & Family Round	71
	Is Mixing Business & Friendship a Good Idea?	75
	Protecting Your Friends & Family	77
	Post-Investment	78
	The Board of Advisors	79
	Government Programmes	80
	Conclusion	85
7	**Business Angels**	**87**
	Preparing to Raise Angel Capital	87
	Finding an Angel	93
	Choosing an Angel	94
	Due Diligence	98
	Valuing an Angel Round	99
	Structuring an Angel Round	99
	Post-Investment	103
	Conclusion	104

PART III: PROFESSIONAL INVESTORS

8 Venture Capitalists — 107
How Venture Capital Firms Operate — 107
Preparing to Raise Venture Capital — 109
Finding a VC — 111
Choosing a VC — 113
The Venture Capital Investment Process — 114
Structuring the Venture Capital Deal — 116
Subsequent Rounds of Financing — 117
The Board of Directors — 120
Conclusion — 126

9 The Venture Capital Deal: Understanding the Term Sheet — 127
Term Sheet Negotiation — 129
Venture Capital Terms Explained — 130
The Close — 155
Conclusion — 156

PART IV: EXITS

10 Public Offerings — 159
Why Go Public? — 160
Preparing for an IPO — 161
Is an IPO the Right Exit? — 162
Where to Go Public? — 166
Post-IPO — 177
Conclusion — 178

11 Trade Sales — 179
Preparing for a Trade Sale — 181
Valuing a Trade Sale — 186
Structuring the Deal — 187
Conclusion — 192

12	**Conclusion**	**193**
	Venturing Forward: The Future of Equity Financing in Ireland	194

APPENDICES

1	Forming a Company in Ireland	197
2	NewCo Ltd Factsheet	201
3	Sample Convertible Loan Terms	203
4	Sample Revocable Proxy	205
5	Ordinary Share Purchase Agreement Terms	206
6	NewCo Ltd Shareholder Update	210
7	Sample Business Plan Contents	213
8	Sample Due Diligence Request	215
9	Sample Notice of Board of Directors Meeting	218
10	Sample Agenda for Board of Directors Meeting	219
11	Sample Minutes of Board of Directors Meeting	220
12	NewCo Ltd Abbreviated Term Sheet	222
13	BVCA Model Term Sheet	224
14	Model Legal Agreements	239
15	Further Resources	241
16	Investor Lingo	244

Index	**251**

FIGURES

1	The Equity Financing Cycle	3
2	NewCo Ltd Initial Capitalisation Table	15
3	NewCo Ltd Pre-money Capitalisation Table	42
4	NewCo Ltd Post-financing Capitalisation Table: Angel Round at €2m Pre-money Valuation	44
5	NewCo Ltd Post-financing Capitalisation Table: Angel Round at €1m Pre-money Valuation	45
6	Common Vesting Schedules	57
7	Venture Capital Terms	130
8	Difference in Proceeds between Convertible & Participating Preference Shares	132
9	NASDAQ National Market Initial Listing Criteria	174
10	NASDAQ SmallCap Market Initial Listing Criteria	174
11	American Stock Exchange Criteria for Listing Foreign Companies	176

DISCLAIMER

The author and the publisher have taken every care to ensure that the information published in this book is correct at the time of going to print. However, neither the author nor the publisher can take any responsibility for any loss or damage caused to any person as a result of acting on, or refraining from acting on, any information published herein. Professional advice should be obtained before entering into any legally binding commitments.

In particular, the sample documents included in the **Appendices** are illustrations only and are intended only to highlight key terms generally included in such agreements. They are not complete documents and may not include clauses, terms, provisions or representations required by local law for specific types of agreement. The documents should not be used in a commercial transaction, nor should they be construed as legal advice. The reader is advised to consult experienced legal counsel to create and draft a legal agreement appropriate for their own particular facts and circumstances.

ACKNOWLEDGEMENTS

When you write books with words like 'equity capital' in the title, it can be difficult to entice friends and colleagues to read, review and edit early drafts (one friend told me he'd rather wait for the movie …). I am very fortunate to have found a group of thoughtful, insightful and experienced reviewers that includes Sharon Bially-Cohen, Suzanne Miller-Farrell, Brad Robbins, Evan Simeone and Nina von Moltke. To them, I owe my most heartfelt thanks.

For the second time, Sinéad Riordan at The Policy Institute deserves credit, recognition and much appreciation for contributing her exceptional editing skills to a book I've written. She edited the entire book and returned a manuscript much improved from the one she received.

Several people contributed their expertise to this book. My career in venture capital has benefited enormously from the experience, knowledge and advice of Harold Bradley at American Century, and Chris Gabrieli at Bessemer Venture Partners. In Dublin, Tim Scanlon at Matheson Ormsby Prentice, Emmet Scully at LK Shields and Joe Tynan at PricewaterhouseCoopers are each experienced advisors in equity financing who contributed their time, assistance and expert perspectives. My gratitude also goes to the many Irish entrepreneurs who agreed to talk with me and to share their own experiences of raising equity capital. Some of their stories are included in the book, although names have been removed and details changed to protect their anonymity.

I must also thank my publisher, Brian O'Kane of Oak Tree Press, for believing that a comprehensive book on raising equity finance in Ireland should be written, and that I was the person to write it. Brian was consistently helpful, enthusiastic and calm both as a publisher and as an editor during the months it took to bring this book from idea to print. I am also grateful to the British Venture Capital Association for permission to reproduce their example of a Model Venture Capital Term Sheet (**Appendix 13**).

My husband Kevin has been an entrepreneur for the past three years and enjoyed telling everyone that this book should really be titled 'Everything my husband should have done better when he started his own business'. The employees at his company welcomed me to their offices, gave me a desk, and provided good company, moral support and lunch companionship during a full summer of writing. Kevin contributed his perspective, ideas and experience to the structure and substance of this book, from the earliest outlines to the very final drafts, and provided valuable and insightful comments all along the way. His enthusiasm, support and many contributions make this book as much his as mine.

Diane Mulcahy
September 2005

FOREWORD

The entrepreneurs who create the indigenous Irish software industry start with a dream, which must immediately be tempered with the need to identify how to fund it. Creating a software company and bringing its business plan to execution will always require funding, by the very nature of the industry we are in – upfront development costs, early customer search and deployment and, in most cases, the need to find some of those early customers from overseas, due to our limited domestic market. Funding the development of an indigenous software company is a journey that can be long and arduous, and one that is impossible to train for, before embarking upon. Not only have we the challenges of needing to play on an international stage at a very early stage of development, but we have a funding industry for the technology sector, which is itself young and not yet fully developed when compared with its counterparts in the US, Israel and some Asian markets. The combination of these factors require world class, execution-focused, entrepreneurial skills in order to build a successful technology company of scale in Ireland.

Many of us carry scars on our backs from facing the challenges that Diane outlines here and, if we don't carry the scars ourselves, we have plenty of war stories from those who do. Diane Mulcahy has done our industry – and Irish entrepreneurs in general – a tremendous service by writing this book. The perspective Diane has written from – that of the experienced, seen it all, done it many times, venture capitalist, still with a passion for the industry, is what makes this book so valuable in the gems it imparts. Diane has clearly identified the challenges that companies create for themselves when trying to secure funding, and given the recipe guide to avoid the pitfalls for the future. I have no doubt it is true to say that, if every entrepreneur followed Diane's advice, there would be a lot fewer scarred entrepreneurs and less wariness, honed by their experiences, good and bad, on the part of those funders on whom we depend – angel investors and venture capitalists.

Funding a company to create scale is a journey. Our industry is still at such an early stage of development that we don't have a huge wealth of experience yet of the route we must take to successfully complete the journey. Diane has given us a map. Thank you, Diane.

Bernadette Cullinan
Chairperson, Irish Software Association

PREFACE

Many entrepreneurs express frustration about how difficult it is to get an idea funded, and want to understand more about why some companies are successfully financed while others are not. There is an impressive amount of information available in Ireland on starting a business, but far fewer resources on financing one. I wrote **VENTURING FORWARD** to help entrepreneurs understand what they must do to make their companies 'investor-ready,' and to provide the knowledge they must have to smartly value, negotiate and structure a 'good' financing.

My previous book, *Angels & IPOs*, discussed raising equity capital in Ireland from a policy perspective. While writing that book, I met too many entrepreneurs who had negotiated poorly structured financings on terms they didn't really understand, with implications they had not fully considered. They had learned, from painful experience, how damaging a badly structured financing can be to a start-up company's development. It was their avoidable errors that prompted me to write this book.

VENTURING FORWARD is geared towards the Irish market but intentionally includes perspectives and practices from the European and American markets that are so critical to the growth and success of Irish companies. Like most Irish industries, equity financing is international. The most successful Irish companies and investors must be prepared to attract capital from abroad, as well as at home. By providing concrete information based on prevailing international investing standards, I hope this book will serve Irish entrepreneurs and their advisors as a truly practical guide to raising equity capital.

Diane Mulcahy
September 2005

1
INTRODUCTION

Vision is not enough; it must be combined with venture.
Vaclav Havel

The best entrepreneurs demonstrate one key common trait. They consistently and aggressively approach the process of raising capital for their company as seriously as the process of growing revenues. They know that the capital required to fund their business plan is as necessary and fundamental to their success as the plan itself.

VENTURING FORWARD is designed to describe and to de-mystify the process of raising equity capital. It will:

- Provide practical guidance on how to structure your company so that it is investor-ready.
- Help you to understand and to negotiate valuation.
- Advise you on the best ways of finding and generating investor interest.
- Better prepare you to value, negotiate and structure an equity capital investment.
- Explain the deal terms you are likely to encounter in equity financing agreements.
- Focus your attention on the importance of planning and preparing for an exit.

Selling your company's potential to investors is actually not that different from selling your product to customers. Both require a strategy, a marketing plan, a sales pitch, a price (investors call it 'valuation'), and the ability to identify, contact and interest the right potential buyers. The difference is that raising equity capital is personal. It's about you, and your management team – about your experience, your ambition and your ability to execute. Equity investors know, or at least believe, that the potential of a company cannot be separated from the promise of its management. It is the people who represent the potential.

Raising equity is also much more about the future. With the exception of friends and family, equity investors make the decision to invest in your company because they believe that, in three or five or seven years, your company will be successful and they will make a significant financial return. They invest for the exit.

Good business ideas often fail because of poor financing strategies and choices. This is not due to bad decision-making, as much as to lack of information. When entrepreneurs begin to raise capital, they don't know what they don't know about sourcing, negotiating and structuring an equity financing. My objective in writing this book is to give you information and advice that will help you avoid some of the most common mistakes that entrepreneurs make when raising capital, and to help you be better equipped to finance your company's growth with equity capital successfully.

WHAT IS EQUITY FINANCING?

At its most basic, equity financing is simply the exchange of ownership for capital. In Ireland, where many start-ups are high-tech companies, equity financing is often the only viable financing option for growth. Debt financing through a bank is usually not an option for high-tech start-ups, since they have insufficient collateral to obtain a loan. While you can always meet the bank's collateral requirements by personally guaranteeing the loan using your own assets, most entrepreneurs resist taking on that level of financial risk.

The Equity Financing Cycle

The equity financing of start-up companies can best be understood within the framework of the equity financing cycle.

FIGURE 1: THE EQUITY FINANCING CYCLE

Entrepreneur → Friends & Family → Business Angels → Venture Capital → Exit

Starting at the left, the figure illustrates that equity financing often begins with the entrepreneur. Many entrepreneurs will invest personal capital into their business during the start-up or 'seed' stage. To finance early stages of growth, the entrepreneur might then seek capital from 'friends & family' (F&F) investors, who will invest relatively small amounts of money (for example, as little as €5,000 to €25,000 per investor, and usually under €100,000 as a group). Larger amounts of capital might then be obtained from 'business angels'. Angels are wealthy individuals, many of them successful entrepreneurs, who are interested in investing in and working with start-up companies. Angels invest individually, or as part of a network, and generally invest amounts of €500,000 or less.

A very small percentage of companies reach the stage where they have the potential to achieve the growth rates and returns sought by venture capitalists (VCs). VCs make equity investments in early-stage, fast-growing and high-potential private companies, with the objective of high returns (usually greater than 20% annual return rates). VCs differ from other equity investors, in that they are intermediaries. They invest capital from institutional investors such as pension funds, banks, insurance companies and foundations, into early-stage companies. VCs typically make equity investments of greater than €1 million, although in Ireland many VCs make much smaller investments.

The last phase in the equity financing cycle is the 'exit', so-called because it allows the investors (and, often, the entrepreneur) to exit the investment and receive the financial proceeds and returns. Possible exits include public offerings (IPOs or 'flotations') for the best companies, a trade sale or management buy-out, or, in the worst case, the company goes out of business and the investors write-off their investment. Any proceeds generated from an exit are available to re-invest and to seed new ventures, thus continuing the cycle.

Each financing is called a 'round', and companies may raise several rounds of financing from the same or different investors over the course of their development.

The equity financing cycle illustrates the types of capital that companies raise, but not necessarily the order in which they raise it. Not every company will raise capital from each type of investor. Some companies raise their first, and only, round of financing from an angel investor; others conduct one F&F round, followed by a VC financing.

What Do Equity Investors Seek?

As a group, equity investors look for specific characteristics in the companies in which they invest. With the exception of friends and family, equity investors look for:

- Rapidly growing companies ...
- Led by strong management teams ...
- With the potential to capture significant market share ...
- In large and emerging markets ...
- Before realising a timely and profitable exit.

If your company meets these basic criteria, you are well-positioned to begin the equity-raising process.

Why Raise Equity Capital?

Raising equity finance is rarely quick or easy. In fact, with the possible exception of friends and family financing, it is definitely a time-consuming and intensive process. Expect to spend a minimum of six months, and as much as a year, raising capital, depending on market conditions. It is challenging to identify, contact and interest investors even to look at your business plan, let alone agree to meet with you. It is also time-consuming to complete investor due diligence, and to negotiate, structure and close a round of financing.

Given its challenges, why, then, do so many entrepreneurs seek to raise equity capital? The reason is that it offers the best, and in many cases the only, way to finance growth. Outside capital provides the cash for young businesses to jumpstart and to increase their growth rate exponentially beyond what they could ever do through

1: Introduction

bootstrapping or through their own resources. And for new businesses in emerging markets, rapid growth is essential for success. To become the market leader, the dominant provider, or the innovator and producer of the next cutting-edge technology, requires much more cash than most entrepreneurs can provide on their own.

Equity capital is attractive to start-up companies for these reasons:

- **No repayments**: Equity capital comes without the burden and cash-flow drain of the monthly repayments required by debt.
- **Value-added capital**: Equity investors can offer, at least in theory, much more value to a company than just capital. Business angels and venture capitalists can bring industry expertise, customer and strategic contacts and proven experience in helping young companies grow.
- **Deep pockets**: Equity investors may be a source of follow-up financing if the business requires it at a later time, adding a sense of financial stability to a growing company.
- **Increased discipline**: External investors can bring a new and higher level of financial discipline, as well as greater requirements for good governance to your business.
- **Enhanced reputation**: An equity investment can meaningfully improve the reputation and status of a company, which can help to attract employees, acquire customers, and interest future investors.

The main disadvantage of equity financing is the reduction of control and decision-making over your business. Even if you sell only a small percentage of your company to outside investors, you will lose some control over decision-making. If you are unwilling or reluctant to sell even minority ownership interests, or to cede any control over decision-making, then raising equity finance is not for you. The trade-off is that your company, without the fuel that outside capital provides, will grow much more slowly and, in the end, will likely be much smaller. You'll own 100% of a small pie, instead of a piece of a much larger pie. For those entrepreneurs who prefer to run a smaller company that provides them with job satisfaction and stability, and the opportunity for moderate growth over the long-term, bootstrapping or debt finance may be preferable options.

OVERVIEW OF THIS BOOK

VENTURING FORWARD is organised into four parts and is designed to guide you through the equity financing process sequentially, beginning with the initial structuring of your company and the earliest rounds of raising capital from informal investors, through to an exit. Within each section, you will find discussion and advice about how to prepare to raise equity finance, how to find investors, and how to value and structure attractive deals. To fulfil the 'practical' promise in the title, samples of key documents and other resources can be found in the **Appendices**.

Although the chapters of this book are organised sequentially to follow the equity financing cycle, each chapter was written to be complete on a stand-alone basis, so you can read them in the order most suited to your own particular information needs.

Part I: Preparing to Raise Equity Capital

Preparing to raise equity capital begins the moment you form your company. Your goal in these beginning stages is to structure your company in a way that will be most attractive to investors. You will need to know how to determine your company's share capital structure, how to find good advisors, and what corporate documents and records investors will ask to see.

This section will discuss and offer advice on all these issues.

Developing a financing strategy at your earliest stages is also discussed in this section. Basically a business plan for raising capital, your financing strategy will help you to determine the amount and timing of capital to raise, and how to maximise your valuation at every round of financing. This section also includes a chapter devoted to valuation – how to think about valuation, how investors approach valuation, and how to negotiate the best valuation for your company.

The final chapter explores the issue of employee equity, helping you to decide whether to offer equity to your employees through a share option or other equity scheme.

Part II: Informal Investors

Informal investors include friends & family and business angels. At the earliest stages of growth, the vast majority of companies will seek financing from such non-professional investors to provide small amounts of capital.

This section provides practical guidance on how to find, attract and approach informal investors. It also offers advice on how to value and structure investments from informal investors, and reviews the key terms and components of investment agreements for both friends and family and angel investors.

Part III: Professional Investors

VCs are intermediaries who invest other people's money, with the sole purpose of generating financial returns. As a result, they seek the most promising companies that offer the greatest potential for rapid growth and large scale. Only a small percentage of companies are appropriate for raising venture capital. For those companies, though, the process of raising venture capital can be challenging to understand and to execute.

This section provides an overview of how venture capital firms are structured and operate, and how best to identify and attract VCs. It then offers a detailed term-by-term explanation of a venture capital term sheet (or 'Heads of Agreement') and advice on which terms are negotiable. The terms discussed in the term sheet chapter will appear in earlier rounds of financing as well, so entrepreneurs raising even the earliest rounds of equity finance will find this chapter (**Chapter 9**) useful.

Part IV: Exits

This section advocates beginning with the end in mind. It is not an exaggeration to say that, from the moment of company formation, entrepreneurs who want to raise equity finance must think about, plan for, and develop a believable plan for an attractive and timely exit. With the exception of friends and family, equity investors are seeking a return on the capital they invest in your company. The better you can communicate how and when an exit will occur, and the projected returns this will achieve, the more investor interest you will attract.

Many Irish companies consistently fail to prioritise or to plan strategically for an exit, and this has contributed to the extremely low rate of public offerings (by far the most lucrative exits) among Irish firms.

This section reviews common exit options and how to plan for, and to execute, them.

PART I:
PREPARING TO RAISE EQUITY CAPITAL

2
IN THE BEGINNING ... HOW TO GET STARTED

The beginning is the most important part of the work.
Plato

As an entrepreneur, you have an enormous number of tasks to focus on, whether it's finalising the development and launch of your new software product or finding distribution channels for your cutting-edge medical device. At the early stages of building and growing a company, you may find it difficult to concentrate on organising the company's administrative structure and processes when you have so many 'business critical' items on your to-do list.

You are not alone. Many entrepreneurs fail to devote the time and attention to the early details of their company's formation and structuring. This is a common mistake that you would be well-served to avoid. The inception of the company is the most critical, sensible and, by far the easiest, time to focus on such issues. Getting the company's structure and processes right from the start will save you time, money and administrative hassles in the end. Investors demand an organised and well-documented corporate structure. Having one will help to attract investors, shorten due diligence and ensure that you maximise your valuation. It will also reflect positively on the execution and management skills of you and your team.

STRUCTURING YOUR COMPANY TO RAISE EQUITY CAPITAL

Your company's initial share capital structure sets the basis for all future financing rounds. The capital structure simply refers to the number and type of shares in your company that you have authorised, issued, allocated and sold.

Companies begin by issuing ordinary shares (also known 'common stock') initially. These are the simplest securities and are usually held by management, employees and directors. Their rights are few and include, at a minimum, the right to participate in shareholder votes, to receive notice of shareholder meetings, and to receive certain financial information. Ordinary shares are also the riskiest shares to hold. They have limited privileges and are the 'last in line', behind preference shares and debt, to be paid in the case of an acquisition, dividends, or winding up of the company.

Each share in your company is a powerful instrument that can be used for a variety of purposes, including:

- A source of voting power.
- A mechanism for allocating ownership.
- A vehicle for raising equity capital.
- An incentive for employee and management team performance and retention.
- Economic participation in the success of the company.

Shares are a valuable commodity that you control and should be carefully managed. Allocate them prudently and thoughtfully. When determining the capital structure of your company, think about how you will be using your shares:

- Are they primarily to be given to the founders and management team as an incentive for high performance and to aid staff retention until an exit?
- Will you be distributing them to the majority of employees in the company?
- Are you planning to sell shares to outside investors to raise equity capital?

The answers to these types of questions will help you determine how many shares to issue and authorise.

Authorising & Issuing Shares

Many entrepreneurs find the process of authorising and issuing shares confusing. They wonder: How many shares should I issue? Of what type? At what value? These are fundamental questions, which fortunately have relatively straightforward answers.

Authorised shares are the maximum number of shares the company can issue to shareholders. Issued shares are a subset of authorised shares and include those securities sold to, or held by, shareholders in the company. For example:

Shares Authorised	1,000,000
Shares Issued	400,000
Shares Authorised but not Issued (can be issued in later rounds of financing)	600,000

The number of shares you choose to authorise and issue is somewhat arbitrary. You can, if you wish, authorise and issue 10 shares or 10 million upon registration. Companies raising equity finance usually authorise more shares than they need initially, in order to have shares in reserve to issue to new investors in later rounds of fundraising. A common consideration that acts to limit the number of shares is the existence of a tax or fee, based on the number of issued shares. In Ireland, shares issued by limited companies incur Companies Capital Duty of 0.5% on the amount paid for the shares.

The value of shares issued, called the 'nominal' or 'par' value, is simply a value declaration required by law and represents the minimum value of the share. It does not bear any relation to the actual market value of the shares or your company, nor does it play a role in setting the valuation of the shares during the initial round of financing. By convention, the majority of firms will issue their initial shares with a nominal value of one cent or one Euro.

How many shares to authorise and issue?

To determine the number of shares to authorise and issue, consider whether you want the company to be closely held by the founder, or if shares will be distributed to employees and investors as part of a broad-based ownership plan. The more shareholders you want to have, the more shares you will likely issue. If your plans include issuing shares to employees as an incentive, you should authorise and issue a higher absolute number of shares than you would if the shares were going to remain closely held. And keep in mind that individuals tend to have an illogical preference for more shares, rather than fewer, even if both choices are worth the same total value. You can see this phenomenon at work in the public market when companies conduct a 'stock split' to reduce the per share price. For some reason, individual investors exhibit a preference for buying 10 shares at €20 each rather than 1 share for €200, even though both are worth the same €200. Therefore, if you plan to distribute your shares widely, you may want to issue a higher quantity of shares to take into account this preference.

If you determine at a later stage in the company's development that additional shares are required, you can raise the number of authorised shares by obtaining the approval of 75% of shareholders through a special resolution, and notifying the Companies Registration Office of the change.

The Capitalisation Table

The capitalisation table, or 'cap table' as it is called, reflects the company's capital structure and is the conventional way to track changes in ownership as each financing round progresses. The cap table is created when the company's initial shares are issued and must be updated and modified each time shares are issued, allocated or purchased. Capitalisation tables are based on shares issued, not shares authorised. Keeping a current cap table is not a legal requirement but is absolutely vital, should you choose to pursue equity financing at any stage. Cap tables are usually maintained by the Company Secretary or by your financial officer, manager or accountant.

A company's initial cap table is simple and reflects the ownership of the founding management team, and often a pool of share options that are set aside to recruit future employees and members of the management team (see **Chapter 5**).

2: In the Beginning ... How to Get Started

There does not appear to be a consistent practice for presenting company capital structure in Irish business plans. A large number of plans present the company's ownership as follows:

Michael Murphy   60%
John Murphy   10%
Seamus Murphy   5%

This is not an ideal presentation, since it lacks information about who the individuals are (company founders, employees or investors), the type of shares the individuals own (ordinary, preference, what Series), the number of shares they own, and the total number of company shares that are issued and outstanding. This presentation is incomplete also in that the percentage ownership does not add up to 100%. Therefore, it is not clear whether the remaining ownership information is missing, or there are other shareholders not listed, or the company has an employee share option pool that makes up the balance.

A better presentation of a company's capital structure is shown in **Figure 2**.

FIGURE 2: NEWCO LTD INITIAL CAPITALISATION TABLE

Owner	Ordinary Shares	Share Options	Percentage Ownership
Michael Murphy MD	300,000		60%
John Murphy Director of Technology	50,000		10%
Seamus Murphy Director of Sales	25,000		5%
Employee Pool		125,000	25%
TOTAL	375,000	125,000	100%

It is helpful to follow the cap table with a narrative that provides further detail, such as the total number of shares the company has authorised, the timing of any capital raised and any other relevant details about the company's capital structure – for example:

> *NewCo Ltd has issued 500,000 of its 1.5 million authorised shares. The core management team owns a total of 375,000 shares, with an employee share option pool of 125,000 shares set aside for award to future hires.*

If there is an employee share option plan, it is also helpful to provide a brief overview – for example:

> *In April of this year, NewCo Ltd implemented a share option plan for all employees and management. The company allocated a total of 125,000 ordinary shares to the plan, which represents 25% of NewCo's total share capital. The exercise price of the share options is €0.10. Management believes that this option pool will provide sufficient equity for employee incentive awards and hiring through to next December.*

Although it is not the most glamorous of tasks, you must be rigorous when it comes to maintaining an accurate and updated cap table. The cap table and the share register represent the ownership of your company, so it is certainly worth tracking. A scrupulously-managed capital structure avoids problems in later rounds of financing, when professional investors and their legal team will comb through your corporate documents and capital structure and require any inconsistencies, errors and sloppy recordkeeping to be rectified. Time that must be spent cleaning up a messy or inaccurate structure can significantly delay closing a financing round, harm the company's cash flow and growth trajectory, and reflect poorly on the company's management team. A structurally-messy deal can also dissuade investors, who do not want to take the time to clean up the company's structure for the equity transaction.

Majority Ownership & the Illusion of Control

When structuring their company and raising equity finance, many entrepreneurs become entirely focused on their personal percentage ownership in their company. If they can't raise financing that allows them to keep more than 50% of the company, then they don't want to accept the capital. They mistakenly believe that a 51% shareholding, and the majority ownership it represents, will ensure their control of the company. This line of thinking fails to recognise the meaningful distinction between share ownership and control.

Majority share ownership does not guarantee control. There are numerous ways for minority shareholders who own less than 50% of the company to secure the power and control to make key decisions about your business. For example, VCs rarely own 50% or more of a company, yet they routinely negotiate (and sometimes exercise) the right to exert tremendous control over the companies in which they invest. They negotiate the right to elect one or more Board Directors, which gives them a significant voice in company decision-making. They obtain veto rights that can allow them to determine unilaterally the outcome of specified decisions, such as whether to raise future rounds of financings. They can also negotiate voting rights that provide them with a disproportionate say on issues that are put to a shareholder vote. Even angel investors who hold ordinary shares but have negotiated a Board seat, by virtue of that seat, will be able to exercise influence and, in some cases, control over key business decisions (for example, if a unanimous vote of the Board is required to make a decision, the angel essentially has a veto right to block it).

Control is dependent on how the ownership is structured, not on ownership *per se*. If you are concerned about maintaining control over your business and its key decisions, pay careful attention *both* to the percentage ownership you sell as well as to the control provisions in the deal you structure.

CORPORATE RECORDKEEPING

Although few entrepreneurs think of it this way, it is not an exaggeration to say that the equity financing process begins the moment you register your company for business. If you intend to raise equity capital to finance the growth of your business, you will benefit enormously by taking the appropriate steps from the beginning to prepare yourself and your company for fundraising.

All equity investors, except friends and family, will want to examine your corporate records before making an investment. The records they will want to see include:

- Company formation documents (such as the Memorandum and Articles of Association). For more information on these documents and on forming a limited liability company in Ireland, see **Appendix 1**.
- Share register and capitalisation table.
- Employee, intellectual property, technology transfer and share option agreements.
- Regulatory filings and tax returns.

Investors have a habit of evaluating the structure and governance of potential investments and classifying them as either 'clean' or 'hairy'.

Clean deals are well-organised, well-documented deals with no major problems to fix. The financials are up-to-date, all employment, share option and shareholder agreements are signed and organised, the intellectual property (IP) ownership is documented, and the company's tax and corporate filings have all been made on time. These deals are attractive, because they are faster and easier to execute and don't require extensive extra due diligence or re-structuring.

A hairy deal can range from being mildly disorganised to an absolute mess. Hairy deals can be hairy for any number of reasons:

- Poor record-keeping and documentation that make the company's capital structure or financials opaque.
- Questionable intellectual property ownership.
- A messy capital structure that must be cleaned up (for example, missing shareholder or share option agreements, share register not up-to-date, etc.).
- A Board composed of inappropriate, unsophisticated[1] or poorly performing directors that must be restructured.

---

[1] The term 'sophisticated', as it is used in this book, is an investment term that characterises a specifically designated type of investor. It refers to an investor with sufficient education, knowledge or investing experience to allow them to be able to accurately evaluate, assess and judge the merits of an investment, and to understand the risks. This definition is used in the US to help determine individual eligibility to make certain types of investments (such as equity investments) under Securities & Exchange Commission (SEC) regulations. I use the term in this book, because it is a handy way to differentiate experienced and knowledgeable investors from novices.

Hairy deals will reflect poorly on you and your team, can reduce the valuation of the investment, and will lengthen the time it takes for the financing to close. They can also cost more in solicitor and management team time to bring the company's books and documentation up-to-date.

For example, on his first venture, one Irish entrepreneur failed to pay attention to corporate housekeeping matters. The company's share ownership records were incomplete, and he did not have signed employment and intellectual property agreements from all employees. He was raising venture capital and had received a term sheet for a €1.5 million round of financing but, when the corporate issues emerged, the investors immediately postponed their targeted close date. The entrepreneur had to spend several unhappy weeks combing through the company's records and emails to ensure he had captured on the capitalisation table, and put in writing, all the verbal promises of equity and share options he had made. He also had to go back and obtain signed agreements from each individual.

The investors remained wary, however. In the end, in order to get the deal closed, the entrepreneur was required to sign a warranty (requiring extra legal time to draft) that, if any other equity was found to have been given away, the amount in question would be taken from his personal equity ownership so the investors would suffer no reduction in their ownership. He then had to convince some of his earliest (and most critical) employees to sign employment agreements to ensure that they signed over their intellectual property rights to the company. This effort was delayed by two weeks, while he waited for an employee he couldn't reach to return from holidays. During that delay, his company exhausted its cash reserves and he had to arrange to borrow money from his brother in order to meet payroll. When the employee returned and signed the agreement, the company's legal documents finally were deemed to be in order, and the investment closed – more than two months later than planned.

This entrepreneur was lucky. His company had access to the cash required to survive the nearly two-month delay caused by his poor recordkeeping, and his investors were willing to work with him to clean up the company's documents and close the round of financing. Others may not be so fortunate. Some investors will just pass on, or kill, a hairy deal. Other investors will lose interest while you are cleaning up your company. During the delay, another competitor could emerge, or your management team could be so busy fixing internal corporate issues that you miss your projections, causing potential investors to lose faith in your ability to meet key milestones.

This anecdote also highlights the importance of keeping agreements with employees current and in order. For instance, if your company's business model includes intellectual property as a critical asset, the first step to protecting that asset is to establish through a written agreement that the IP belongs completely and solely to the company. Any claims that an individual, such as a founder or other employee, has on any IP must be transferred to the company. A technology transfer agreement should clearly state that any and all intellectual property rights (for example, to patents, trademarks, etc.) are transferred to and belong to the company. It should also state that any future inventions or intellectual property made during the course of employment will belong to the company. The company's standard employment agreements should also contain such a clause, so there is no doubt that the company, and not any one employee, has full rights to all proprietary developments. These agreements are critical, since so much of the value of a start-up technology company can be contained in the intellectual property. Clear ownership of IP is also a key concern of outside investors, so establishing a clean and unambiguous record of such ownership from the start is the easiest and best approach for positioning the company to raise equity capital.

Corporate housekeeping may seem trivial but, if badly done, the consequences can be significant. No investor wants to take the time to clean up a messy or poorly structured company. Therefore, if they do, the cost of that effort will most certainly be reflected in a lower valuation, increased legal expenses and a longer time to close the financing.

THE IMPORTANCE OF ADVISORS

No entrepreneur sets out to create a hairy corporate structure or to conduct a messy, complicated and badly-structured financing. These situations come about because entrepreneurs don't raise money every day, so they are inexperienced and, in most cases, they are uninformed when it comes to the details and nuances of fundraising. They don't realise that they have structured their company incorrectly, or closed an unattractive financing, until a later investor tells them. For those reasons, the only way to ensure that you have a clean company and well-structured deal is to work with experienced advisors.

It is hard to overstate the benefits of an experienced team of advisors. Competent advisors, with experience of doing equity financing deals, can contribute significant value to your company. A good working relationship with a top advisor will often facilitate access to their network of investors, entrepreneurs and other industry contacts that could help your business grow. Good advisors can offer timely market information about average valuations and normal deal terms, since both can vary tremendously with general market conditions. They can also help you to understand the proposed deal structure and terms, and to evaluate how company-friendly or investor-friendly it is. This inside market information is very valuable, since it will help you to avoid accepting an overly-aggressive term sheet or, on the other hand, asking for excessive valuations or terms that are generally considered unacceptable. Working with well-respected and experienced advisors is likely to have a positive reputational effect on your business. The expert and professional company you keep will only enhance the perception of your company.

At the early stages of your business, you should seek a solicitor and accountant who have already established expertise in working with small growing companies and in conducting equity financings. You will obtain the best value from your advisors if you begin working with them early. It is much cheaper to pay an advisor to prevent a problem than to fix one.

One successful Irish entrepreneur, when reflecting on his own company's beginnings, said that the smartest things he did when he started his business were to find good advisors, namely a law firm with an excellent reputation in the VC community, a top accounting firm, and a small, hungry public relations firm that was willing to work hard for a modest retainer. He raised his first and only round of capital from VCs. In preparation for the financing, he negotiated delayed payment of the law and accounting firm fees, so that they did not have to be paid until the fundraising was complete. He was also able to negotiate a discounted fee from the law firm. The entrepreneur found that the law firm offered the most assistance during the financing round – helping him to understand and negotiate the term sheet, ensuring that the deal documents accurately reflected the term sheet, and, most importantly, playing the 'bad cop' in negotiations so that the entrepreneur could be the nice guy and maintain good relations with his investors-to-be. He believes that his relationship with his investors is much better than it would have been had he been forced to conduct most of the negotiations on his own. He also credits the law firm with helping him to get what he views (even in hindsight) to be fair investment terms.

To close a complicated round of financing, such as a venture capital round, it is reasonable to expect legal fees in the €10,000 to €40,000 range. Simpler financings will cost less. Don't be afraid to negotiate with advisors on price. Many experienced solicitors and accountants, who have made a decision to work with promising young companies as clients, will negotiate reasonable prices for defined services. They may agree to defer payment for services until after the company has successfully raised financing. Or they may agree to work for no fee or a small fixed fee in advance of a fundraising to help the company prepare, based on the understanding that, if the company raises financing, the legal transaction work will be given to the firm. For simpler financings, it may be possible to agree on a fixed fee to close the transaction.

It is unfortunately an extremely common error in judgment for entrepreneurs to be 'penny wise and pound foolish', when it comes to devoting their scarce financial resources to obtaining good legal and accounting advice. They either take a 'DIY' approach, or look for low cost advisors (for example, friends, neighbours, and the local solicitor who helped them buy their house) as a way to save money. This is a truly foolish approach, since working with a bad, or even mediocre, advisor can be more expensive in time and mistakes than the cost of the up-front investment required to obtain expert advice. It can cost you in lost investor meetings or lower valuations because your deal is sloppy, unprofessional, and needs work to restructure. The time it takes to make changes in the company's structure or processes can delay the closing of a round of financing, and negatively affect the cash flow of your company. A solicitor who doesn't know the current market standards of equity financing can give you well-intentioned, but misleading, advice that may cause you to give away too much of the company or too much control. Even more importantly, bringing a poorly-structured or messy deal to investors reflects badly on you and your management team's ability to identify and execute smartly the critical steps necessary to best prepare your company for financing and growth.

Overseas Advisors

Given our island location, it is important for Irish companies to think early about how best to access advisors in overseas markets, where much of your growth and business will take place. International advisors are necessary to help you reflect your financials according to local conventions, and to ensure that your tax and reporting obligations are fulfilled accurately and in a timely manner. They can also ensure that your intellectual property is protected, and that you are in local compliance with corporate, employment, environmental, and health and safety laws wherever you do business.

There are two options for finding an overseas advisor. One way is to seek out local firms in the markets in which you do business. If you have an office in London and much of your business and sales in the UK, retain a British law firm. Local firms can be an excellent source of local business and finance contacts. They can also help you to access capital or to explore exit opportunities locally, both of which are important options in helping you to increase the chances of creating a competitive round of financing. The second option is to seek Dublin-based advisors with international offices and partners. This may be more suitable if you don't have a concentrated market of business in any one overseas location, or if you conduct a significant percentage of your business in Ireland.

How Do You Find Good Advisors?

To identify accounting and law firms that have developed expertise and experience in working with early-stage companies:

- Talk to successful entrepreneurs, angels and venture capitalists about which advisors they use.
- Check with the Irish Venture Capital Association (www.ivca.ie) or the Irish Software Association (www.software.ie) for members who, by joining, have already demonstrated an interest in working with emerging businesses.
- Identify the firms that sponsor and speak at conferences and other networking events for young companies and that have specific staff who specialise in small business development.

The same rules apply for finding overseas advisors. Talk to other entrepreneurs, use the local venture capital association as a starting point to find firms interested in working with small businesses, and attend events geared towards start-up companies.

A good rule of thumb is always to interview at least three or four different advisors to get a concrete sense of their capabilities and experience and to gather enough information to competitively evaluate price and services.

CONCLUSION

When it comes to raising equity capital, the old adage is true. If you fail to prepare, you are preparing to fail. From the beginning, it is critical to organise, structure and maintain your company to be attractive to future investors. Start with your company's capital structure. Keep it simple and manage your company's shares as carefully as you do your company's cash. They are just as valuable. As you set up your company, pay attention to corporate recordkeeping. Create and maintain complete and up-to-date share ownership records, corporate documents and written and signed agreements. Finally, the best way to get started is to work closely and early with experienced advisors. Better to pay them now to prevent problems than pay them later (and more) to fix them.

3
DEVELOPING A FINANCING STRATEGY

Lack of money is the root of all evil.
George Bernard Shaw

A number of Irish entrepreneurs describe an investing environment in which companies are 'drip-fed' capital at their early stages of growth. They are able to obtain small amounts of capital from investors, but must repeatedly return to both existing and new investors to raise additional funds. The result is that the entrepreneur must engage in a series of intensive, time-consuming fundraisings. Entrepreneurs say that investors seem to view drip-feeding as a way to minimise their risk and to maximise their control over their investments.

How do you avoid being drip-fed? One way is to develop a financing strategy that anticipates your company's capital needs in advance, and plans fundraisings around the accomplishment of key corporate milestones. Armed with such a strategy, you have a much better chance of presenting to investors a compelling and attractive plan for raising the full amount of capital you need during a financing.

One concept that is generally not explicitly considered by entrepreneurs is that subsequent rounds of financing are not independent events. The terms, structure and price of each financing round influences the terms, structure and price of later rounds. This is why it is important to think strategically about the amount, price, terms and structure of each capital raising, such as:

- Is the round appropriately valued given the company's stage, performance and market conditions?
- What will the next set of investors look for and what will make this company an attractive investment for them?

- Are there any unusual terms in this financing and what is the justification for them?
- Is this financing round well-documented and organised for the next round?

Because they are inter-related, each financing should be conducted with the next round in mind.

WHAT IS A FINANCING STRATEGY?

Think of a financing strategy as a business plan for capital raising. It outlines how much you plan to raise, as well as when, and what you plan to accomplish with the capital. Like a business plan, it can always be changed, modified or updated based on market conditions or company performance.

A financing strategy typically addresses and answers questions such as:

- How much capital does the business require?
- How much must be raised now, and how much in future rounds of financing?
- How many rounds of financing do you expect to raise? What is the expected timeframe for each round?
- What milestones will be achieved in each financing round?
- How will the value of the company be increased significantly between financing rounds?
- What is the likely exit, and when?

A financing strategy is simply a roadmap to get your company the money it needs when it needs it. It summarises the company's capital requirements over time and outlines a fundraising plan organised and executed around value-creating milestones.

3: Developing a Financing Strategy

A financing strategy could look like this:

> *NewCo Ltd is seeking to raise €1.0 million from private investors. This capital will be used to launch Release 1.0, obtain our first reference customers, hire our core sales team in three key markets, and begin development of Release 2.0. Next year, the company anticipates raising a €2.5 million venture capital round of financing in order to launch Release 2.0, significantly expand our sales and marketing functions, and open our US office in New York. We also anticipate hiring a Director of Sales and a Chief Financial Officer, and increasing the size of our technical staff to develop Product #2. A final round of €5 million in two years' time will provide us with the expansion capital to enter London and Frankfurt markets, develop a 24x7 customer service operation, and release Product #2. To significantly increase revenues, we will also be focused on developing an indirect distribution channel. We expect to be well-positioned for a possible trade sale exit in three to four years' time.*

The plan is not intended to provide specific dates and metrics, but rather an overall strategy about general timelines that are tied to key corporate accomplishments. The main goal of a financing strategy is to ensure that the company will always have adequate cash available to accomplish its business plan objectives. An equally important goal of the strategy is to increase the valuation of your company at each successive round of financing.

Why is increasing valuation so important? Besides the obvious objective of creating wealth through ownership in an increasingly valuable company, growing value between financing rounds maximises the amount of ownership you can keep. Entrepreneurs sell less ownership at higher valuations, for any given investment amount. Increasing the valuation of your company is also important in order to attract more investors in later rounds of financing – it sends out a positive signal about the company's performance, ability to execute, and growth potential. It also avoids the need to raise future rounds of finance at a lower price than the last round. 'Down rounds' are unattractive and usually unpleasant and many investors will avoid them entirely. Without an increasing valuation, then, it can be very difficult to raise later rounds of capital.

Many entrepreneurs fail to develop a compelling financing strategy and, instead, make the mistake of raising money in response to short-term needs for capital. They raise enough capital to get them through a specific time period (for example, the next year or 18 months) without explicit regard for what milestones will be accomplished during that time period. Such an approach fails to address the two key issues that all investors have:

- What specific milestones are you going to accomplish with the money I invested?
- Why, and how, will the valuation increase in the next round of financing?

As a result, when the money from the financing runs out, the entrepreneur does not have a compelling story that describes their last round of financing and what they accomplished, nor do they have a convincing basis for a higher valuation in the next round. Investors are justifiably unimpressed, which can make it difficult for the company to raise additional capital. A persuasive financing strategy will address such investor issues and will present a convincing plan to raise capital at strategically attractive times in the company's growth.

WHEN TO RAISE CAPITAL

The best time to raise capital is before you need it. The timing of each round of fundraising is the most critical component of the financing strategy. With the possible exception of a friends and family round, equity fundraisings are never short and sweet. Expect that each round will take six to nine months to complete. It is a lengthy process to identify and interest investors, schedule meetings and other presentations, conduct due diligence, negotiate and close the transaction and receive the money. The cost of waiting too long to start the fundraising process falls entirely on you. Investors are rarely in a rush to complete a deal, and their patience affords them negotiating leverage if the company is in desperate circumstances and requires an urgent injection of capital. There is no good reason to put your company at a disadvantage by waiting until you need the cash to raise it. By the time you need the money, you've already lost most of your negotiating leverage. Be smart. Start the capital-raising process well before you need the money.

A successful Irish serial entrepreneur has taken this point to heart. He had raised a large round of venture capital for his current start-up and knew that he would need to raise a second round of financing within the next year. It was after the market crash and the financing environment was poor, so he decided to begin his fundraising very early. He still had several million Euros in the bank, which would get him through about 12 months, when he began approaching existing and new investors for additional capital. His current investors offered to do a financing, but on terms that the entrepreneur found unattractive. He declined their investment offer and, because he had the time and cash available, was able to begin the process of attracting new investors. He was able, ultimately, to raise a second round of venture financing with an external investor leading the round. He closed the round within nine months, on more favourable terms than his existing investors had offered.

HOW MUCH CAPITAL TO RAISE

It is challenging to decide the right amount of capital to raise. Forecasting your company's performance is an inexact science, and actual performance will almost certainly differ from what was projected. That said, it is important that the amount of capital you raise is as close as possible to what you need. Raise too much and you will have sold too much of the company too early and too cheap. Raise too little and you will run short of cash or, worse, run out of cash altogether. A good rule of thumb is to raise enough capital to cover the projected losses (conservatively projected) to get you to the next milestone that significantly increases your company's valuation. Then add a cushion of three to six months to get you to the closing of the next round of financing.

Raising Too Little Capital

As most entrepreneurs are sensitive to reducing their ownership percentage, they tend to err on the side of raising too little capital.

In just one example, a promising early-stage technology company run by two industry veterans had successfully raised about €600,000 from an impressive group of private investors, many of whom were previous work colleagues of the founders. The founders thought this capital would be sufficient to get them through their technology launch and obtain their first customers, which would position them well to raise a €2 to €3 million round of venture capital financing. The company's technology was developed and launched on schedule, but it had trouble securing its initial customers. The sales cycle was longer than it had projected, and its early customer prospects demanded some additional features that took time to develop and to add to the current release of the product. The company had already begun its next round of financing and was in discussion with several venture capitalists. But, without the customer revenues it had projected, the company began to run short on cash.

The founders approached the most interested VC and discussed the possibility of a small interim financing of €200-300k, but thought the valuation the VC offered was much too low. The founders stopped taking their salaries in order to conserve some cash, and then went back to their existing angels and approached an even wider circle of industry colleagues in hopes of attracting a few new private investors. Based on the founders' reputation within their industry, and the promise of their technology, they were able to secure an additional €250,000 in financing from private investors at the same valuation as their prior round. This capital gave them the time to obtain two paying customers, one of whom was a blue chip reference customer.

These founders, due to their experience and reputation, narrowly avoided having to accept a down round of financing that would have been dilutive to their existing investors and would have set a much lower price for their next round of financing. They learned the hard way that they needed to project more conservatively their company's ability to achieve its goals and to raise capital based on projections that realistically include the inevitable delays, mishaps, mistakes and setbacks that most early-stage companies encounter.

As this example also illustrates, raising insufficient capital exposes you to the risk of running out of, or falling short of, money and being forced to raise additional capital based on an urgent need and before key milestones have been achieved. In that situation, the chances are

3: Developing a Financing Strategy

that you would be forced to raise capital at the same valuation as your most recent financing (called a 'flat round'), or at a lower valuation (called a 'down round'). Flat and down rounds are best avoided. They can demoralise management teams and weaken investor confidence and enthusiasm, which makes it more difficult to raise future rounds of financing.

Another example that didn't turn out so well illustrates the common occurrence of a company that raised too little capital at too low a valuation. This is a fatal combination. The entrepreneur sold 35% of his early-stage revenue-producing company for €200,000, which was enough capital to get him through six months, but not enough for him to conduct the sales and marketing activities the business needed, or to hire the staff he should have. The funding was insufficient to achieve the milestones needed to increase valuation. When it came time to raise an additional round of financing, he was unable to attract additional investor interest. He had too little performance to show from the prior round, and another round at the same valuation would leave the management team with too little equity to remain appropriately motivated. The company ended up being liquidated.

These examples also illustrate that raising too little capital can result in your company having to seek financing more frequently than expected, which incurs tremendous time costs for the company. In the worst case, insufficient capital puts the company at risk of going out of business because it simply runs out of cash and can't obtain any additional financing in time.

Raising Too Much Capital

Less commonly, companies without a clear financing strategy can make the mistake of raising too much capital at too early a stage, with the consequent drawback of selling too much equity too soon. This is not a fatal mistake, so it is of much less concern to most entrepreneurs. And in fact, although you may sell more equity than you needed, extra capital can sometimes provide a needed financial cushion to weather a period of under-performance, or a market downturn.

CONCLUSION

Your financing strategy is your roadmap to raise capital, just as your business plan is your roadmap to grow revenues. A thoughtful financing plan will help you to identify how much capital to raise, when to raise it, and will allow you to avoid the common, and sometimes fatal, mistakes of raising capital too little or too late. Implementing a financing strategy that outlines a defined plan to achieve key milestones and to increase valuations is also likely to impress investors, increase your negotiating leverage, and reduce the risk that you will lose control of your financing to 'drip-feeders'.

4
VALUATION

In what does the objective measure of value lie?
Friedrich Nietzsche

Valuation is the issue that strikes fear into the heart of most entrepreneurs. You probably feel that you don't know how to calculate it, you're not quite sure how to think about it, and you are convinced you won't get the best valuation you deserve.

Think of valuation as the 'price' of the deal. During any fundraising round, entrepreneurs attempt to maximise the value of their company, thereby minimising the amount of ownership they sell. In contrast, investors look for lower valuations to maximise the upside potential between the price they pay at the time of investment and the proceeds they receive at exit. While other nuances come into play during actual deal negotiation, this fundamental tension exists in every equity financing transaction.

The first step in arriving at a price for the deal is to understand what is being priced or measured. By researching competitors and publicly-traded companies in your sector, you should be certain to understand how the value of your company is measured – what metrics and milestones are important? How are they weighted? These are the performance indicators on which to concentrate, in order to build value consistently between financing rounds and to maximise value during each round. For example, if you are running a retail-based company, such as a chain of coffee shops, traditional retail metrics such as store growth (how many new shops are you opening each quarter and year?), same-store growth (within existing shops, how much are sales growing), average revenue per transaction and sales per square metre are important. For every industry, there are metrics like this that investors use to measure and signal performance. Build your business around them.

THE VALUATION MARKET

Like any price, valuations fluctuate based on the current supply and demand. Supply and demand factors can include how 'hot' the sector is, how many investors are interested in the company, and the appetite of the trade sale and public markets for companies in your industry and sector. The Internet boom presents an exaggerated, but fundamentally true, illustration of this. A booming stock market, increased demand from investors with large amounts of cash to invest and a limited supply of good deals drove valuations to historical highs. After the crash, demand dried up. The Internet sector went from hot to cold, investors lost interest in funding Internet e-commerce deals and the public markets were all but closed. Valuations plummeted.

Valuation is a snapshot in time. It reflects the market conditions, and supply and demand, at the time the company was being valued. Over time, valuations will fluctuate, based on general market conditions (like stock market booms and busts), on industry performance (like the Internet bubble), and even geography (valuations in Europe are almost always lower, on average, than in the US), so it is important to research and to obtain current and local market information on the potential value of your company.

Getting a market-based valuation for each round of financing is critical. If early rounds of financing are priced too low, you will sell too much of the company for too little. In addition, later investors will have to address the risk of diluting the management team to the point where they have little or no equity incentive to work hard to develop the company. It is very difficult to recover from early excess dilution. An under-priced early round can also make it difficult to negotiate the valuation upwards significantly in later rounds, because the starting point for negotiations (the price of the last round) is so low.

In contrast, if early rounds are priced too high, it sets a floor for later rounds that investors may view as over-priced. Of course, later investors have the option of offering a lower price or 'down round' but, in reality, down rounds are demoralising to management, difficult for early investors to accept, and challenging to obtain Board and shareholder approval for. It is also an unappealing way to start a partnership between the investor and the company. For these reasons, then, down rounds to fix an earlier overvaluation are rarely done. And, if they are done, they are rarely pleasant.

VALUATION METHODOLOGIES

While there are several quantitative methods for calculating valuations, such as the comparables analysis or discounted cash flow methods discussed below, the reality is that valuing early-stage companies is an art much more than a science. Investors are experts in the industries and sectors in which they invest. They see a dozen or more business plans and meet with several emerging companies every week. They talk to their co-investors, attend industry conferences, and track industry data on trade sales and public offerings. They understand what types of companies command which prices, and why. They know their market. When you walk in the door, the investor already has a comprehensive and detailed picture of the industry dynamics and market in which you operate. Based on this detailed and current industry knowledge, the investor already has a good idea of the general market valuation range for your company.

Let's exaggerate the process for simplicity and take a non-venture capital example. If I buy fish every day, I know, compared to last week, last year or five years ago, whether the fish trade is booming or busting (industry and market conditions). I know which types of fish (sectors) are in demand and which ones are not. If I'm looking at buying a particular type of fish, such as salmon, I can evaluate a catch that has just come in and determine whether it is exceptionally good, mediocre or poor, based on specific criteria such as colour, texture, weight, and size (company-specific factors). I think about the price at which I know my restaurant customers and the public will buy it (exit price), build in my profit, and then make my bid (pre-money valuation). I don't need a spreadsheet, I know my market.

This is a very exaggerated example, since fish are commodities and companies are not. There are certainly more nuances and much more expertise that comes into play when evaluating a cutting-edge high-technology company than when trading a piece of salmon. Trading commodities also doesn't involve the human element that setting a valuation on a company invariably does. Fish don't have a strong management team, a promising founder, or a difficult Board to impact the price. They don't have personality or fit or chemistry, and they haven't been referred to me personally by the smartest Managing Director I know. But, simple as it is, the example drives home the basic point that valuations are market-based and that investors know their market. If you want to have a substantive and credible conversation about valuation, do your homework, conduct your research, and learn as much you can about your market.

Comparables Analysis (What the Market is Paying Now)

Comparables analysis is the assessment of market valuations of similar companies. It is trying to determine what other investors are willing to pay now for your type of company (based on industry, sector, and stage). Investors conduct comparables analysis to confirm a general valuation range. They are looking for companies in the same industry with a similar business model and growth prospects.

For instance, take the fictitious example of an Irish coffee shop chain with 30 domestic stores and growing operations in the UK and the US. A comparables analysis would include other multinational coffee chains, perhaps looking at *Coffee Republic* and *Costa Coffee* in the UK, *Timothy's Coffee* in Canada, *Starbucks, Seattle's Best Coffee, Caribou Coffee* and *Peets Coffee* in the US. To widen the range, the analysis might also include coffee and food retailers such as *Pret à Manger* in the UK, *O'Briens* in Ireland, or *Einstein Brothers Bagels* in the US. Investors find comparables information by researching the financial and valuation ratios of publicly-traded companies, and by talking to financial analysts and industry consultants, as well as to other investors.

You are well-served to do your own homework by gathering financial and valuation information and learning everything you can about publicly-traded competitors in your sector. The public market is always a good place to start a comparables analysis, since it will generally provide the high end of the valuation range, and because it is a good way to become familiar with standard metrics that companies similar to yours use to report their performance. Public filings can also be a good source of prices that public companies paid to acquire privately-held firms, and how those transactions were valued.

Exit Scenario Modelling (What the Market will Pay Later)

With this methodology, investors price your company today, based on its potential return at an exit. Exit scenario modelling involves trying to determine what other investors (either a corporate buyer or the public) will pay for your company in the future.

Investors gather exit values, based on existing data of IPO valuations and recent trade sales in your industry. This data is used to estimate the potential future value of your business. This future value is then discounted back to the present, using the investor's targeted return rate. An investor who knows they are seeking a 30% or higher return on their investment in your company can use that rate of return to discount back to the present and arrive at a pre-money valuation. This methodology is clearly much more art than science, since it relies heavily on investor judgment to determine:

- The type of exit the company is likely to realise (IPO or trade sale).
- The probable timing of the exit, which reflects underlying assumptions about the company's expected growth rate and financial performance.
- The projected value of the exit, which reflects the investor's view of the trade sale and IPO markets' expected future performance.

To continue with the coffee shop example above, investors would evaluate two different exits. First, they would look at the valuations of small to medium-sized coffee retailers that are currently publicly-traded or have recently conducted a public offering, to assess a potential valuation that might be reasonable for your company. They would then discount that valuation back using their required rate of return (and possibly some other discounts), to get an estimate of a reasonable 'pre-money valuation'. The investor would also model a potential trade sale exit. Because the large public coffee companies have a history of conducting acquisitions, the investor could gather information on the prices paid for small to medium-sized privately-held coffee shop chains and the metrics upon which those prices were based. Using that information to estimate a potential future valuation for your company, they would again discount the valuation back using their preferred rate of return.

Discounted Cash Flow

Discounted cash flow (DCF) is the finance-textbook method for valuing businesses but in the venture capital industry, it is rarely used. Discounted cash flow, as its name suggests, calculates the value of a company's projected future cash flows and then discounts this value back to the present to arrive at a current valuation. The discount value is often the weighted average cost of capital (WACC), but any number of discounts can be used and, depending on which one you select, the results can vary tremendously.

Because of its dependence on accurate future cash flow projections, which don't exist in early-stage companies, DCF is much better suited to the analysis of stable companies with a solid financial track record and steady growth opportunities. It is unusual indeed for an early- or growth-stage investor to rely on DCF to establish a valuation, because cash flows are too uncertain and which discount rate you use makes too much of a difference to the outcome of the analysis. If you receive a valuation based on DCF, worry about the investor's experience in making early-stage investments, but appreciate that you have an opportunity to make a more compelling valuation case, based on analyses more relevant to an early-stage company.

GETTING THE BEST VALUATION

With all the art and negotiation involved in establishing the valuation of an early-stage investment, how do you know what the 'right' valuation is for your company? Well, there is no real 'right' valuation, only relatively better or worse ones. But, when you walk in the door to meet an investor, you want to have done your valuation homework and be prepared to argue for the best valuation you can get.

To do that, consider the following steps:

1. **Know your sector**: Do what the investors do. Research the public and private companies in your sector that compete with you and are similar to you. Understand their valuations, what drives their performance and price, and how both the IPO and trade sale markets value these companies.

2. **Know your metrics**: From public company filings, industry reports, press releases of competing companies and industry

4: Valuation

associations, understand how companies like yours are measured. What metrics are used to measure and signal performance? What are some industry averages and ranges? How does your company compare? If the metrics currently used don't really apply to your company, which ones are you suggesting that will signal performance, and why?

3. **Develop a valuation range**: You want to begin to develop a range of valuations for your company, based on both the sector and metric information you've evaluated so far. You will also need to educate yourself about what the 'going rate' valuations are in your market. Talk with other entrepreneurs and advisors about current valuations, and keep up with IPO and acquisition valuations in your local market. You should decide where within that range you would feel like you got a good valuation. This helps you have a number in your head when you meet with the investor.

4. **Build your case**: Conduct your own valuation analysis of your company and be ready to present a well-researched and factual argument about your company valuation. Incorporate specific comparable valuations and performance metrics into your case, as well as company-specific factors that can justify a higher valuation, including:

    ◊ A strong and experienced management team (most important).
    ◊ The existence of other investors who are interested in / bidding on the deal.
    ◊ Being in a 'hot' sector or market.
    ◊ Strong IPO or trade sale markets with high valuations.
    ◊ Having paying customers (particularly one or more blue chip customers).
    ◊ A strong sales pipeline to support revenue and growth projections.
    ◊ Intellectual property ownership or other competitive advantage / barrier to entry.

    Value killers are all the opposites. Other common value depressors are:

- ◊ A hairy deal.
- ◊ An over-priced earlier round.
- ◊ Difficult early investors or Board members.

5. **Negotiate**: While the old adage 'you get what you negotiate' applies here, there are factors beyond your negotiating skill that will influence your ability to obtain a higher valuation. There are several factors that can increase your negotiating leverage:
   - ◊ Generate interest from more than one investor.
   - ◊ Generate interest from more than one investor.
   - ◊ Generate interest from more than one investor (it is hard to emphasise this enough!).
   - ◊ If you are a serial entrepreneur, your credibility is your currency and you will have better negotiating outcomes than a first-time founder.
   - ◊ Raising capital early, before you need it, gives you negotiating leverage, since you have the advantage and ability to walk away from a mediocre deal and the time to create other alternatives.

No matter how strong and compelling and airtight your case is, you will ultimately only get a valuation that an investor is willing to pay. In general, equity investing is, and will remain, a buyer's market. Nonetheless, doing your homework and preparing to argue for the best valuation you can justify will help you avoid a mis-priced round, impress investors and contribute to your financing strategy.

PRE- AND POST-MONEY VALUATION

Understanding the 'deal maths' of how to calculate valuation, percentage ownership and price per share can help you to model the impact of different valuations on your company's capital structure. When investors talk about valuation, they are referring specifically to the valuation of your business today, right now, before you raise a round of equity finance. This is called the 'pre-money valuation'. As discussed above, the pre-money valuation is not arrived at through calculation but through a combination of market conditions, company factors, and negotiation between the company and investors.

4: Valuation

The price per share is determined by dividing the pre-money valuation by the shares outstanding prior to the investment:

$$\text{Price per share} = \frac{\text{Pre-money valuation}}{\text{Shares outstanding}}$$

After the equity investment, the value is referred to as the 'post-money valuation', which mathematically is the pre-money valuation plus the amount invested:

$$\text{Post-money valuation} = \text{Pre-money valuation} + \text{Investment amount}$$

To determine the percentage of equity you are selling in different valuation scenarios, use the formula:

$$\text{Percentage equity sold} = \frac{\text{Investment amount}}{\text{Post-money valuation}}$$

The actual number of shares purchased can be calculated by:

$$\text{Number of shares purchased} = \frac{\text{Investment amount}}{\text{Price per share}}$$

The percentage ownership of any individual or group once the financing closes can be calculated as:

$$\text{Percentage ownership} = \frac{\text{Shares owned by individual / group}}{\text{Post-money shares outstanding}}$$

With that understanding of deal maths, you are ready to use a cap table to model investment and valuation scenarios, and to calculate dilution.

DILUTION

To demonstrate more concretely the impact of company valuation and the importance of increasing it over time, you will need to understand dilution. Dilution refers to the reduction in existing shareholders' percentage ownership in the company that results from the issue of new shares. Dilution is minimised when the value of a company increases with each round of financing. During a flat or down round, dilution effects are greater. A cap table is the perfect place to illustrate the impact of dilution, and how sensitive it is to valuation. A more detailed discussion of dilution, and the anti-dilution protection that equity investors seek, can be found in **Chapter 9**.

Returning to the same initial cap table as presented in **Chapter 2**, **Figure 3** is an example of a cap table for start-up company, NewCo Ltd, with the following pre-money capital structure:

FIGURE 3: NEWCO LTD PRE-MONEY CAP TABLE

Owner	Ordinary Shares	Employee Options	Percentage Ownership
Managing Director	300,000		60%
Director, Technology	50,000		10%
Director, Sales	25,000		5%
Employee Pool		125,000	25%
TOTAL	375,000	125,000	100%

The company had authorised a total of 1.5 million shares, and has issued 500,000 (375,000 + 125,000) so far.

Assume NewCo has raised an angel round of €500,000 based on a pre-money valuation of the company of €2 million.

$$\text{Price per share} = \frac{\text{€2m pre-money valuation}}{\text{500,000 shares}} = \text{€4.00 per share}$$

$$\text{Post-money valuation} = \text{€2m} + \text{€500,000} = \text{€2.5 million}$$

$$\text{Percentage equity sold} = \frac{\text{€500,000}}{\text{€2.5 million}} = 20\%$$

4: Valuation

$$\text{Shares purchased} = \frac{\text{€500,000 invested}}{\text{€4.00 per share}} = 125{,}000 \text{ shares}$$

The company issued 125,000 new shares to the angel investors, which brings the total issued shares to 625,000. Of its 1.5 million authorised shares, there are still 875,000 remaining and available to issue in future rounds of financing. The post-money cap table is shown in **Figure 4**.

To illustrate the impact of valuation on dilution, take the same NewCo Ltd and assume it raised the same €500,000 round, based on a lower pre-money valuation of €1 million, instead of €2 million. The calculations now are:

$$\text{Price per share} = \frac{\text{€1m pre-money valuation}}{500{,}000 \text{ shares}} = \text{€2.00 per share}$$

$$\text{Post-money valuation} = \text{€1m} + \text{€500,000} = \text{€1.5 million}$$

$$\text{Percentage equity sold} = \frac{\text{€500,000}}{\text{€1.5 million}} = 33\%$$

$$\text{Shares purchased} = \frac{\text{€500,000 invested}}{\text{€2.00 per share}} = 250{,}000 \text{ shares}$$

Due to the lower pre-money valuation, the investors receive more shares at a lower price, and thus the existing shareholders suffer greater dilution. The revised cap table is shown in **Figure 5**.

Figure 4: NewCo Ltd Post-money Capitalisation Table: Angel Round at €2m Pre-money Valuation

Owner	Ordinary Shares	Employee Options	Percentage Ownership	Amount Invested	Ordinary Shares	Percentage Ownership
Managing Director	300,000		60%			48%
Director, Technology	50,000		10%			8%
Director, Sales	25,000		5%			4%
Employee Pool		125,000	25%			20%
TOTAL Employees			**100%**			**80%**
Angel A				€20,000	5,000	1%
Angel B				€30,000	7,500	1%
Angel C				€50,000	12,500	2%
Angel D				€85,000	21,250	3%
Angel E				€140,000	35,000	6%
Angel F				€175,000	43,750	7%
TOTAL Angels				**€500,000**	**125,000**	**20%**
TOTAL	**375,000**	**125,000**	**100%**			**100%**

Options are listed as ordinary share equivalent
Amount invested   € 500,000
Pre-money valuation   € 2,000,000
Price/share   € 4.00
Post-money valuation € 2,500,000
Total shares o/s   625,000

FIGURE 5: NEW CO LTD POST-MONEY CAPITALISATION TABLE: ANGEL ROUND AT €1M PRE-MONEY VALUATION

Owner	Ordinary Shares	Employee Options	Percentage Ownership	Amount Invested	Ordinary Shares	Percentage Ownership
Managing Director	300,000		60%			40%
Director, Technology	50,000		10%			7%
Director, Sales	25,000		5%			3%
Employee Pool		125,000	25%			17%
TOTAL Employees			**100%**			**67%**
Angel A				€ 20,000	10,000	1%
Angel B				€ 30,000	15,000	2%
Angel C				€ 50,000	25,000	3%
Angel D				€ 85,000	42,500	6%
Angel E				€ 140,000	70,000	9%
Angel F				€ 175,000	87,500	12%
TOTAL Angels				**€ 500,000**	**250,000**	**33%**
TOTAL	**375,000**	**125,000**				**100%**

Options are listed as ordinary share equivalent
Amount invested   € 500,000
Pre-money valuation   € 1,000,000
Price/share   € 2.00
Post-money valuation € 1,500,000
Total shares issued   750,000

As a comparison of **Figure 4** and **Figure 5** illustrates, the management team is able to retain significantly more ownership (80% versus 67%), if they can develop a financing strategy and achieve milestones that create an additional €1 million of value before seeking external investors.

The most dilution occurs at the earliest rounds of financing, when the company's valuation is relatively low. To avoid excessive dilution, many companies turn to 'bootstrapping'. Almost a forgotten art during the tech market boom in the late 1990s, bootstrapping is back in vogue and a sensible way to maximise cash flow. Bootstrappers focus on growing their businesses as much as possible using revenues from paying customers. Such companies are very market-driven and customer-oriented. Not all companies have a product development cycle that allows them to start selling at a very early stage in their growth but, for those that do, an early strategy of growth through revenues can result in a valuable base of reference customers and a strong case of market validation.

CONCLUSION

A key challenge of equity financing is to balance carefully your company's capital needs with valuation and dilution concerns. Maximizing valuation in each financing round minimises dilution of existing shareholders. Valuation is the price at which investors are willing to buy a percentage ownership in your company. Like all prices, it is subject to supply and demand and general market conditions. It is also partly dependent on a number of company-specific factors and your negotiating leverage.

The best ways to get the highest valuation is to bring the credibility of a serial entrepreneur or the interest of other investors to the table. Absent that, research your sector and performance metrics, learn the 'going rate' of valuations in your local market, and build the strongest case you can, based on the merits and the market, to negotiate an attractive valuation.

5
SHOULD EMPLOYEES BE OWNERS?

No person will make a great business who wants to do it all himself.
Andrew Carnegie

One of the first, and biggest, challenges you will encounter when starting your business is recruiting and building a good team. Companies that award equity ownership to their management team and employees do so because it helps them hire and retain the best people. Equity ownership can be a very effective way to attract, retain and motivate key employees. For high-technology companies in particular, equity ownership is often a necessary part of a competitive remuneration package. Individuals who join start-up companies are willing to take the risk that such employment entails, but frequently seek the potential to be rewarded commensurately through equity participation.

SHOULD YOU ISSUE EQUITY TO EMPLOYEES?

Determining whether to include your management team and employees as part of the ownership structure of your company is a weighty decision. When you allocate equity to someone else, they have legal ownership and voting rights in your business that cannot be revoked easily, simply or cheaply.

In Ireland, certain business decisions are statutorily subject to the vote and approval of the company's shareholders – therefore, the people to whom you allocate equity will have an ongoing say in critical choices taken in relation to your business.

When evaluating your choices about allocating ownership and shares, consider the following factors:

- What purpose would the equity awards serve? Are you trying to create an ownership culture? Are they intended to be a long-term performance incentive, a one-time lump benefit as part of a quick exit, or a boost to morale?
- What does an equity award programme offer to your employees that a cash-based incentive bonus programme would not?
- Is the equity to be allocated only to key employees and management, or are you interested in offering an ownership stake to the majority of your employees?
- Assess your management team and employees. Are they financially sophisticated? Can they understand and handle the level of risk that may be involved in your business? Do they understand the benefits and risks of share options? What will be the initial and ongoing education needs of your employees, if you implement an equity participation plan?
- What would you do if the equity awards fell dramatically in value (for example, if share options became worthless, or if your share price fell)? Do you feel that offering equity brings with it the obligation to insure awardees against the downside of significant falls in value? If not, how will you deal with the reduced morale that such a decline can induce?
- On the other hand, if the value of your shares increases, how will you handle requests to cash-out or exit?
- What is the competitive environment regarding equity compensation? Are companies similar to yours offering equity participation? What percentage of the company is reasonable to offer in your market, in order to attract and retain good people in key management positions? Will you need to attract employees and management in international markets? What are the equity compensation norms there?

A surprisingly common mistake made by entrepreneurs is to give excessive share allocations to management and employees. The result of such extreme awards is that too much of the company is given away for too little performance. It leaves little room for future incentives, or for awards to new hires. Equity is a scarce resource within your company, and it is definitely worth questioning whether a 'one for everyone in the company' plan is required. It is prudent practice to award little equity to few people early in the company's development. Approach awarding equity slowly and cautiously. You can always award more equity later, but it is impossible to take excess equity away.

TYPES OF EQUITY AWARDS

There are a number of different ways in which companies can provide equity compensation to employees including: share options, restricted shares, and equity-like awards. Each is discussed below.

Share Options

Share option plans are attractive for companies to implement because options are generally understood and perceived as valuable by employees. Also, in Ireland, they are relatively cheap for the company to award, since usually they are not required to be expensed in the company's financial statements – however, international accounting standards increasingly require share options to be expensed at the time of issue, which makes them less attractive to companies that plan to raise finance outside Ireland.

Share options give the employee the right to purchase ordinary shares at a fixed price (called the 'exercise' or 'strike' price) in the future. Option holders are not actual shareholders until they exercise the option and purchase the underlying shares. Therefore, option holders do not receive any of the rights awarded to the company's ordinary shareholders (such as the right to vote, or the right to attend shareholder meetings).

In Ireland, companies can implement Revenue-approved or unapproved share options schemes. The main difference between the two is that approved share schemes must meet a number of specific conditions, and must be 'widely held' within the company. Depending on which type of scheme you choose, the tax impact on the employees when they exercise and sell their shares will vary. This is a matter to review with your financial advisors / accountant to determine which type of scheme makes the most sense, given the level of distribution of equity and the characteristics of your company.

Share option volatility

Entrepreneurs have learned the hard way that equity awards can be a double-edged sword – providing incentives and rewards in good times, but causing employee problems and discontent in bad times.

Options are derivative instruments (in that they derive their value from the value of the underlying stock) and, like most derivatives, they are both risky and volatile. When the stock market crashed after 2000, the volatility of share options became fully evident. Options can provide significant financial rewards in a bull (up) market, or within a rapidly-growing company. But their value can also fall to zero in a bear (down) market or in a poorly performing company. For example, if the company's share price falls below the exercise price of the option, the options become worthless. The options will remain worthless, unless and until the share price increases to a point higher than the exercise price.

In addition, many companies realised that the equity they had awarded to employees in the form of share options to encourage performance and retention quickly became a disincentive once the options lost value. Once employees believed that they had 'lost' money (even though these were only losses on paper, not losses on cash invested) through the decline in the value of their equity, their motivation and morale was affected and, in some cases, employees felt entitled to compensation to make up for the paper loss. Some firms responded to this pressure by re-pricing the options so the exercise price was below the market price, while others simply issued additional options at a lower price. Each of these options is expensive for companies. Re-pricing options has become more costly, as new accounting rules increasingly require a charge against the company's expenses when re-pricing occurs, while issuing additional options at a lower price dilutes the ownership of all existing shareholders.

Creating a share option pool

If you decide to issue share options to the management team and employees, the best and standard practice is to set aside an employee pool of options to be awarded. Determine the size of the pool by estimating the shares that you think will be required to attract and reward the employees you need in the short and medium term – 18 months is a good guideline for early rounds. Local executive search and recruitment firms are an excellent source of information on the market rate for equity compensation. Consult with them to project how much equity you will need to offer your key hires. From this data, you can estimate the size of the option pool you will need to complete your projected recruiting. A good guideline to keep in mind is that employee option pools of early-stage companies typically represent 15-25% of the company's capital, not including the Chief Executive Officer (CEO) / Managing Director (MD).

There are two main benefits to allocating a share option pool. First, it avoids frequent unpleasant and awkward conversations as the existing team members face continuous reductions in their ownership from the equity awarded to new employees as they come on-stream. It is much easier to set aside a pool up-front that provides sufficient shares to attract high quality employees and ensures that existing key employees retain a steady percentage ownership until the first financing from an equity investor. Second, it eliminates the share option pool as a negotiating issue during later rounds of financing. If the employee pool is not already included in the initial capitalisation table, some angels and all VCs will generally want it included in the pre-money valuation of the company. If the full allocation of the pool is not ultimately required to build the management team and attract employees, the shares can be re-allocated to the existing team or back to the company at a later time.

Awarding share options

Although employee equity awards and the size of the option pool are discussed in terms of percentage ownership, be aware that few employees think about share options that way. When you present the awards, most employees will think about them in terms of the number of shares they receive, not in terms of percentage of ownership. The standard presentation therefore would be to indicate:

> 'Seamus, we are awarding you 100,000 share options – congratulations!'

not:

> *'Seamus, please accept our award of .004% of the company, based on fully diluted shares outstanding.'*

Although a percentage ownership presentation is probably a more accurate statement about the value of the award, employees most commonly think about their share option awards like this:

> *'If I have 100,000 options and, in a few years, the company's share price goes up to €5.00, I'll have half a million Euro! Even if it only gets to €3.00, I'll have €300,000!'*

For management, this thinking can be much easier to deal with, because the number of shares awarded always remains constant. There is therefore little ongoing need for education and communication about changes in the award. If employees were awarded options on a percentage ownership basis, they would need to be educated about, and understand, the fact that later rounds of financing or additional equity awards will reduce or dilute their ownership over time.

Restricted Shares

Options still remain a popular post-crash incentive, but some companies are turning towards awarding actual shares instead of options as a way to provide ownership to employees. Restricted shares are attractive both to companies and employees, because they are characterised by much less volatility than share options. In perhaps the most visible example, Microsoft has reported eliminating its share option programme altogether, in exchange for a programme that grants employees restricted shares that vest over a five-year time period. Restricted shares are ordinary shares in the company that are granted to employees and are 'restricted' in the sense that they vest over time or have other conditions of ownership attached to them. The shares are valued at the time of issue and can be sold once vested.

Companies increasingly find restricted shares an attractive choice, since they reduce volatility from the equity portion of employee compensation. Unlike share options, restricted shares allow employees to retain some equity value if the company's share price falls. In the case of a decline in the company's share price, employees remain better off with a share award. While an option becomes worthless (goes to zero) if the share price falls below the exercise price, share awards always retain some value.

For instance, if you grant an employee share options with an exercise price of €10, and the value of the company's share falls to €5, the option is worthless, since it costs more to exercise it than the share is worth when sold. But, if instead you granted shares to employees at €10 per share and the value falls to €5 a share, the employee can still realise €5 a share if they sell the stock.

Equity-like Awards

Both share options and restricted shares are designed to give the employee ownership in the company. What if you like the idea of providing equity ownership incentives to your employees, but are reluctant to take on the legal obligations and regulatory requirements of additional shareholders? Fortunately, there are ways to structure equity-like rewards that allow you to realise the financial benefits of equity awards but to avoid granting an ownership stake in the company. Both 'phantom shares' and 'stock appreciation rights' (SARs) are rare in Ireland, but they represent a creative choice for companies that wish to reward employees based on their share price, but don't want to give them a percentage ownership in the company.

Phantom shares

Phantom shares are not actually shares, but are simply a cash bonus plan designed to deliver the same financial rewards as shares. The phantom shares are not real physical shares, are not actually issued, and do not grant ownership in the company. Instead, they mirror the financial performance and movement of the company's ordinary shares. Phantom shares are granted at the same valuation as the current ordinary share price. The price of the phantom shares then moves in tandem with the price of the ordinary shares. Employees can 'sell' their phantom shares at the current price of the company's shares and receive a cash payment. The current price can be determined as either the current valuation of your company stock (based on an auditor's opinion or recent round of financing), or based on a valuation formula that is specified in advance.

Stock appreciation rights

Another choice to reward employees as if they had equity, but without providing any ownership, is stock appreciation rights. SARs grant employees the right to receive a cash bonus that is tied to the appreciation in your company's shares over a fixed period of time. So, at the time the SARs are granted, they are 'priced' at the current value of the ordinary shares. For any increase above the price at which the SARs are granted, employees receive a cash bonus.

For example, if the value of your ordinary shares in January is €5.00, you would grant SARs to employees at that price. In December, when you were getting ready to award bonuses, you would review the ordinary share price. Let's say it had increased during the year to €6.00. Therefore, employees would receive a €1.00 cash bonus for each SAR they held.

There is tremendous flexibility in how phantom stock and SARs can be structured. The awards can vest over time, just as share options or restricted shares do, and the company can secure the right to buy them back and cash-out the employee at specified times. Alternatively, some companies limit cash-out opportunities to an exit event such as a sale or merger.

Again, while phantom shares and SARs offer similar benefits to regular equity shares, the tax effects of each choice can vary for the employee. To maximise the benefit of the award you choose, work with an accountant to make sure you understand the likely impact on your employees.

THE SHARE OPTION AGREEMENT

Regardless of which alternative equity structure you select – options, restricted shares, phantom shares or SARs – you will need to develop and sign a written agreement that describes the terms of the equity or equity-like award granted. Since share options are by far the most popular method for granting equity to employees, we will focus here on the share option agreement.

The purpose of the share option agreement is to describe the number and price of the equity award, any vesting or exercise conditions and any other terms that are specific to your business. A key objective of the share option agreement is to allow the company to keep control over its shares by:

- Outlining a process for dealing with employee shareholders who leave the company.
- Limiting share transfers.

At a minimum, a share option agreement should cover the following key areas:

- Vesting schedules.
- Employee departures.
- Share transfers.

Companies that are not disciplined about getting signed share option agreements can find that ex-employees, advisors and others involved in the early stages of company development can come back at a later time and assert that verbal promises were made about share option awards or pricing. These alleged liabilities can be both very difficult to disprove and expensive to make go away. It is for your protection, then, that all agreements with employees and others involved in building the company are maintained in writing and documented with signed originals that are kept in the corporate minute book or in appropriate files.

One Irish solicitor described how common such 'informal promises' of options or shares are. He has been involved in several cases, in which the lack of documentation has become an issue in employment disputes, particularly with departing employees. In those cases, the employee and the company each have different understandings about what (if anything) was granted, and on what terms. With no agreement to clarify the dispute, it has to be resolved through negotiation, usually with solicitor involvement and expense. If the company has a consistent practice of documenting share option awards and obtaining signed agreements, it can be much harder for an employee to assert that an exception to that practice occurred and that the company instead made a binding verbal promise to them.

For instance, one founder of a software company had been extremely disorganised about his corporate recordkeeping when he formed the company. He had not obtained any shareholder agreements from any original employees, some of whom had left and gone onto jobs at other companies. One of the company's former employees had departed (he claimed he was dismissed; the company claimed he resigned) and had since been contacting the founder, claiming he was owed money for share options he had been promised. The company denied ever issuing shares to the employee and the exchange continued for several months. About that time, the company was approached about being acquired. Upon hearing that, the former employee contacted the company's solicitors and Board to negotiate a resolution. Because of the impending acquisition (and detailed research they knew the potential acquirer would conduct), the company knew it would have to resolve this outstanding issue. In the end, the company paid the former employee cash for the options he claimed he was awarded, as well as all the legal fees (for both sides) incurred during the dispute resolution and drafting of the settlement agreement.

If you have been giving out equity awards with no share option agreements, the solution is to talk with an experienced solicitor about drawing up an agreement and to approach your option holders immediately to obtain signed agreements.

Vesting Schedule

Share options are usually granted to employees, subject to a vesting schedule that specifies how and over what time period the employee obtains ownership of the shares. Options that are vested are owned by the employee, while unvested options are still owned by the company.

5: Should Employees Be Owners?

Typically, a specified percentage of an option award will vest each year. The first vesting usually occurs upon the employee's one-year anniversary, and then continues linearly after that on either a quarterly or annual schedule. It is always a good idea to wait to begin any vesting of equity awards on or after the employee's first anniversary with the company. Working for a start-up company is demanding, exhausting and usually characterised by long hours and travel. Some employees, even members of the management team, will find that they either can't or won't achieve the level of performance and stamina required to work in a new business. Keeping the first year of employment free from any equity ownership makes it easier and less complicated to part ways if there is a mismatch of expectations or performance.

Standard vesting schedules

A standard vesting schedule is to vest the options equally over five years (although, during the technology boom in the late 1990s, vesting schedules were often accelerated to three years in order to recruit employees). 'Cliff vesting', in which employees remain unvested for an initial time period and then a substantial portion or all of the shares vest at one time, is an attractive schedule for start-ups. Employees must stay with the company for a significant time period before any portion of their equity award vests. **Figure 6** illustrates how the most common vesting schedules operate.

FIGURE 6: COMMON VESTING SCHEDULES

	Vests equally over 5 years	Vests equally over 3 years	Cliff vesting after 3 years
Year 1	20%	33%	0%
Year 2	20%	33%	0%
Year 3	20%	33%	50%
Year 4	20%		25%
Year 5	20%		25%
TOTAL	100%	100%	100%

Vesting schedules are an important tool for employee and management retention. Traditionally, vesting schedules have been based on years of employment and have served as a 'golden handcuff' to keep employees at the company. To strengthen the retention incentive, companies grant further employee options annually, so at any point in time there are significant numbers of unvested shares to encourage the employee to stay.

Vesting based on time or performance?

Stock options that vest according to time provide maximum incentives for retention, but do little to incentivise performance. For stock options that vest over five years, for example, employees are provided with an incentive only to stay employed at the company for that length of time to obtain full ownership of their options. Companies that are more focused on performance than retention are increasingly tying vesting to overall company performance, or to specific accomplishments. For example, one company has tied the vesting of its equity awards to its ability to attract and satisfy customers. The advantage of this method is that it sends a message and develops a company culture that clearly prioritises performance and achievement, rather than seniority. The disadvantage is that, although all employees are interested in seeing the value of their stock options maximised, it can be difficult for employees in even small companies to discern what their particular position or job contributes to overall company performance. Without a clear understanding of – and link with – this, the performance incentive of stock options for employees is compromised.

There is also the possibility of combining the two incentives. One entrepreneur structured his company's vesting schedule to include both time and performance measures. This company was a new start-up, and needed to raise a round of financing to develop and launch its software product and to be able to hire additional staff. The entrepreneur, therefore, structured the first vesting of options to occur upon the closing of the round of finance, with the remainder to vest annually in equal amounts over the next four years. The share option agreement was written so that employees hired after the initial financing was complete vested annually on a normal five-year time schedule.

Accelerated vesting

There are circumstances in which vesting schedules can be accelerated. This means that employees obtain full ownership of their share options on a faster timeline than originally promised. Accelerated vesting most often occurs in the case of the company being acquired or merged with a larger firm (also referred to as a 'change in control'). Because Irish companies most frequently achieve exits through trade sales, the topic of accelerated option vesting is particularly relevant. At issue is whether to provide accelerated vesting and, if so, whether the acceleration should be automatic or discretionary. There are many sides to this debate and how you resolve it is likely to be determined by your philosophical opinion, a variety of tax considerations, and the underlying structure of your option plan (specifically how many employees it covers and how substantial the awards are). How much time you spend contemplating this issue will also be directly proportional to how likely you think a trade sale exit is for your company.

Proponents of acceleration argue that, in the event of a trade sale, the acceleration clause protects employees, many of whom rely on equity as a significant portion of their compensation, against the financial loss of potentially forfeiting their unvested options. Other supporters view it as a just reward for employees, who have worked hard to help make the company an attractive acquisition target. Detractors of the acceleration option point out that acceleration can be an impediment to an acquisition, since it forces the acquiring company to come up with a new set of 'handcuffs' (or incentives) for key employees. This will usually result in a lower purchase price offer, to the detriment of all shareholders. If the option plan is big enough, an acceleration clause could even serve as an obstacle to a possible acquirer.

Of course, the acceleration of any options can be structured to have a more moderate impact. For instance, the share option plan could give the Board of Directors the right, but not the obligation, to accelerate the vesting schedules for share options. This provides negotiating leverage and flexibility. Another option is to provide acceleration to all employees except 'key employees', or to all employees who are made redundant as part of the transaction. This protects lower-level employees, or those who are not offered employment by the acquiring firm, but ensures that the management team's 'handcuffs' remain in place. For key employees, a partial acceleration (of, say, 50% of their total share options) can serve as a reward for hard work to date, while still providing the acquiring company with comfort that the employee is motivated to stay on and to continue contributing to the company's growth. Again, seek the advice of an experienced solicitor to help structure a vesting schedule that best suits the characteristics and circumstances of your company.

Handling Employee Departures

Every share option agreement must include a description of what happens to the option awards when an employee stops working at the company. Departure clauses are critical because they deal with the virtual certainty that, for a variety of reasons, employees will leave the company. Not all employees who start building the company with you will have the capability, interest, stomach or energy to continue with you. It is a much simpler, and less contentious, process for them to leave if the impact on their equity holdings has already been determined and agreed in advance and, most importantly, in writing.

A comprehensive share option agreement will include clauses that outline what happens to the employees' equity awards in four standard cases (which I call the 'Four Ds'), depending on whether the employee:

- Dies.
- Becomes disabled.
- Departs (is a 'good leaver').
- Is dismissed (is a 'bad leaver').

Vested and unvested equity are always handled separately in each situation. Dealing with unvested shares is simple. Any unvested shares or options still belong to the company, so employees, once they leave the company, retain no right to them. The shares or options remain owned by the company, and are returned to the employee pool where they are available for re-issue. Again, it is worthwhile to postpone any vesting until at least one full year of employment has been completed, in order to ensure that there is a good fit between the employee and life in a start-up.

For vested options, the employee is usually given a short time period (for example, 30 or 60 days) in which to exercise the options. If they fail to do so, the options expire and the employee relinquishes all rights to the award. If the employee decides to exercise the option, they then become a shareholder in the company.

5: Should Employees Be Owners?

Buyback provisions

Few companies relish the idea that former employees continue to hold shares and voting rights, so most agreements include a provision that gives the company the right to purchase, at a specified price and within a defined time period, any shares the employee holds. This provision should be written so that the company can buy back the shares itself, from its own reserves, or, if the company does not have the capital available to purchase the shares, gives it the right to find buyers for the shares (including from among other shareholders in the company). Securing the buyback right allows you to maintain control over who owns shares in your company.

One high-technology start-up company that was founded during the technology boom wrote its share option agreement a little too optimistically and failed to include a buyback provision for departing employees. About 15 months into the venture, the founder and the Chief Operating Officer (COO) had an enormous falling-out about some significant strategic issues related to the company's growth. The COO left the company on bad terms with the founder, but also left with a nearly 5% shareholding in the company (since this was during the technology boom, the company's vesting schedule was shorter and more employee-friendly than would be the case today). The founder had no choice but to provide the former COO with annual financial data, and to solicit his vote during general shareholder votes. Worse, about a year and a half later, the company was aggressively pursuing a trade sale and the founder had to prepare himself to distribute a significant portion of the trade sale proceeds to the former COO, who had not been involved in the company in over 18 months. It was an expensive mistake indeed.

Another start-up company, founded a few years before the boom, had a different experience. This was a consumer services company that was founded by three business partners. They successfully raised a round of venture capital financing and were growing very rapidly when the Operations Director just burnt out. He had been with the company since it was an idea, and it was now over four years into the venture and the pace and work demands were still increasing. He was exhausted, his family was becoming less supportive of the time and energy the venture took from him and he saw no end in sight. He resigned (as a good leaver), and the company re-purchased all his vested options at the market price, as this had been a clause in the original agreement. The buyback worked well for everyone. The director realised significant value by selling, at a price set during the last venture capital financing, the options he had been granted at a very low price when the company was only an idea. The company purchased the share options from its own reserves and added them back to the employee option pool, which gave it a much-needed boost during the aggressive growth phase the company was entering. And the original three founders went forward on good terms.

It is important to emphasise that these buyback terms give the company the right, but not the obligation, to repurchase employee shares. Therefore, your Board always retains the ability to exercise discretion about whether to allow some employees to remain shareholders by not requiring the sale of their shares. This may be appropriate in the case of a key employee or founder, who has left the company or retired after contributing significant value over a number of years.

Buyback purchase price

The purchase price at which the company buys back the shares from ex-employees may also vary. Standard agreements specify different prices depending on whether the employee is considered a 'good leaver' or a 'bad leaver'. Those who are dismissed are considered bad leavers, whereas good leaver status is awarded to the remaining three Ds (although, in some cases, a voluntary resignation within a certain time period may be considered a 'bad leaver').

The purchase price for shares of good leavers typically is the current market price of the shares. Bad leavers normally are offered the *lower of* the market price or the original exercise price. The market price is often defined as:

- The price at which the shares are currently being awarded to employees, or
- The price at the last outside round of financing, or
- A pre-defined formula, or
- An auditor's valuation.

The market price should be defined as clearly, simply and concretely as possible in order to avoid protracted discussions, disagreements or even a dispute with a departing employee. Defining it by an existing price or pre-defined formula are the best options. It is rarely a good idea to define the market price based on an auditor's or accountant's valuation, since such valuations can be expensive and somewhat time-consuming to obtain, particularly in comparison to the value of one departing employee's shares.

One company, founded by three partners, structured its share agreement very simply. The purchase price for bad leavers was set at the original exercise price at which the option was awarded. For retention purposes, the company included a clause declaring that, if any of the founders left the company (for any reason except death or disability) within the first five years, they would be considered a bad leaver. After two years, one of the founders needed to relocate to his home country for personal reasons. Although the company had raised a round of financing from angels and was worth significantly more than when the original options were issued, the founder, after two years of work, walked away with only a nominal amount of cash from selling his options.

Share Transfer Restrictions

A useful and important way of maintaining control over share ownership is to restrict the transfer of shares by existing shareholders. In the absence of such restrictions, an employee could arrange a private sale of their shares to a competitor, to a third party unknown to the company, or to another shareholder (which could allow one shareholder, or a group of shareholders, to build up a significant ownership position within the company). Therefore, most share option agreements restrict the transfer, sale or assignment to anyone but the employee to whom the option was granted.

CONCLUSION

The decision of whether to compensate employees through equity is a weighty one. It is also a personal one. There are no 'right' answers about whether or how much equity to award to employees. The decision is one of personal preferences and philosophy.

Equity is perceived as very valuable by employees. Equity awards are attractive to companies because they can help you attract, retain and reward the best employees. Historically, share options have been the most popular equity award, since they were relatively cheap for the company to award. This may change as companies increasingly are required to record options as an expense. Other forms of equity awards, such as restricted shares or equity-like awards, may become popular in the future. The risks of equity awards are that they can be volatile, and that many companies make the mistake of awarding too much equity too early.

The most prudent approach, if you decide to award equity to employees, is to do so slowly and to a small number of employees initially. This mitigates the risk against the common tendency to over-allocate shares. It is easy to award equity later, but impossible to take away. Consider carefully why you want to award equity and what your specific objectives are. You may be able to accomplish your goals through less cumbersome cash bonuses.

Regardless of what type of equity you award, how much or to whom, it is imperative to document the awards through a written and signed agreement. The agreement should include a description of the price and terms of the award, and detail the vesting conditions, how departing employees are handled, and share transfer restrictions. Employee departures are inevitable. Get all awards in writing from the beginning to avoid disputes, the involvement of solicitors, or the need to settle with employees who could later claim promises of equity.

PART II:
INFORMAL INVESTORS

6
FRIENDS & FAMILY

*He who loses money loses much.
He who loses a friend loses much more.*
Eleanor Roosevelt

The good news is that friends & family (F&F) money is the easiest capital you will ever raise. You will not be grilled with detailed questions about your business model, prospects, customers and financials. You not be reference-checked, poked, prodded and asked to produce a landfill-sized pile of documents to substantiate everything you say. And most importantly, your potential investors already like you. The process for raising friends and family capital will be quick – usually only a few weeks. So kick back and enjoy. It only gets harder from here.

PREPARING TO RAISE FRIENDS & FAMILY CAPITAL

Friends and family capital typically comes at a critical time in a company's growth, and obtaining this first round of financing can be a decisive milestone for a young start-up. Before raising F&F capital, most entrepreneurs invest some of their own personal capital into their business. Investing your own capital will allow you to reach some early milestones without selling equity, and will make a more compelling story to investors. Investors are always interested in how much 'skin in the game' an entrepreneur has, relative to his resources. Has he been taking a market rate salary, or none? Has he put his own money in? How much? There is no magic number that investors seek, rather it is a relative sense of how much the entrepreneur has invested given his resources. It makes a more compelling selling story to external investors, if it is clear that you have significant personal investment in the company.

At the same time, financial prudence dictates that you should be careful not to invest all your assets, or even the maximum that you can afford, into the company. Having too much invested can leave you paralysed with fear about losing everything and result in risk-averse decision-making that can ultimately harm both company growth and returns on your investment. If your business fails, you don't want to be in a position where you lose everything.

Similar to your own money, F&F capital is relatively easy to raise, and quick to obtain. Although raising friends and family capital is the least rigorous of all external financing rounds, some preparation is still required. While it is true that Aunt Mary always loved you best and is going to invest no matter what, written information about your business and investment opportunity helps to provide clear documentation and to avoid problems later. Also, as you approach a wider circle of potential investors outside your immediate family, they will likely be interested in receiving more conventional information.

The F&F round is the perfect time to hone your business pitch. It may seem obvious, but many entrepreneurs cannot communicate clearly and concisely to potential investors what they do and why. Particularly for friends and family, who may not be sophisticated investors, a clear description of your business is required to help them evaluate whether an investment in your business is appropriate for them.

In order to develop this description, think about the following:

- What is your product?
- What exactly does it do?
- What problem does it solve?
- Why does the customer want to buy it?
- Is the problem a high priority for the customer? Is your product a 'must have' or a 'nice to have'?

To provide more detail on your company, it is advisable to create and distribute at a minimum the following documents:

- A one-page company fact-sheet (see **Appendix 2**).

- A brief description or summary of your business idea (an executive summary or business plan).
- A written disclosure of the risks your business faces.
- Summary financials with projections.
- An investment agreement, such as a share purchase agreement for ordinary shares, or a convertible loan agreement if the valuation is not being set during this round (see discussion on page 71).

Once you have this information prepared, consider organising a dedicated event to present the investment idea formally to your group of interested friends and family. Invite them to your offices or place of business and give a short presentation about your company. Describe the investment and its risks, and take questions and answers. Explicitly identify, orally and in writing, the risks and assumptions of the investment and the possibility of failure. When in doubt, disclose. Such an event presents the investment opportunity professionally and is a good way to communicate information consistently to all potential investors and to address any questions or concerns. It also gives the management team valuable practice in conducting such events for potential investors, and a sense of what types of questions arise and any additional information that should be included in the presentation.

FINDING FRIENDS & FAMILY INVESTORS

The investment decisions of friends and family tend to be personally motivated and relationship-based. They invest in people they know and care about. F&F investors are usually approached to make relatively small equity investments (often less than €25,000) but, of course, this depends on the relative wealth of your friends and family circle as well as the cash needs of your business. For some entrepreneurs, it isn't even an option to ask friends and family for capital; for others, it can represent meaningful amounts of funding. Even modest individual investments, however, can represent a critical mass of early-stage capital when added together.

There is no reason to limit yourself to your closest and most personal relationships during this round. Instead, use your immediate circle to find other individuals who might be interested and able to invest. Consider friends of friends, acquaintances, neighbours, work colleagues, and people who vaguely remember you from school but now have lots of spare cash. Think very broadly about who you can approach to participate in this earliest round of financing. The wider the circle you approach, the more likely you are to raise the capital you seek.

For example, one entrepreneur was only a few months into starting his new company when he exhausted his own very limited financial resources. He knew he needed to raise over €500,000 to accomplish the milestones that would prepare him to raise the next round from VCs, but his company was currently at such an early stage of development that he was not even ready to approach angels. Unfortunately, his family did not have the money to invest a significant amount and, because this entrepreneur was young (late 20s), most of his friends did not have the spare cash to invest either. Instead, he asked his immediate circle of friends and family for referrals to other individuals who might be interested and have the cash to invest. He also contacted a wide circle of acquaintances that included his college professors, work colleagues and ex-clients. In the end, he successfully raised over €600,000 from 14 individuals, only one of whom was a personal family member (his parents invested €30,000) and none of whom were close friends.

There is a risk in any F&F round that individuals who want, or can only afford, to invest very small amounts of money will seek to participate in the financing. This is an unattractive proposition for you, because large numbers of very small shareholders are administratively burdensome and generally unappealing to later investors. It can also be cumbersome to manage such small shareholders when shareholder consents, signatures and votes must be gathered from each shareholder. You can control this problem by selling shares in 'lots' of a minimum amount (say, €5,000 or €10,000), with subsequent fixed increments (of, say, €1,000). This policy allows you to graciously turn away tiny investments that contribute little to the capital needs of the company and will only prove administratively costly to manage in the future. In addition, by setting a 'floor' on the investment amount, you also implicitly discourage from investing those who can't afford the minimum amount.

VALUING & STRUCTURING A FRIENDS & FAMILY ROUND

There are two ways to approach valuing and structuring a F&F round:

- Postpone setting a valuation on the round and structure the financing as a convertible loan.
- Set a valuation for the round and structure it as a typical purchase of ordinary shares.

Convertible Loans

The challenge of setting a valuation during a F&F round is that most likely you will have to do it yourself, based on your assessment of 'going rate' valuations, as well as your company's past performance and future potential. After all, your F&F investors are not likely to band together and determine the appropriate valuation to pay, and it simply is not worthwhile at such an early stage of your company's development to pay an accountant for an 'official' valuation to price a small, early round.

Because of fairness concerns, and the possible conflicts of interest inherent in setting a valuation for an investment made by a personal friend or family member, entrepreneurs commonly postpone pricing the F&F round. Instead, they rely on the next round of financing, in which more experienced angel or VC investors are involved, to set the price. The F&F round is then retroactively priced at a discount to the later angel / VC round. Depending on the stage of the company and the expected time to the next round of financing, the discount is generally in the 10-25% range. The discount guarantees that friends and family investors will pay the lowest price of all investors, and ensures that they are compensated for taking the additional risk of investing at an earlier stage than angel or VC investors.

If you value the F&F round at a discount to the next round of financing, the most common way to do so is through a loan that can be converted at the discounted price to ordinary shares upon the closing of the next financing. This is known as a 'convertible loan'. Typically, the full loan amount is used to purchase shares at the discounted price upon the closing of the next round of financing. Many investors will specify that the loan converts only upon a financing of a certain size (for example, €250,000 or higher), since a larger financing round offers more protection against mis-pricing. A sample convertible loan agreement is included in **Appendix 3**.

For example, assume that a group of friends and family investors provides a convertible loan of €250,000 to the company and that, nine months later, angels invest €500,000 to buy 500,000 ordinary shares at €1 per share. The €250,000 F&F loan would then convert into ordinary shares at 80 cents per share, which is a 20% discount from the €1 the angels paid. The F&F loan would therefore be converted into 312,500 ordinary shares.

A convertible loan is attractive for the company because it removes the risk that the F&F round of financing will be mis-priced, the convertible loan agreements are relatively simple, and this type of financing can be done quickly. Investors find them attractive because they provide upside potential through the conversion to equity at a discount to the next round, but downside protection since the loan is a debt instrument that must be repaid ahead of any capital to shareholders in the case of a liquidation. Most importantly for all parties, discounting is a common strategy that will be acceptable to later stage investors.

If the company does not raise the round of financing, or is liquidated, the loan does not ever convert but instead remains a debt obligation of the company. In that case, the capital must be paid back to the investor, with interest, according to the term that was specified in the agreement (usually the term is 12 months). Practically speaking, however, few seed-stage companies have the capital available to pay back the loan if the company liquidates or is unable to raise additional financing. It is helpful to determine in advance what will happen if your business does not have the resources to pay back the loan. Are you personally willing, and able, to compensate your investors? Or is there a risk that they may lose their investment entirely? By offering a loan structure, you introduce the expectation that the capital invested will be repaid in full, so reflect carefully about whether this is feasible, and manage the expectations of your investors accordingly.

Ordinary Share Purchase Agreement

If you decide instead to set the valuation of the F&F round at the time it takes place, your investors will purchase ordinary shares with their invested capital. They will need to sign a simple share purchase agreement that outlines the terms of their investment. Your F&F round will likely be the only round of financing in which you have the opportunity to structure the investment terms. Take advantage of this and work with your advisors to keep it clean and simple. Because of the personal relationship issues inherent in F&F financing, it is even more essential to pay the most careful attention to how the transaction is structured and conducted. Your goal is to maximise both the existence and appearance of fairness, professionalism and prudence.

F&F rounds are normally structured as a purchase of ordinary shares. Friends and family investors do not contribute the expertise or value to justify the rights and privileges awarded to preference shareholders nor does the small amount of capital they invest support the more complex structure of preference shares (see **Chapter 9** for more detail on these).

A brief share purchase agreement for the F&F purchase of ordinary shares is all that is needed to keep the deal clean and professional. The agreement would generally include the following key clauses:

- **Voting rights**: Ordinary shareholders have one vote per share and typically vote together as a class to elect one member to represent their interests on the Board of Directors.

- **Proxy voting**: A less common clause that is worth considering is a proxy voting term. Under such a term, the shareholder transfers their voting rights to the company's management. The transfer of voting rights can either be permanent (an 'irrevocable proxy') or temporary until the shareholder revokes it (a 'revocable proxy'). Since the company management and the F&F shareholders both hold ordinary shares, their interests should be aligned in any shareholder vote, so there is every reason to believe that allowing management to vote F&F share votes should not introduce any conflicts. From the company's perspective, obtaining proxy voting rights can be faster and more convenient than tracking down individual shareholders for a vote or signature, particularly if the F&F round consists of many individuals, or of individuals located in several different geographic locations. Proxies are often drawn up in a very brief separate agreement, particularly if they are revocable. A sample revocable proxy agreement can be found in **Appendix 4**.

- **Pre-emption right**: Irish company law awards pre-emption rights to ordinary shareholders automatically, unless the company 'dis-applies' this provision in its Articles of Association. The pre-emption right gives investors the right (but not the obligation) to invest in later rounds of financing up to a level that allows them to preserve their percentage ownership in the company. If the right is dis-applied, the investors theoretically can be excluded from later rounds of financing. In practice, even if you dis-apply the pre-emption right, you still have the choice (but not the obligation) to offer investors the opportunity to invest in later rounds.

  Pre-emption rights can be cumbersome if you have a lot of small investors, since the implementation of this right will require you to provide specified amounts of time for investors to consider the investment, make their decision, and respond to the company, which can slow down a financing. On the other hand, most entrepreneurs look for as much participation in future rounds of financing as they can get, so they don't mind awarding this right. Base your decision on whether to award pre-emption rights on the number of investors you have and their interest and likelihood of participating in a later round of financing.

- **Restriction on transfer of shares**: This is an important term for the company. The ability to transfer ordinary shares is usually restricted, since the company's interest lies in limiting share ownership to known parties. With the exception of certain transfers required by law, such as to a deceased shareholder's estate, ordinary shareholders should be severely restricted in their ability to sell or assign their shares to other third parties.

- **Information rights**: Ordinary shareholders are entitled under Irish law to receive a copy of the annual financial statements that the company must submit to the CRO. Of course, the company can award additional rights that would allow investors to receive other financial information, although it is usually not worth the administrative burden to do so. The company is always free to provide additional information, and it is less cumbersome to have the choice to do so, rather than the obligation.

The ordinary share purchase agreement usually also will include standard representations and warranties. A more detailed outline of ordinary share purchase agreement terms can be found in **Appendix 5**. A much more detailed discussion of these and other investment terms can be found in **Chapter 9**.

IS MIXING BUSINESS & FRIENDSHIP A GOOD IDEA?

The main drawback of F&F capital is that it requires mixing personal relationships and business, which is never simple and often inadvisable. The risk of a ruined relationship, or a family dispute over money, can be enough to prevent some entrepreneurs from even approaching their close friends or family. Raising money from friends and family requires a delicate balance of business and personal concerns.

F&F investors are usually unsophisticated investors, insofar as they generally have little or no experience in making private equity investments. Therefore, the onus is on you to assess and invite into the F&F round only individuals who accept that they may lose their investment, and, more importantly, can afford that loss. Be particularly wary of taking capital from friends and family who may want to help, but for whom an investment is a real financial strain or sacrifice.

Because your friends and family probably won't have the investment experience to assess accurately the risks of the investment, it is essential to deal openly and candidly with the possibility of business failure. While no one expects or hopes for anything but success, you and your F&F investors must be able to live with the very real possibility that the business may not succeed. It is your job to manage their expectations to include the possibility of failure. Your friends and family must be prepared to accept the financial consequences of the loss of their investment, as well as the more personal impact of anger, guilt, disappointment and resentment that might follow failure. Although it may be difficult to temper your enthusiasm for your new venture, it is important not to be overly optimistic to your friends and family, who believe in you and will be inclined to take you at your word.

Even if your investors are reasonably sophisticated, mixing your business and personal relationships may not be a good idea. For example, one entrepreneur began his first venture with a round of F&F capital. During the round, he was able to raise capital from several former colleagues, who he assumed had a good understanding of the industry and the risks of investing in a start-up. His company made very promising progress, raised venture capital and was considering an IPO, before it fell victim to an industry downturn. Ultimately, the company was sold for a fire sale price that did not return any capital to investors. One of the entrepreneur's colleagues, who was a successful industry consultant, has not spoken to him since. The colleague holds the entrepreneur personally responsible for losing his investment, and blames him for the failure of the company. Because of a €7,500 investment, and a misunderstanding about risk tolerance, their friendship is over.

One of the most important things to realise is that accepting an investment in your business from friends and family will affect the dynamic of your personal relationships. By accepting F&F funds, you establish a legal shareholder relationship between each individual investor and your company. That relationship gives them a series of legal rights, and imposes on you a series of legal obligations. When it comes to business, you will need to treat Aunt Mary the same as Moneybags Venture Capital Fund. In some cases, this contractual element can be an awkward, and not an altogether welcome, change to a previously social or familial relationship. Consequently, you will likely want to limit the extent to which your new legal and business relationship can encroach on your existing personal relationship. Setting boundaries about when (for example, not at family dinners and weddings) and how much is acceptable to discuss business issues can offer a way to keep the two different dynamics somewhat separate.

Also be aware of the more subtle and unspoken expectations that can emerge after you take money from your friends and family. That new Mercedes you bought may make them question where the money they invested is going – into your pocket or into growing the business.

Similarly, the three-week wine tour in South Africa may seem excessive to your friends and family who feel, rightly or wrongly, that their money is paying for it. And, they may wonder, why aren't you working harder instead of taking a holiday? While no one sets out to look over your shoulder at every personal and business financial decision you make, it can happen, and when it does, it can be awkward for both parties.

The bottom line is that seed-stage investing is risky. If you feel significant concern over someone's investment, for either personal or financial reasons, you must seriously consider whether to accept it. A good litmus test of F&F investing is to have both parties ask themselves whether this investment passes the 'Christmas dinner' test. Will you be able to sit down at the holidays year after year with the people from whom you've accepted money and have everyone feel comfortable and good about the investment, no matter what the outcome? Only if the answer is 'Yes' should you proceed.

PROTECTING YOUR FRIENDS & FAMILY

The nature of ordinary shares leaves few safeguards that an entrepreneur can realistically offer F&F investors. If the company does poorly, ordinary shareholders face the real risk of losing their entire investment. Many entrepreneurs want to guard their friends' and family's investment and seek to structure terms that offer additional protections. Rarely is this a good idea, since unusual provisions attached to ordinary shares are likely to become the subject of negotiation in later rounds, and may have to be eliminated. In addition, most companies taking F&F investments have little in the way of cash to pay even creditors if the business is not performing – consequently, protective terms are generally not useful.

However, there are a few ways that are commonly used to offer a minimum level of protection to F&F shareholders that will not be onerous to later investors, including:

- ♦ Personally guaranteeing their investment by paying back the amount of their investment from your personal resources if your business fails.

- Deciding that you will not personally receive any cash from a liquidation or other exit until your F&F investors have been paid in full (or as close to full as possible).

If your friends and family have the capital and interest to invest in later rounds, providing a pre-emption right that gives your F&F investors the right to preserve their percentage ownership in the company can offer protection against dilution in later rounds. It also can give your F&F investors a way to purchase preference shares with more rights attached.

POST-INVESTMENT

After the investment closes, it is a very good idea to continue to manage the expectations of your F&F investors and keep them informed of the company's progress. Because of your relationship with them, F&F investors are likely to exhibit a higher interest in your company's development than the average investor. It is more effective to manage their curiosity, and your time, with regular proactive communications rather than responding to *ad hoc* requests for information and updates.

A bi-annual or, at minimum, annual, 'shareholder update' can be a useful way to communicate updates to F&F investors. A shareholder update can be a simple three- or four-page summary document sent out by email or hard copy that gives early investors an update on the company's progress, recent sales wins, key hires, anticipated financings and a summary financial snapshot. You can attach copies of any press releases, press coverage or other media the company has received, or a sample of the company's brochure or marketing materials. A sample shareholder update can be found in **Appendix 6**.

If, later on, you raise additional rounds of financing, you should again consider organising a dedicated event to bring your F&F investors together with other ordinary shareholders and your solicitor to give them an overview of the company's progress and proposed round of financing.

THE BOARD OF ADVISORS

Beyond the two Directors required by law, few companies at this early stage see the need to develop a formal Board of Directors. Unless you have exceptional friends and family with relevant experience and expertise, it usually doesn't make sense to put your Aunt Mary and your neighbour on the Board. Particularly if you plan to raise additional rounds of financing, it makes sense to keep your Board very small until later fundraisings, when investors will want to obtain seats.

But, this start-up period is an excellent time to consider creating a Board of Advisors (BoA). A BoA allows you to benefit from the assistance of experienced experts, without the administrative burden and formality of a Board of Directors. The BoA is usually composed of a group of individuals who have agreed to contribute their experience and time to the company on an 'as-needed' basis. They serve as an *ad hoc* resource for the company's management team and do not assume the legal obligations and responsibilities of a Board of Directors. However, the influence of a BoA should not be too comprehensive or ongoing, as individuals who are deemed to provide ongoing advice that the company is 'accustomed to' following may be deemed to be a 'shadow director',[2] which subjects them to all the liability risks of an actual Director.

The BoA is usually formally created and named, but it does not have regular or formal meetings, and may not have any meetings together at all. Entrepreneurs often work with advisors on an *ad hoc* basis over the phone or by email. Advisors can be chosen for any type of experience they bring to the company. They can offer not only their own experience and expertise, but also contacts and referrals to industry experts, customers or investors. A strong BoA adds credibility and reputational weight to your start-up. The BoA is the perfect place for academic or government experts, who would not be suitable for Board of Director seats but could contribute value to your company. Because the BoA is an informal structure, most arrangements do not involve cash compensation, but could include reimbursement for any expenses. However, BoA members generally receive a nominal award of share options.

---

[2]   For more information on shadow directors, see www.odce.ie.

GOVERNMENT PROGRAMMES

For the past decade, the Irish Government has been very involved in the equity financing of domestic small businesses. Government programmes geared towards seed- and early-stage companies offer a way to complete or supplement a F&F round of financing. Key government programmes that you should consider for assistance include:

- Business Expansion Scheme (BES).
- County & City Enterprise Boards.
- Enterprise Ireland (EI).
- EquityNetwork / InterTradeIreland.
- Seed Capital Scheme (SCS).

Some of the agencies provide other services to start-up companies in addition to financing, as noted below.

Business Expansion Scheme

The BES is a source of very early-stage financing that has been in existence since 1984. Companies can obtain up to €1,000,000 of equity capital from a BES fund or BES investors. To be eligible to participate in the BES scheme, your business must meet the criteria for being designated a 'qualifying company', you must receive the money from 'qualifying investors', and you can only sell ordinary shares in a BES financing (called, you guessed it, 'qualifying shares'). Finally, you must use the capital raised for one of several approved purposes. Detailed conditions for BES participation can be found and reviewed at www.revenue.ie.

BES investors are private individuals who can receive up to €31,750 in annual tax relief for their participation in the BES. The investors can invest in companies directly, or can invest through a Designated Fund (for example, the Davy BES Fund), which will then invest in a portfolio of BES qualified companies. BES investors must hold their investment for a minimum of five years to avail of the full tax relief, so most investors will seek an exit after that time period has passed.

Companies taking BES funding should be aware that there can be significant exit pressure, including redemption, from individual investors and from BES funds, once the five-year mark has passed and there are no further tax benefits. The BES is currently expected to run through to December 2006.

County & City Enterprise Boards

Ireland's 35 County & City Enterprise Boards are focused on helping very early-stage companies with fewer than 10 employees. They offer a range of grant programmes for selected early-stage companies, as well as low interest loans. The 'equity financing' offered by the Enterprise Boards typically takes the form of redeemable preference shares, which are an equity investment that gives investors the right to 'redeem' (demand repayment of) their investment. In practice then, these equity investments function more like loans.

In addition to financing, the Enterprise Boards offer business mentoring, start-up assistance and classes, networking events, case studies and resources for entrepreneurs. More information is available at www.enterpriseboards.ie.

Enterprise Ireland

Enterprise Ireland offers grants and equity financing for manufacturing or internationally traded services companies, as well as for 'high potential start-ups' (HPSUs), primarily in the technology industry. Before EI will make an equity investment in a company, it requires that its capital be matched or exceeded by one or more private equity investors, which can include the management team, the BES, friends and family, angels or VCs.

EI also funds a number of venture capital firms through its 'Seed & Venture Capital Programme'. Historically, these venture capital firms have invested in high technology companies located in Dublin. Of investments made under the Seed & Venture Capital Programme, over 80% were in the software and communications industry and over ²/₃rds in Dublin-based firms. Be aware that some of these funds are very small in size (less than €25 million of investible capital) and, because of that, have a lower probability of surviving over the long term. For instance, of the 15 funds established under the 1994-1999 Programme, 40% (six of the funds) are no longer making new investments as of mid-2005. This introduces a risk to the company that the venture capital firm will not have sufficient funds to invest in later rounds of financing. In addition, if a venture capital firm is no longer actively investing, it also means that it is likely to be unavailable to offer the company any of the 'value-added' services that venture capitalists provide such as strategic help, operational assistance, or access to the firm's network of contacts.

In addition to financing, EI offers a rich and valuable selection of other services to young companies. Many entrepreneurs sing the praises of EI's network of 34 international offices. Located in key cities like New York, Tokyo, Sydney, Shanghai and Silicon Valley, they provide assistance with introductions to potential customers, partners, suppliers and advisors as well as marketing and sales assistance. Several of the offices have office space that is available to Irish companies to rent for limited periods of time. For more information, see www.enterprise-ireland.com.

EquityNetwork / Inter*Trade*Ireland

Following research which showed that promoting private equity is the key to accelerating business growth among new ventures, small and expanding businesses and inward investors, Inter*Trade*Ireland developed EquityNetwork, a detailed education and awareness programme on the benefits and availability of private equity.

EquityNetwork provides the following services:

- ♦ An island-wide education programme to raise the awareness and use of private equity for accelerating business growth.
- ♦ Free advisory services to businesses to assist in making them 'investor-ready'.
- ♦ Signposting and advice for businesses seeking equity finance.
- ♦ The promotion and development of a comprehensive island-wide non-executive director network available to businesses.
- ♦ An island-wide Centre-of-Excellence on private equity and related matters.

On an all-Ireland basis, Inter*Trade*Ireland frequently sponsors events geared towards start-ups. It is a partner in HaloNI, a business angel match-making service in Belfast. It also sponsors the annual All-Ireland Seedcorn Competition, which awards up to €100,000 for the winning business plan. More information can be found at www.intertradeireland.com.

Seed Capital Scheme

The Seed Capital Scheme provides a tax subsidy to entrepreneurs. It applies to entrepreneurs who invest their own capital in a 'qualifying company', in which they are a full time employee or Director. Those entrepreneurs can claim back their own previously-paid personal income tax for the past six years, up to the amount they have invested in their company. The total relief they can claim is limited to either the lower of:

- Total personal income taxes paid by the entrepreneur in the past six years, or
- An overall income cap of €182,240.

Companies in which the entrepreneur invests must be certified by one of several designated authorities as being a 'qualifying company'. 'Internationally traded services' companies, such as most high technology firms, must meet the additional requirement of having already received grant aid or an equity investment from an Irish industrial agency, such as EI. Detailed information on the full guidelines and requirements for the SCS can be found at www.revenue.ie. The SCS is currently scheduled to continue until December 2006.

Other Government Programmes

There are many more examples of both Government and private sector supports for small businesses. The menu of Government programmes available to help young companies changes over time. New initiatives are introduced and old ones fade away. To keep up with recent changes, check www.startingabusinessinireland.com.

Another possible source of support are the Enterprise Platform Programmes in Cork, Dublin, Dundalk and Waterford. The M50 Enterprise Programme is one of these and is run by four academic institutions located on the M50 corridor (Nova/UCD, DCU and the Institutes of Technology in Blanchardstown and Tallaght). Based at IT Tallaght, it is a 12-month programme offering office space, mentor and coaching resources, training opportunities, and financial assistance in the form of a small stipend of €550 per month. It is designed for early-stage 'innovative and knowledge-based' businesses.

Companies in Dublin can also apply to the Digital Hub, a Government-sponsored office incubation space with reasonable lease terms and rental rates. The Digital Hub is a Government initiative to create a 'Digital Enterprise Area' in Dublin city centre and to support the development of digital media enterprises. As of September 2005, more than 50 companies are currently located there.

Pros & Cons of Public Capital

Availing of Government financing offers a number of clear advantages:

- It is relatively easy to access.
- Once you obtain the financing and become a client, you have access to all the other resources of the agency, such as grants, loans and invitations to events organised for entrepreneurs and small businesses.
- The Government is a passive investor that will rarely seek a Board seat or position of control within the company.
- Public investors are also patient investors. They will seldom press for a short-term exit or minimum returns.

On the other hand, obtaining equity from Government programmes can be a cumbersome and bureaucratic process that takes considerable time to complete. It may require working with staff who possess little or no investment and business experience and add little value besides capital to your venture. It can require lengthy forms and approval processes that fail to acknowledge the urgency and pragmatism that characterise most start-ups.

Because Government financing programmes don't focus solely on generating financial returns, public equity can introduce competing objectives such as economic development, regional growth, or a focus on narrow metrics like increases in employment that are not meaningful to developing companies. One entrepreneur who was raising public capital was surprised at how often he was asked how many jobs he planned to create and where in the country the jobs would be located. He had come prepared with information and projections of revenue and sales growth, and customer adoption but went away feeling that the funders were much more concerned with regional jobs growth, to the exclusion of traditional business metrics.

Accepting capital from the Government may also have a neutral to negative effect on your company's reputation. Because the Government is not a sophisticated or dedicated investor, there is little cachet or reputational benefit that accrues to the company from taking public capital.

CONCLUSION

Friends and family capital is a critical source of seed- and early-stage financing for start-up companies. At the very earliest stages of your company's development, the relatively small amount of capital you can raise from friends and family can make a critical difference to your ability to finance growth. The F&F round of financing is the easiest and quickest capital you will raise. Yet it is important to take the time and care to:

- Think broadly but carefully about whose money to accept.
- Conduct the fundraising professionally.
- Consider setting the valuation at the next round of financing and structuring this F&F round using a convertible loan.
- Contemplate the possible consequences of mixing business and personal relationships.

Your goal upon closing this round of finance is to obtain the capital you need to continue financing the growth of your company, while structuring a clean, simple and reasonably-valued round that will be attractive to later investors.

7
BUSINESS ANGELS

O, What may man within him hide, though angel on the outward side!
William Shakespeare

'Business angels' are like actual angels – great in theory, but hard to find in real life. Angels are wealthy individuals, many of them former entrepreneurs, who invest their own capital in emerging companies. They invest for predominantly financial returns, but many angels are also interested in actively working with the company and 'giving back' some of their experience and knowledge to help a new business get off the ground. They are frequently referred to as 'smart money', in recognition of the valuable business expertise they can bring to a start-up or early-stage company.

If your company is too early and small for VCs, but too large for all but the wealthiest friends and family, seeking angel financing is probably the right strategy. Angels invest alone or as part of a group, usually in amounts that can range from €10,000 to €500,000. Internationally, angels are by far the most common source of financing for early- and growth-stage companies.

PREPARING TO RAISE ANGEL CAPITAL

Angel financing represents the first round of financing in which you will be evaluated based on the merits of your business, rather than your personal relationship with individuals. This clearly calls for some degree of professional preparation. Although angels are not as comprehensive and standardised about their company research as VCs, you must still be prepared to make a compelling presentation and back it up with a credible and concrete business plan.

Investors regularly complain about reading a business plan or sitting through a presentation and still not clearly understanding what the company *does*. They key to a good pitch is: clarity, clarity, clarity, followed by conciseness.

Your goal is to communicate your business opportunity and objectives. Say what you do, who is going to pay you for it, and how much. Note who your potential customers are and what pain point you solve for them (it is always much more compelling if your customers need, rather than want, your product). Add a sentence or two about the management team and finish with a line about the exit strategy and expected return. Leave the detailed technology discussion to the business plan.

To prepare to meet angel investors, you will need:

- An executive summary of your business and its accomplishments.
- Description of the management team.
- Business plan.
- Competitive analysis.
- Full financials.
- Financing strategy.
- A plan for an exit.

Angel investors do not have the due diligence infrastructure and staff that VCs do, so the more information you can provide pro-actively to help them to evaluate your company, the faster the decision-making process will be.

What Angels Seek

To be successful, companies seeking equity financing beyond the F&F round must possess a number of minimum key characteristics that equity investors seek:

- Strong and experienced management.
- An attractive and timely exit.
- Large and growing market.
- Very rapid growth and potential for scale.
- A unique and proprietary product.

There are many other qualities investors require but, without these critical elements, which are described in more detail below, your business is unlikely to be successful in attracting the interest of potential equity investors.

Strong and experienced management

If real estate investors look for 'location, location, location', then it is an equal truism that equity investors seek 'people, people, people'. From this round forward, your management team will be the most important driver of investor interest. Your executive summary and business plan should detail your team's background, experience and expertise.

Present yourself and your team as if answering the question 'Why should *you* run this business?'. Particularly in the early stages, it is likely that you will not have a large management team. It is perfectly acceptable for your team to be small initially, consisting of only two or three members, but you should be able to present job specifications and a recruiting plan for future hires, to convince investors that the strategy to build a management team exists and has been carefully and thoughtfully prepared. If the experience you need is not available in Ireland, be prepared to recruit from abroad, or in one of the key markets that you do business.

Why is management so important? Primarily because execution – that is, actually getting the job done – is the most crucial factor for the success of any young business. Conventional wisdom holds that good ideas are a dime a dozen but that good execution is rare. Therefore, investors seek people who have demonstrated experience in successfully executing a business plan. Investors are also aware that businesses rarely grow according to plan and that new and rapidly-growing markets are inherently unstable. Attractive management teams demonstrate that they have the skills to respond to changes and to engineer the inevitable mid-course corrections that will continue to drive a company to success. Therefore, serial entrepreneurs represent the ultimate in 'investible' people.

In addition to demonstrable experience, intangible characteristics like ambition, drive and passion are also important to investors, as these qualities inspire confidence that the team has the desire and attitude to make the business successful.

An attractive and timely exit

Investors are ultimately in the business of realising returns on their invested capital. To realise returns, they need a way to exit or sell their investment and to get their money out of your company. As part of their investment decision, equity investors assess the possibility and probability of an attractive and timely exit. You should be aware that an exit is the key investor objective and be prepared to explain the type and timing of exit that you expect. Investors are ideally seeking the probability of high returns through an IPO or trade sale exit within three to seven years (depending on the stage of your company at the time of investment).

Not every entrepreneur is interested in driving towards an exit. Many enjoy running and slowly growing their own business in a way that provides an attractive income and lifestyle for themselves and their family. Investors refer to these as 'lifestyle' businesses and, while they may be profitable, they are not appropriate for equity finance.

A large and growing market

Think big. The market in which your business operates should be growing and potentially very large. As a general rule, equity investors seek company growth that comes from identifying and dominating attractive *new* markets, not stealing market share in existing markets.

Investors are interested in understanding the specific market into which you are selling and must be convinced that you possess a detailed and expert knowledge of it. Entrepreneurs very frequently botch this opportunity to present a compelling market story by calculating their market size using the entire market, defined in its broadest terms, and projecting a small percentage share to capture. A common statement in business plans goes like this:

> *The chocolate bar market in the UK is a €1 billion market and, if we get just 1% of it, we will have a €100 million company!*

Be warned that investors will view such calculations as inaccurate and superficial and, worse, as a signal that the management team does not have a strong and deep understanding of their market. All large markets are highly segmented, whether by geography, price, type of customer or a variety of other factors, and an accurate assessment of potential market penetration must take such factors into account. So, a better assessment of the market from the example above might say:

> *The chocolate bar market in the UK is a €1 billion market overall, and our niche of gourmet handmade organic chocolate bars is currently a €150 million market, growing at 30-40% per year.*

It is critical to demonstrate that you understand how your market is segmented, your customers, the growth rate of your niche, your price point, and where you fit in the overall market space before approaching investors.

Very rapid growth and scale

Equity investors are not seeking the stability of steady cash-flow or an ongoing stream of dividends. Instead, they are looking for tremendous increases in revenues in the first three to five years of a company's growth, and the potential to develop into a large-scale company. For Irish companies, the size and scale of growth that will interest investors will not come from the domestic market alone, but from significant international sales as well. Therefore, your plan to investors will need to include details of your plan for establishing a presence in overseas markets.

When preparing to meet angels, define how you will reach and attract customers in your market. Be concrete about how you plan to identify, contact and win customers:

- Are there customers you will target for beta testing?
- Who are they?
- How will you reach them?
- Who are the first 10 customers you will target for sales?
- Do you have a process for tracking and managing your sales pipeline?
- What is your pitch?

The more precisely and realistically you describe your current or expected sales process, then the more likely it is that your growth and revenue projections will be perceived as credible.

If they say that actions speak louder than words, then the market speaks louder than any business plan. At this point in your company's growth, any concrete market validation of your product is enormously advantageous. The best proof of your product is a customer. Ideally, the customer pays for your product, but even a beta customer who is interested enough to test it is a compelling endorsement.

A unique and proprietary product

Investors look for cutting-edge products that offer an innovative solution to a demonstrable customer problem. Be prepared to tell investors about the 'pain point' your customers experience and how your product solves it. Intellectual property protection, proprietary technology, exclusive agreements with key customers or suppliers, or other significant barriers to entry faced by competitors, all contribute to a product's uniqueness and will capture investor attention.

A competitive analysis is an excellent way to demonstrate the value and uniqueness of your product or technology. An extremely common mistake made by entrepreneurs is to say that they have no competition. Unfortunately, this is almost never true and saying it can ruin your credibility with investors. Direct, indirect and potential competition exists in every market and your competitive analysis must address all three.

Some questions your competitive analysis could address include:

- Who are your direct and indirect competitors?
- How do they identify and approach customers?
- What is their price point?
- What features and benefits do they offer?
- What level of service?
- How does what they offer differ from your product?
- Who are the existing players in your industry who could follow into your market with a competing product?
- What is the financial and marketing position of these companies? Could they afford to subsidise their offering or initiate a price war?

- How quickly could a new entrant develop and sell a similar offering to yours? Where would this potential competition originate?

Demonstrating a detailed understanding of the competition is essential to impressing investors, and will convince them that you have done your homework and can successfully position and sustain your product in the market.

FINDING AN ANGEL

Finding an angel can be difficult – after all, it's not like they advertise. Serial angels report that they rarely do deals that come in to them 'cold', without a referral from a credible source that they trust. Therefore, the best way to identify and contact an angel is through personal or professional referrals such as friends and colleagues, accountants, solicitors and other entrepreneurs in your industry. Industry consultants, professional associations and other companies are also good sources of introductions. Former entrepreneurs in your industry who have moved away from the daily management of a growing company (for example, retired or taken on a chairman of the Board role) are another possibility for angel capital or referrals. Perhaps the easiest way to find angels is through your relationships with the advisors that you have selected to help grow your company. Because they work on fundraisings and other equity deals, accounting firms and law firms can be an excellent source of referrals.

One Irish entrepreneur successfully raised angel financing by working with his banker to raise capital from a group of investors in the bank's private client group. He was able to raise a total of €220,000.

Angel investors are generally parochial about their investments and prefer to invest in local deals close to home. Given the very limited supply of angel capital in Ireland, you may have to turn to local angels in the overseas markets in which you have offices. There can be strategic advantages to working with angels in other locations. They are a good source of introductions and referrals to local VCs, which can help create a competitive bidding situation during your next round of financing. Investors located in the geographic areas where you do business can also assist your company by referring you to potential customers, suppliers, or employees with industry experience.

Finding an Angel Network

Angel networks are easier to find than individual angels. They will often have a website or be a member of an angel network association, such as the European Business Angel Network (www.eban.org) or the British Business Angels Association (www.bbaa.org.uk).

Angel networks or syndicates are groups of angels who have joined together, formally or informally, to invest together in deals, share due diligence and expertise, and pool their pipeline of potential deals. Working with a network can be easier than working with individual angels since a network will usually have:

- Clear investment criteria.
- A professional process for evaluating opportunities.
- Greater amounts of capital to invest than individual angels.
- Prior investment experience that can be reference-checked.
- A track record of doing reasonable and professional deals that appeal to later investors.
- More experience in making early-stage investments and working with young companies.

Since there are no formally-organised angel networks in Ireland, consider the possibility of finding a network in other markets in which you have significant operations. For example, if your company has a London office or does a fair amount of business in the UK, refer to EBAN to identify possible investor networks in England and Northern Ireland. In the US, there are a variety of angel networks across the country that can be identified by state through the Angel Capital Association.

CHOOSING AN ANGEL

Angels are like snowflakes – every one is unique. Unlike VCs, whose motivations are consistently focused on generating returns, angels bring a variety of motivations, objectives and even eccentricities to their investment activities.

In my experience, there are several types of angels:

- **The technology guru**: Angels with industry expertise, who love your technology or product and want to work with you to help it succeed.
- **The teacher**: These angels are often former entrepreneurs who have successfully built and exited their own companies. They are often seeking an active mentoring role with a young company, or a way to 'give back' to a fellow entrepreneur.
- **The status-seeker**: Angels who are cashed-out or retired entrepreneurs may bring an ego component to their investment decision, in that they are looking for the 'status' of taking a Board seat or actively working with a start-up.
- **The investor**: Angels for whom the decision to invest contains no emotional component and is strictly a rational investment decision, based on their assessment of the financial returns they expect from your deal.
- **The portfolio manager**: Angels who have no entrepreneurial experience in building a company or running a business but are simply wealthy individuals, who believe that investing in private companies as an asset class is a good financial strategy.
- **The 'virgin angel'**: New angels, who have never before made an investment, are commonly called 'virgin angels'. These angels are risky to work with, since you won't be able to obtain any references for them as investors. Their behaviour will be more unpredictable than serial investors'.

What is more important than the type of angel you target or attract is the relationship you develop. Once the deal closes, the personality of your investor and the chemistry between you will become increasingly important. The most productive investor relationships are based on the premise of a partnership. You are looking for an investor whom you respect, trust and like, and who understands and agrees with your own objectives and values for the business.

One founder of a medical technology company, for instance, raised his angel round of €700,000 primarily from 18 angels, who purchased 27% of the company. Twelve of the angels were doctors who had a strong belief in the potential medical application of his technology, but no experience as entrepreneurs or in business. They were all 'virgin angels'. Nonetheless, this entrepreneur was fortunate, as the physicians turned out to be very good angels. They provided excellent industry references, and two of the doctors were able to convince their hospitals to become customers of the company. When the company raised its next round of financing from venture capitalists, the doctors were very helpful and co-operative to the new investors and several chose to participate in the financing.

Another entrepreneur of a start-up technology company had a much different experience. He raised his angel round of €250,000 from three individuals in the construction business, who had no entrepreneurial or industry experience, and no history of investing in private companies. The investors obtained 50% of the company for their investment, and two Board seats. The angels were a convenient source of capital, but did not provide any additional help to the company after their investment. Moreover, when the company began raising a second round of financing, the angels became unco-operative and obstructionist. Because it is extremely difficult (and usually impossible) to attract new investors to a company in which existing investors are hostile and difficult, the angels were able to hold the company hostage over the new round of financing and demand that their investment terms be renegotiated before they would co-operate. They refused to give up their Board seats, and insisted that their investment be made redeemable, on terms that guaranteed them a very substantial return. It became clear from their demands that they were only interested in their own investment, not in helping to build the company. This new deal structure and the antagonistic and selfish attitude of the angels has made it very challenging for the company to attract new investors, and may even render it unable to raise future capital. The company's angels could kill the business. As of this writing, the company is still, after eight months, trying to raise its second round.

Evaluating Angels

While there are positives and negatives to working with each type of angel, the key is to identify and know your angel investor, so that you can understand:

- Their motivations and objectives for making the investment.
- Their likely future behaviour.

To assess this, you will have to undertake your own reference-checking on your potential investor. This does not imply a formal or rigorous process, but rather calling and talking to entrepreneurs of companies in which the angel has previously invested, to evaluate their post-investment involvement, attitude and behaviour. For instance, you may want to ask:

- To what types of situations / issues have the angels brought the most expertise and assistance?
- What value have they added? Have they provided introductions and referrals to investors, customers or suppliers? Or are they just a source of capital?
- How have they behaved when the business has not gone according to plan or the company has missed its projections?
- Did the company need follow-on capital and did the investor provide it?
- Have they been supportive in later rounds of financing? Do they participate in follow-on rounds?
- Are they active or passive investors? To what level are they involved in the company's operations? On the company's Board?
- Would you work with this angel again?

It is also helpful to gauge the size of the investment in your company, relative to other investments the angel has made. If your company is the first, or the largest, investment the angel has made, and things go sideways or poorly, you may have an inexperienced and nervous investor on your hands.

Similarly, evaluate how deep your angel's pockets are. First, you want to understand their capacity to participate in follow-on investments. Second, you want to assess your risk that the angel will have liquidity problems that affect their behaviour as an investor in your company. The angel whose house renovations have gone over budget, and left him feeling a little pinched, could renege on promises to provide follow-on support in later rounds, or push prematurely for an exit. Finally, angels who have liquidity issues, and are faced with losing a significant percentage or all of their investment can become greedy, obstructionist and difficult if your company experiences below-plan performance, or is forced to consider a liquidation.

The point of this reference-checking is for you to learn about what types of behaviour your angel may exhibit as an investor. If you have an idea about what to expect, you can talk in advance with your angel about similar situations, or you can work with your solicitor to try and prevent through the deal structure the angel's ability to exert a negative influence.

DUE DILIGENCE

Angels tend to be much less standardised and rigid in their pre-investment research than professional investors, but most will want to conduct at least some due diligence on your company prior to investment. To expedite the process, put together a basic due diligence binder that you can provide to interested angels and thus jumpstart the process.

The basic binder should include:

- Corporate documents and a capitalisation table.
- Detailed management biographies and full CVs.
- A full set of financial statements: any historical and 3-year projected.
- Competitive analysis – a competitive analysis matrix, table or other review of the competition.
- Detailed information on your product / technology – patents, research / white papers, and market data / research.
- An up-to-date sales / distribution pipeline.
- Information on any customers.

7: Business Angels

This information will get the potential investor working on your deal, while you respond to any specific requests they may have for more information.

VALUING AN ANGEL ROUND

Since the angel round is often the first financing that sets a firm valuation on the company, it is extremely important for entrepreneurs to avoid the frequent mistake of selling too much equity too early. A very common error is for young companies to take the first terms they are offered, without seeking market validation of the price, or legal review of the terms. As a result, they sell so much equity in the early rounds that there is too little left during later rounds to motivate the management team.

As a rule, sophisticated serial angels and angel networks are more familiar with local investing norms, including acceptable deal structures and valuations. With less experienced angels, valuing a round of financing can be more difficult and the risk is higher that the deal will be mis-priced. The best solution, if you are dealing with a novice or infrequent angel investor, is to validate the proposed valuation with other entrepreneurs and advisors. If it is your first round of capital, you can consider valuing the round at a discount to an expected future round of financing from VCs, through the use of a convertible loan. This option is much more attractive to VCs than restructuring and fixing a deal that was mis-priced. Again, educating yourself about local market conditions and working with an experienced advisor are your best protections against doing a badly-priced deal.

STRUCTURING AN ANGEL ROUND

Angel financing terms are often proposed by the company. In that case, you and your solicitor will create the investment terms and deal structure. Your goal is to structure the angel investment to be simple, uncomplicated and standard by local norms. It is important to manage the structure of the investment so that it presents no impediments or obstacles for future rounds. A badly-structured angel deal could discourage professional investors from making a later investment.

Sophisticated serial angels or angel networks are more likely to propose an investment with their own deal terms and structure. Generally speaking, the more experienced the angel investor, the better the structure of the deal because they are more aware of, and experienced with, the requirements of later rounds of financing.

Ordinary Share Deal

The best structure for an angel round is the purchase of ordinary shares. It is simple, clean and attractive to later investors. A clean angel deal for a group of individual angels would consist largely of the same ordinary share purchase and terms as a F&F round (see **Appendix 5** for a detailed outline of ordinary share purchase agreement terms), although the terms might be slightly modified, as described below, for an angel round:

- **Voting rights**: Ordinary shareholders receive one vote per share. They also vote along with all other ordinary shareholders as a class to elect a Director to the Board.

- **Board of Directors:** At this stage of your company, it is appropriate to have a small Board of three Directors to oversee governance issues. An ideal structure for the Board would be one or two executive, or inside, Directors (such as the CEO and founder) and one outside independent Director. This structure allows you to begin to hold Board meetings and establish good corporate governance practices and oversight, while also allowing space for the addition of investor Directors or other outside Directors as the company continues to grow.

    If you have been fortunate enough to receive an investment from an experienced angel in your industry who could provide valuable operational or strategic assistance to the company, it may be appropriate to appoint that angel to the Board, or to grant the angel investors the right to elect their own representative to the Board. If your angels are simply wealthy individuals with no real expertise to bring to your business, do not grant them a Board seat, and try to avoid awarding them the right to appoint a specific Director to the Board.

- **Proxy voting rights**: Angel investors are usually wealthy individuals with a lot of other activities going on in their lives.

They are often busy successful people, who travel frequently and can be hard to reach on short notice. As a result, it is wise to negotiate and sign a revocable proxy voting agreement that allows the company to vote the angel shares along with the company (see **Appendix 4** for a sample revocable proxy agreement).

- **Pre-emption rights**: If you have not dis-applied these rights in your company's Articles of Association, all the angel investors automatically will have the right (but not the obligation) to participate in each subsequent round of financing up to an amount that maintains their percentage ownership in the company (this is commonly referred to as *pro rata* participation). If you have dis-applied the pre-emption right, you have the choice (but not the obligation) to offer the investors the ability to participate in future rounds.

  You might also consider limiting the pre-emption rights through a 'play or pay' clause (described further in **Chapter 9**), which says that, if the angels do not invest in any subsequent round of financing, they lose the right to invest in any other future rounds. This provides the incentive to participate in every round, in order to maintain their percentage ownership.

- **Restriction on share transfers**: As with F&F investors, severely restrict the angel's right to sell or transfer shares in the company.

- **Information rights**: With the exception of annual financials required to be filed at the CRO, private companies are not required to disclose financial information, even to their investors. Some angels may request the right to receive ongoing financial information that allows them to monitor the company's progress. Usual requests for information include unaudited quarterly financials, an annual budget, and unaudited annual financials within 30 days of year-end.

  If you do award additional information rights, ensure that you can fulfil the obligation by sending the information electronically (which saves the company the time and cost of a mailing). Also require the investors either to sign a confidentiality agreement about the information they will receive or to waive their rights to additional information.

What does a badly-structured angel deal look like? Most commonly, it is mis-priced. If the angel round has been over-priced, with too high a valuation, later investors will be dissuaded from investing. If they believe the deal is over-priced, they will not want to pay the same or higher valuation, and few new investors find the idea of initiating a down round attractive. If the deal has been under-priced at too low a valuation, the angels will own so much equity that the next round of financing introduces the risk that management will have insufficient ownership to remain motivated.

A badly-structured angel deal is also one in which angels have too much control over key business decisions. For instance, the angels may have secured veto rights over certain decisions (such as approving a subsequent round of financing), or they have 50% or more of the Board seats. A final red flag is an angel round that is comprised of inexperienced and unsophisticated angels or includes unusual or complex terms.

Preference Share Deal

In the eyes of a VC, there is more tolerance for structuring an angel deal with preference shares if the investors are experienced former entrepreneurs, serial angels or angel networks. Even in those cases, however, the deal should be structured so the preference shares are very simple, with limited rights and privileges. Otherwise, excessive rights could become the subject of a renegotiation, or even an obstacle, in later rounds.

In addition to the voting, proxy voting, pre-emption and information rights above, preference terms that are reasonable to include in an angel round are described below. A much more detailed description of each term, and how they can be structured, can be found in **Chapter 9**. The key terms are:

- **Dividends**: Preference shares almost always have the right to receive dividends, yet start-up companies rarely declare and pay them. Therefore, angels should not be granted dividend rights that are mandatory (that is, rights that must be paid).
- **Liquidation preference**: The liquidation preference is a critical term. It gives preference shareholders the right to receive their capital back ahead of ordinary shareholders, in the event of a

winding up or sale of the company. A modest liquidation preference that gives the angels the right to their original investment amount back is reasonable. A very detailed discussion of liquidation preferences, and how they work, is provided in **Chapter 9**.

- **Anti-dilution protection**: This protection limits the percentage ownership the angel investor can lose in a subsequent 'down round' financing. Either no, or moderate, anti-dilution protection (called 'weighted average' and described further in **Chapter 9**) is acceptable. If the angels are awarded moderate protection, the right to that protection should be contingent upon their continued investment in future rounds of financing. If they choose not to participate in a future round, then their anti-dilution protection should be automatically waived in later rounds.
- **Board of Directors**: Unlike ordinary shareholders, preference shareholders are almost always awarded the right to appoint a Director to the Board. Unless you have an exceptional group of experienced and credible angels that have the potential to add tremendous value, they should be granted the right to appoint a maximum of one Director to the Board.

Finally, a standard conversion term that specifies under what conditions the preference shares convert to ordinary shares must be included. As much as possible, avoid awarding angels significant control provisions, particularly the ability to block a later round of financing or the ability to force an exit.

POST-INVESTMENT

As with F&F investors, it is a good idea to create and implement a regular shareholder update to provide information pro-actively to your angel investors (see **Appendix 6** for a sample). This helps to keep the angels informed of the company's progress and aware of opportunities for which they might provide assistance. It also helps investors remain assured that the company is making productive and good use of invested capital. A brief three- or four-page letter sent on a quarterly basis that outlines the key accomplishments of the quarter (sales, revenues, customers won, management hires) and provides high-level financials (balance sheet, profit and loss account and cash flow) is sufficient. These reports should not be time-consuming and elaborate – instead, they should contain key metrics and information that can easily be filled into a standard template format on a regular basis. For lead investors who may have contributed the majority of the angel capital, more detailed or frequent contact, such as a monthly telephone call, may be more appropriate.

CONCLUSION

Angels are a good source of capital for amounts under €500,000. Angels evaluate a business much the same way that a professional investor would, although there is an element of personal motivations and objectives in most angel investments. To raise angel capital, you will need to be prepared with a business plan and presentation and ready to undergo a moderate amount of due diligence.

The primary challenge is to find angel investors. Most angels are found through professional or personal referrals. Irish entrepreneurs are well-advised to seek angel capital in the overseas markets in which they do business. The presence of well-established angel networks and a greater supply of angel investors can make raising capital in the UK or US an appealing option. In Ireland, the supply of angel capital is relatively low and there are no formally-organised domestic angel networks.

The experience, helpfulness and personality of angel investors can vary dramatically. Attracting an experienced entrepreneur with strong industry experience and an accessible network can be hugely beneficial for a young company. It is important to understand, through reference-checking and talking to other investors and entrepreneurs, your angel investors' investing history, business experience, and prior behaviour working with start-ups. Bad angel deals in which the investors are controlling, obstructionist and value-detracting are unfortunately quite common and can be very difficult to fix.

As with the F&F round, structure the simplest and most basic investment agreement you can, preferably with the purchase of ordinary rather than preference shares.

PART III:
PROFESSIONAL INVESTORS

8
VENTURE CAPITALISTS

The Golden Rule: Those who have the gold make the rules.
Anonymous

Venture capitalists (VCs) differ from friends and family and angel investors in that they enjoy the privilege of investing other people's money. They are professional investors, whose job is to generate high returns for their investors. Their success is determined by how well their investments perform, and their reputation is created and maintained by continuously backing successful companies. This pressure to perform drives the venture capital industry.

When you approach a VC, understand that their focus is on generating returns. You must show them how your company can help them do it. Accept and address the fact that their primary interest is making money for their Limited Partners, whose capital they invest.

HOW VENTURE CAPITAL FIRMS OPERATE

Traditional venture capital firms are organised as Limited Partnerships. Within that partnership structure, the venture capitalists are the General Partners (GPs), who manage the daily operations of the firm and make investments. VCs raise money every three to five years from institutions such as pension funds, insurance companies, banks and private investors. These institutions become the firm's Limited Partners (LPs). (Entrepreneurs should enjoy the thought that VCs have their day on the fund-raising side of the table).

With the capital from their LPs, the venture capital firm forms a fund, normally structured to have a lifespan of 10 years. The year that the fund is formed is called its 'vintage' year. A venture capital firm, at any given time, will have several funds active (usually imaginatively named Fund I, Fund II, etc.), each from different vintage years. During the fund's 10 year life, the VC partners source deals, make new investments, take an active role in working with their portfolio companies to help them develop, make follow-on investments, and finally, exit or liquidate the investments. VCs are serial investors. Like serial entrepreneurs, they live off their results. VCs use the returns generated from prior funds to attract LPs to invest in their next fund. If they don't generate competitive returns, they will be unable to attract LPs to invest in their funds, and their firm may cease to exist.

After raising capital from LPs, the next challenge is putting all that money to work, investing it. VCs are under constant pressure to create and maintain good 'deal flow' or a pipeline of investible, high-growth companies seeking investment. To generate the best returns, a VC firm must attract the highest quality entrepreneurs and the most promising companies, have access to the best deal flow from well-respected advisors, and keep successful serial entrepreneurs coming back for repeat investments. VCs cultivate deal flow primarily through their reputation from prior investments. Over time, VCs develop reputations for their ability and willingness to offer entrepreneurs fair investment terms, to act constructively throughout the company's growth cycle, and to provide value-added services such as contacts and referrals. It is worth keeping in mind that a VC's reputation matters and is an important component of their long-term success.

VCs are paid based on their performance. A VC's most significant compensation comes from taking a percentage of the profits of their investments. This compensation is called 'carry' or 'carried interest', and usually amounts to 20% of the profits from any portfolio company exits. The remaining 80% is returned to the fund's LPs. For example, an investment of €5 million into a company that later sold for €25 million would return a net profit of €20 million. The proceeds of that investment would be split so that €16 million (plus the €5 million cost base) is returned to the LPs and €4 million (20%) goes to the VCs for distribution among the VC firm's General Partners.

VC compensation also includes a management fee of a fixed percentage of the capital raised in the fund. Management fees are typically between 2% to 2.5%. For example, a venture fund that raised a €100 million fund would draw down €2 million per year to pay for their offices, salaries, travel, due diligence, conference attendance and other overhead expenses.

PREPARING TO RAISE VENTURE CAPITAL

Raising capital from VCs is a rigorous process. Unlike informal investors, who bring personal motivations and objectives to their investment decisions, VCs will evaluate your company as an investment opportunity, purely on the basis of potential financial return.

One of the first concerns expressed by entrepreneurs preparing to raise venture capital is maintaining the confidentiality of their idea, and whether potential investors will enter into a Non-Disclosure Agreement (NDA). In general, investors will not sign NDAs and some firms even have a policy to that effect. Because individual VCs specialise in specific industry areas and constantly see business plans and talk to entrepreneurs all in the same market space, it is just too risky to sign an NDA. Most entrepreneurs realise this and ultimately send their business plan without the NDA.

Allocate Sufficient Time

Prepare to raise VC by allocating sufficient time to the process. Assume that raising VC will take at least six months and require considerable management time. By far the most common mistake that entrepreneurs make is to significantly underestimate the time it will take to raise and close a round of financing.

For instance, one Irish entrepreneur was raising his first round of venture capital, having raised one small F&F round prior to that. He was about four months into the financing, and was in discussions with two VC firms. The entrepreneur did not anticipate that the financing would take more than one fiscal quarter and was beginning to run low on cash. He approached the most interested VC to discuss the possibility of a small convertible loan to help him cover the next few payrolls until the financing closed. The VC was unwilling to extend a loan to a company in which they weren't 100% certain they were going to invest. Panicked, the entrepreneur was able to raise a portion of the cash he needed from some of his existing F&F investors, but had to borrow the remainder from equity in his house. The VC round took another two and a half months to close.

The consequences of not allocating sufficient time to raise capital fall entirely on you. You sacrifice negotiating leverage and introduce the risk that you may run out of cash if you wait too long to begin raising finance.

Writing the Business Plan

Most VC firms have a section on their website that indicates what they look for in a business plan submission, which is the best place to look. If the investor has taken the time to outline exactly what they want to receive, you are well-served to provide it. For firms that don't provide an outline, there is a sample business plan table of contents in **Appendix 7** that outlines the most commonly critical topics to cover.

The most common complaints VCs have about business plans are that they do not clearly state what the company does and that they are too long. In fact, US venture capital firm Sequoia Capital directly challenges entrepreneurs to develop a clear and concise explanation of their business that they can fit on the back of a business card. While this is a challenging exercise, it does drive home the point that time spent refining your business plan and pitch about what your company does is well-spent.

Investors generally do not read business plans cover to cover. Instead, they tend to go right to the most important parts of the plan:

- **Page 1 of the business plan / the Executive Summary**: Investors go here first, to learn what the company does. This section must be very clear and concise. In order to convey best what your company does, you may find it helpful to include graphical explanations and diagrams. They can capture investor attention better and present your company's product or market niche more vividly.
- **The description of the management team**: Investors are looking for the credibility and experience of the management team, as well as how balanced the team is, both in terms of expertise and in terms of responsibilities and leadership. This section should include detailed bios with past experience, education, and current responsibilities.

- **The financials**: The fundamental tension in projecting and presenting your company's financials is to make them look attractive, yet reasonable. Aggressive and linear revenues, and sales growth projections that are not supported by a solid customer pipeline, are not reasonable. The cost structure should also be very lean, yet realistic. For instance, projecting below-market salaries for new hires is impractical, since VCs know that good talent isn't cheap.

If their interest is still sustained, VCs will look next at the market and competition sections. When writing your plan, focus on developing and refining these key sections.

FINDING A VC

The best way to meet a VC is through a referral. The VC business is relationship-driven and, by their own admission, few VCs end up making investments in companies that come in 'cold' without any personal or professional introduction. There are many ways to find introductions or referrals to VCs. Ask your advisors about investors they have worked with in the past, talk to other entrepreneurs and companies in your industry and ask where they received their funding. If you have raised angel financing, find out who your angel investors know. Ask around and see who the 'friends of the firm' are. At minimum, attend conferences and workshops that VCs attend and make connections in person.

Don't limit yourself to domestic VC firms. The Irish VC industry is small, and Irish companies conduct so much of their business abroad that it makes sense to seek out investors in those locations in which you intend to do business. Geographically, investing has become much more pan-European, and a company formed in Ireland but with significant turnover in the UK, for example, would be an excellent candidate to approach UK investors.

The most critical step to take when beginning a fund-raising is to create and maintain the largest pool of potential investors you can. Ideally, you want to generate the interest of several investors and receive multiple investment offers from which to choose. Yet surprisingly few entrepreneurs conduct a round of financing in a way that is consistent with that objective. It is stunning how frequently entrepreneurs will find one interested investor and cease all other investor-generating activities. A few weeks or months later, if the deal falls through, or the price is low, or the deal terms are onerous, the entrepreneur is left panicked, running out of cash, and with no other options readily available.

One Irish entrepreneur began raising venture capital and obtained a referral to a local venture capitalist. The initial contact was successful and the VC began some preliminary due diligence. During this time, the entrepreneur did not continue identifying or obtaining referrals to other investors, either in Ireland or in the UK, where his company also had an office. A few weeks later, the VC offered the entrepreneur a three-page term sheet with a 45-day exclusive. The entrepreneur signed the term sheet and began working closely with the VC on detailed due diligence. After 30 days, the VC determined that he did not want to make the investment. The entrepreneur had just wasted two-and-a-half months working only with this VC, and had not developed any contingency plan. He was faced with beginning the financing process again, right from the start. This time, the entrepreneur approached the process much more pro-actively – developing a list of investors, seeking several referrals, and aggressively following-up on any interest. In the meantime, he had to significantly slow his company's development in order to conserve the cash needed to make it through the next four to six months that the financing would take. He pushed back the timeline on his company's product launch, put off making any new hires, and tried to keep his customer leads warm until the company began going full throttle again. By the time the financing closed, the entrepreneur had spent close to one year fundraising.

Unfortunately, situations like this happen all the time. To avoid a similar outcome, your objective must always be to attract as much investor interest in your company as possible, and to generate more than one investment offer. You will need to be relentless about identifying, contacting, cultivating and following up with as many investor leads as you can throughout the financing.

CHOOSING A VC

If you are successful at attracting the interest of more than one investor, there are other factors besides price and deal terms to consider when choosing among them. Entrepreneurs who take on equity financing enter a long-term partnership with their investors that will last for several years, until an exit occurs. Therefore, select an investor you think will be a good partner, and one with whom you have good chemistry and rapport. You'll be working together through all your company's ups and downs, so you want to pick an investor that you respect, can trust, and feel like you can talk to candidly. Also look for VCs that bring more than money to the table. The best VCs have a successful investing history. They bring expertise about your industry, and have an excellent network of potential customers, suppliers, investors and employees.

Reference-checking is the best way to get an accurate sense of your investor and any good VC will encourage it. A few phone calls to the investor's portfolio companies and co-investors is all it takes and the results can be extremely illuminating. Yet, surprisingly few entrepreneurs make the effort to reference-check their potential investors. Even if you are desperate for the cash and are going to take the investment no matter what, reference-checking can provide you with some good information about your investor's working style, their non-capital contributions to company development, their level of involvement, and their behaviour in different circumstances. These insights may also help you think about how to structure the deal with regard to voting, Board and other control provisions.

Finally, if you have investment offers from more than one VC, a possible option is to avoid choosing among them and, instead, explore whether there is a way to convince the top two or three VCs to invest as a 'syndicate'. Syndicates can be advantageous for the entrepreneur because they represent more capital around the table should further financings or a follow-on be required. A syndicate also prevents one VC investor from dominating the Board or controlling the deal, and gives the company access to the contacts, networks and resources of more than one VC firm. In a syndicate, there will be one 'lead investor' who will step up to co-ordinate and manage the due diligence process, draft the term sheet, and assume most of the document-drafting responsibilities.

THE VENTURE CAPITAL INVESTMENT PROCESS

Once VCs have identified an attractive company that fits their investment criteria, the venture capital investment process itself is well-defined, and generally consists of several sequential steps:

- Conducting due diligence.
- Making the investment decision.
- Deal structuring and negotiation.
- Ongoing oversight and management (Board membership).

In general, VCs invest with a portfolio mindset, in which the risk of failure and probability of success is spread across multiple investments. Investors know that not every deal will be a success. This portfolio approach is most commonly illustrated through an example portfolio of 10 companies. Within that portfolio, VCs expect that 1 to 2 deals will be 'home runs', with returns of 10 times or more of the original investment (represented as a '10x' return). Three to four investments will generate decent to good rates of return (two to five times the original investment), and the rest will be breakeven or write-offs. Industry data shows that venture capital fund returns are largely driven by a few top performers and that it is the one or two 'home runs' in any VC's portfolio that are responsible for generating the majority of overall venture capital returns.

Due Diligence

VCs have a reputation as being risk-takers. To a certain extent, they are. But the due diligence process will be your first peek at how effectively VCs work to mitigate the risk in every deal they do. The term sheet will be your second.

The purpose of due diligence is to allow investors to verify information that you have given in your business plan, and to identify other risks that require mitigation or monitoring once the deal has closed. Depending on the stage and complexity of the deal, the due diligence process can continue for between six and 12 weeks. During due diligence, investors will request and review a variety of legal, financial and business information from the company (a sample due diligence request list is attached in **Appendix 8**). They will also make a series of due diligence calls to prior investors, existing and potential customers, and management references. The investors generally will be most interested in the business and people checks, while a solicitor will manage legal due diligence and the review of all key agreements.

By far the most effective approach to dealing with due diligence is to pro-actively assemble a due diligence binder (either electronic or hard copy) of documents that are likely to be required, or have already been requested, such as:

- The business plan with detailed historical and 3-year projected financial data.
- Incorporation and other corporate documents.
- Board minutes.
- Copies of all significant agreements, leases and contracts.
- Management CVs and references.
- Customer list and contact information.

That way, when a potential investor is ready to begin due diligence, you can hand over the pre-prepared binder to get the process going, then fulfil other customised requests for information, as needed. Due diligence is clearly an intensive and intrusive process but, if the management team is prepared, they can minimise the disruption to the company's day-to-day business.

The Investment Decision

If the due diligence results look positive, the VCs will begin their own internal investment decision process. This process can vary among VC firms in terms of time, level of formality and detail.

Before the final decision is made, you will usually be asked to make a presentation to the entire VC partnership. Know that this meeting is as much, if not more, about evaluating you and your team as about your business. The VCs are interested in assessing your team dynamics and leadership, and evaluating your performance and presence. Can you control the meeting? Can you state clearly what your business does? Do you present a compelling story? How do you handle questions? Are you nervous or confident? Do you know the operational and financial details of your business or do you have to refer to others for answers? It is a good idea to bring at least one or two strong team members to showcase your team's interactions and to demonstrate the complementary skills and expertise of team members.

The investors are also looking for a number of other key characteristics. A track record of success is the most compelling trait of any entrepreneur. Relevant experience, the ability to attract, build and retain a good team, and a deep knowledge and understanding of the market and competition are also critical. Investors will also be looking for intangible qualities such as energy, passion, ambition and commitment, as well as your motivation for starting and running your business.

After the presentation, due diligence and an investment recommendation from the sponsoring partner, the investment decision made is based on a general consensus or a partnership vote. If the vote is positive, due diligence may still continue, but you will also begin the process of negotiating the deal and drafting documents required to close the deal.

STRUCTURING THE VENTURE CAPITAL DEAL

The next chapter in this book is dedicated to a detailed term-by-term review of a VC deal and a discussion about negotiating a VC term sheet.

SUBSEQUENT ROUNDS OF FINANCING

Once you've raised your first round of venture capital, raising subsequent rounds can either be a buoyant or distressing situation. If your company is doing well, is on target and growing full steam ahead to an exit, an 'up' round of financing, in which you obtain a better valuation than the previous round, is a positive development. In that case, manage the process just like any other round of financing. Start early before you need the cash, and work hard to attract as much investor interest as you can.

'Down' rounds occur when the company is not performing to plan and needs an additional cash infusion in order to reach the next milestone. Investors believe that the company still holds promise, and are willing to invest additional capital, but at a lower price. Down rounds are never fun for anyone and, without careful managing, they can quickly become very contentious.

How to Manage a Down Round

As an entrepreneur, there are a few things you can do to manage a down round in order to keep the process from degenerating into a greed-driven free-for-all.

At the top of the list is keeping control of your Board. The Directors of your Board have a fiduciary responsibility to act in the interests of the company as a whole. Remind them of this and make sure they act in a way that is consistent with that duty. For example, in any subsequent financing, the terms upon which the current VCs invested become subject to re-negotiation. If a new investor comes in and is looking to invest, existing investors may find themselves under pressure to re-negotiate some of their rights or privileges in order to attract the new money. A new investor could express interest in investing in your company and present a term sheet that requires prior investors to waive their anti-dilution rights for the round, or to reduce their liquidation preference going forward. An investor sitting on the Board must vote whether to accept the deal based on whether that financing, compared to other defined alternatives, best serves the company's interests, not the interests of their personal investment.

Second, tightly manage your existing investors. You will need to go through the term sheet and share agreements that you signed with your existing investors and understand precisely what rights and controls they have in the down round. You need to understand whether you are dealing with simply an unhappy investor, or with one who has the technical or legal power to block the financing. A powerful investor will require a lot more attention and compromise than a merely unhappy one, so establish early which one you're managing. The other point to remember is that the easiest way for existing investors to avoid the loss of rights and privileges is to participate in the current round. In that way, they actually secure, through the purchase of the new preference shares, the same rights and privileges as the new investor. Encourage your existing investors to participate in the down round as a way to mitigate its negative impact.

Third, keep your team focused on running the business. During a down round, any hopeful news – a key customer win, an exclusive agreement that gets signed – can improve the mood or help to break an impasse.

Finally, remember that investors have reputations to protect amongst other investors, advisors, and the entrepreneurial community. Few investors are interested in being known as obstructionist, difficult, greedy and unhelpful when the company is going through a difficult time. A gentle reminder that everyone around the table has a broader image to protect may be enough to prevent the most egregious behaviours.

Investor Participation in Subsequent Rounds

Another trying issue of later rounds of financing is investor participation. It is standard practice in the VC industry for existing investors to support their companies by participating up to their *pro rata* amount in later rounds of financing. If they don't, it can be interpreted as a signal that the company's prospects are deemed unattractive. New investors will look to existing investor participation levels as a signal about how the company is really performing. While it won't kill the deal if your mother doesn't pony up for the later rounds, a sophisticated angel or a VC who passes on a later round of financing can send a very damaging signal about your company's prospects to new investors. Therefore, prior to raising a later round of capital, you will want to get your existing investors interested and committed to contributing at least their *pro rata* share, in order to signal expectations of good future performance.

It does happen that sometimes an investor is not able to participate in a later round of financing, even if they would like to. A small-sized fund may not have the capital available to continue providing follow-on investments. After the bubble, many new funds and angel networks found that they had not set aside a percentage of their capital to follow-on or support existing portfolio companies, and had no money left to invest in later rounds. Other VC funds decided after the tech crash to change their focus, which left individual partners who were advocating for their companies unable to obtain approval for follow-on rounds. Unfortunately, corporate venture funds and investors have developed a reputation for unreliability during market downturns. When corporate profit margins are down or redundancies are under consideration, the capital allocated to venture investments is too often the first cut to be made, which leaves nothing for corporate investors to invest in follow-on rounds. There is little you can do to address investors who can't participate, except to make sure other potential investors understand that their lack of participation is not a negative signal about the company.

Then there are investors who are able to participate, but choose not to. They really are sending a signal about their view of the company's potential. To be successful, a VC must become an 'efficient killer' of deals that look like they won't make it. They must be disciplined about continuing to invest capital and time only in deals that show promise for future success. It is a truism of investing that companies that are going to fail, fail early, while success takes time (this is sometimes called the 'lemon law' of venture capital investing). The decision to not continue to invest in a portfolio company is certainly one of the most difficult an investor has to make.

'Vulture Capitalists'

It is an unfortunate reality that, in the worst case, investors can take advantage of a down round or underperformance by acting like 'vulture capitalists' and offering onerous terms for continued financing. The most common situation in which this happens is when the company is raising a down round but cannot attract new investors. In that case, an 'internal round' of financing, in which existing investors are the only participants, is the only option. In fact, down rounds are frequently internal rounds, since it can be hard to attract a new investor to a distressed or underperforming company.

There are a few ways for you to mitigate the potential damage of an internal round. First, if the company is not too far off-plan and the amount being raised is small relative to prior rounds, the investors may agree to valuing the down round at a discount to the last round. Second, if the company plans on raising capital from external investors and is already in discussions to do so, existing investors could structure a small 'bridge loan' that converts to equity at the new investor's valuation. Bridge loans are so-called because they are meant to 'bridge' the company to a future round of financing that is considered imminent. Therefore, a bridge loan is usually appropriate only if a company has a very high probability of closing an external round within a few months. Finally, the valuation of the internal round will need to be sufficient to ensure that the management team retains enough ownership to remain motivated.

THE BOARD OF DIRECTORS

Professional investors will negotiate at least one Board seat, so if you have not formally formed a Board, this VC financing round is the time to start considering Board issues. The Board of Directors exists to provide advice, assistance and oversight to your company's operations and management team. A good Board is a valuable asset to you in terms of providing strategic assistance and attracting potential investors; a dysfunctional Board can be disastrous. Another compelling reason to carefully reference-check potential investors is that you are accepting your next Board Director when you accept an investment.

It can be challenging to attract knowledgeable and competent directors to boards of young companies as they tend to be time-intensive and there is a personal risk of liability and reputational risk for the Directors, if the company does not do well.

Members of the Board of Directors have a legal fiduciary relationship with the company, which means they are required by law to act in the best interest of the company as a whole. In all decisions, they must place the interests of the company ahead of their own personal interests, or the interests of employees, creditors or other investors.

Directors have specific duties they must assume while sitting on the Board. Specifically, they must:

- Exercise their powers in good faith and in the interests *of the company as a whole*.
- Not make an undisclosed profit from their position as Director.
- Carry out their functions with due skill, care and diligence.

There may be occasions when one or more of your Directors will be tempted to act in their own interests, or in the interest of protecting their own investment, rather than in the interest of the company as a whole. It is your job to manage your Board and ensure that the decisions it makes are consistent with the company's interests.

For example, one company's Board was composed of two angel investors (one of whom was a successful former entrepreneur) and two of the company's executive management team. The company was raising a second round of financing and it was clear that it was going to have to accept a down round valuation. No investors were offering to match the price the company had obtained in the prior round. Unfortunately, the angel investors (led by the more sophisticated former entrepreneur) became extremely difficult and obstructionist about the new financing. Technically, though, the angels had no basis to influence the decision about the new financing. They did not control the Board, did not have a veto right that allowed them to block the new financing, and did not control the ordinary shareholder vote. That didn't stop them. Instead, they decided to exert their influence by throwing a fit at the Board level, which was certain to alienate the potential new investors.

The entrepreneur was uncertain how to handle the situation and intimidated by the angels' actions. He brought in his solicitor to help renegotiate the terms of the angel deal, in exchange for obtaining their approval for the new financing. A better course of action would have been to force the issue at the Board level. The Directors had only one offer on the table for a new financing and, if they refused it, the company would be required to liquidate. Therefore, their crystal clear fiduciary obligation to the company would have forced them to vote for the financing. There is also an obvious reputational risk for the angels (particularly the former entrepreneur from the same industry) that could have been leveraged. Blocking the only deal on the table puts them at risk of being characterised as a greedy, difficult and unsophisticated investor.

The new investors, too, could have used their leverage to insist that the angels go forward or threaten to take the deal off the table. It is unfortunate, but true, that a new financing and 'what the new investor wants' often provides much-needed leverage to aggressively manage obstructionist early investors. VCs understand this and, very often (much more often than you would think), provide their first value-added service to a company by helping it sort out existing dysfunctional dynamics on its Board or management team, prior to closing the investment.

Board Composition

Boards of Directors for early-stage companies have little reason to be larger than five members, of which a maximum of two are company insiders. It is far preferable to have a very small board initially, as a small Board is much cleaner and more attractive for investors, than having to restructure a large or inappropriate board. From the company's perspective, it is always easier to add Directors later than to remove them. Boards are usually structured with an odd number of Directors to avoid voting ties.

There are two broad categories of Director. Executive Directors are involved in the day-to-day management or running of the company. For example, a Managing Director who sits on the Board of his own company would be considered an Executive Director. Non-executive Directors are also called independent or outside directors. They do not work for the company on whose Board they sit, so are more distant from the daily management of the company. The function of a Non-executive Director is to bring a more objective and independent perspective to company debates and decisions. A Non-executive director could be an industry expert or a venture capitalist.

The type of Board members you want should be identified and their experience defined in advance, based on your company's need. Identify the expertise that would most benefit the company, and which best complements the experience of the management team. When soliciting Board candidates, confirm that they have sufficient time and interest in your company to commit. Young companies are time-intensive for Board members, since they tend to meet every month in the early stages, which requires significant preparation and attendance time. Board members also serve at some risk to themselves, as their fiduciary responsibilities allow them to be held personally liable for losses resulting from their own negligence. The company can mitigate these risks by providing Directors and Officers (D&O) liability insurance to Board members. This insurance protects Directors against liability claims, except in cases of fraud.

Directors of early-stage companies are rarely compensated with cash, simply because cash is so scarce. Outside Directors instead are usually offered a small share option award that vests over time, to compensate them for their input. Investors in the company, including venture capitalists, are considered compensated for their Board input through the equity position they hold in the company. It would be extremely unusual for an investor to be paid cash fees, or awarded additional equity, for serving on the Board. It would be just as unseemly for them to ask.

To ensure ongoing flexibility, it is helpful to structure the Board so that each Non-executive Director has a defined term of service, at the end of which they must be re-elected in order to continue to serve on the Board. This allows the entrepreneur and investors to eliminate poorly-performing Directors gracefully or to reduce the size of the Board at regular intervals. It also allows companies to replace directors and to bring on new members as the company requires different types of expertise, as it grows. For instance, in the early stages, the company may benefit greatly from a Board member who has expertise and contacts that will help raise early-stage capital. During the later growth stages, the company may prefer a Board member who has the expertise and networks to help it acquire key large customers, or recruit a management team of scale.

Keep in mind that your Board members are not required to serve out any kind of minimum term, and can resign at any time. For example, one company that had been underperforming was unable to raise a much-needed round of financing. It was facing the prospect of a fire sale of the company's assets, or a liquidation. As the situation became evident, the entrepreneur was surprised to see three of his four Non-executive Directors resign from the Board. When Directors resign, they relinquish their fiduciary responsibilities to all shareholders, which can make it easier to protect their own investment in a troubled situation. Since it was a five-person Board, all that was left was the entrepreneur and one Director. Without a functioning Board to make decisions and give advice, he had to rely much more heavily on his solicitors to guide him through the transaction. Ultimately, the liquidation never happened, but the company ended up being acquired at a fire sale price.

Board Meetings

Part of your job as an entrepreneur and founder of a company with investors is to organise and conduct regular Board meetings. Board meetings are used both to review a variety of corporate issues and to approve specific company actions. There are standard processes and rules that are followed when organising and conducting a Board meeting. Board meetings are often scheduled in advance at regular intervals (for example, the 15th of every month, or the first Tuesday of every month) and held at the same time so that members can put them in their diaries for the entire year. Prior to the meetings, Directors are sent notices of the meeting as a reminder (see **Appendix 9**). At least a week before each Board meeting, the company must send to each Director (usually by email, but can also be hard copy) a 'Board Book' that typically includes:

- ♦ A written agenda for the Board meeting that includes the order in which items will be addressed, as well as the approximate time each item will take, and any motions / proposals for Board approval (see example Board agenda in **Appendix 10**).

- The Minutes of the last Board meeting (see example Board minutes in **Appendix 11**).
- Any supporting attachments.
- Any information to be discussed or reviewed by the Board but that does not require Board action (for example, regular monthly financials, sales pipeline, etc.).

Directors are expected to come to each meeting having read the Board Book, and having asked for additional or clarifying information in advance of the meeting. For Board members to be effective, the company's management team must focus on providing them with the appropriate information (which is distinctly different from overwhelming them with data) to enable them to fulfil their fiduciary responsibilities. Companies make the common mistake of providing Board members with the full detail of the company's monthly and YTD financials, when that data is best provided as a supporting attachment to several key graphics or visuals that summarise the company's financial performance to date and provide information about the company's actual performance against their business plan.

If an entrepreneur is inexperienced at running meetings, it can be helpful to appoint a chairman of the Board to assist in making sure the meeting runs according to schedule, on time, and gets through the agenda. At each meeting, a secretary or member of the Board should be appointed to take notes, record votes, and be responsible for preparing the written Minutes of the Board.

Common issues discussed at Board meetings of young companies include financial and operations reviews, sales and business development updates, and strategic discussions about the company's future, anticipated fundraisings, key management hires, and exit options. Boards will rarely become involved with issues such as day-to-day operational issues of the company or normal employment issues.

Board Performance

There is significant debate about what constitutes good Board performance, and how entrepreneurs can best manage Boards to maximise performance. Companies have the right to expect that any member who has agreed to serve on the Board will have sufficient time and interest to devote to the company, will attend Board meetings (some companies quantify this commitment and stipulate that Directors attend at least 80% of all Board meetings or be deemed to have resigned), and will come to the meeting having read the Board Book, having asked in advance for any additional information, and be prepared to discuss and decide upon the agenda items. For young companies, implementing short and defined terms of one year for each Director is the best way to manage performance with the least effort, since it provides the option to replace directors every 12 months.

CONCLUSION

VCs are in the business of generating returns on their invested capital. Their return requirements are high and, to meet them, VCs seek to invest in only the best, fastest-growing and most promising companies. If you receive an investment offer from a VC, it represents a meaningful milestone in your company's development and endorsement of your business model and prospects.

Raising venture capital is a rigorous process. You will need to prepare thoroughly, seek referrals to individual VCs and present a compelling business plan for your company's growth. Before making an investment decision, VCs conduct extensive due diligence that is designed to review, examine and analyse every part of your business. Preparing for this process in advance can help minimise its disruption on your business.

Once you accept venture capital, your job description expands to include managing and working with your investors during subsequent rounds of financing and on your Board of Directors. A company's Board is extremely influential. A good one can be a tremendous asset, and a bad one can do a lot of damage. Choose your investors carefully, keep your Board small, and manage it tightly to ensure it makes the best decisions in your company's interests.

9
THE VENTURE CAPITAL DEAL: UNDERSTANDING THE TERM SHEET

Let us never negotiate out of fear, but let us never fear to negotiate.
John F. Kennedy

Receiving a term sheet is a good sign. The term sheet (or 'Heads of Agreement') is the first real step to closing a VC round of financing. It outlines the price and proposed structure of the financing and offers a starting point for negotiations. Once the term sheet has been finalised, it will serve as the basis for drafting the legal documentation required to close the investment. This chapter is dedicated to walking you through the major terms that are included in a standard VC term sheet. Each term is described and explained. If the term sheet you receive omits some of these, you will want to clarify their status with the investor.

A term sheet is not a legally-binding document, and receiving one does not guarantee that the financing will ultimately close. At any time during the process, investors can 'pull' the term sheet and withdraw from the negotiation process. Few investors make a habit of this, as it is considered an unsavoury business practice within the VC industry. Instead, the term sheet is generally considered to be a true and serious indication of investor interest, and good faith negotiations with full intent to close the deal generally proceed from it.

Term sheets can differ quite substantially in length and level of detail. Some VCs prefer a detailed term sheet (six to eight pages) that outlines each of the key terms in specific language. This type is most helpful to you, since it allows you to understand and evaluate accurately the deal being proposed. It also allows the two parties to reach fairly specific agreement about key terms, which can save time and costs once the lawyers become involved in drafting the detailed agreements. Other VCs present two- to four-page term sheets that do not comprehensively outline all the key terms and do not provide enough information to evaluate the deal.

For instance, one software entrepreneur who was raising a round of venture capital finance had been in discussions with one VC for about 10 weeks. He received a three-page letter from the VC that included a term sheet. The term sheet was two pages long and only included an outline of six terms: type of shares, price per share, liquidation preference, anti-dilution protection, the Board of Directors and conditions to close. It also included an eight-week exclusivity clause. The entrepreneur should not have signed this document in its current form. The exclusivity clause was too long and, therefore, too risky for the entrepreneur. And there was no way to evaluate the real deal being proposed. The VC did not include key terms on dividends, conversion, redemption, or any veto provisions, which made it particularly difficult to determine the level of control they would be awarded over key business decisions.

The real danger of such abbreviated term sheets is that the complete set of terms, some of which could be real deal-breakers, will only emerge after you have frittered your time and remaining cash away on what could be an ultimately unattractive deal, and when your other investor leads have gone cold. Without a reasonable level of detail on each of the key terms, you risk your company's limited time and cash resources in pursuing a deal you do not understand. The risks of moving forward with a deal based on a sparse term sheet are borne entirely by you.

If you receive a term sheet that does not outline the full structure of the deal, go back to the investor and ask for more detail. Arrange a time to walk through and discuss the major terms, so you can gain an understanding of exactly what the VC is proposing. Then, if the deal seems interesting, ask for a revised term sheet that includes more detail. Any reputable investor will be happy to clearly explain the proposed terms of their investment offer. If not, you have bigger issues of communication and trust on your hands. Examples of both abbreviated and complete term sheets are included in **Appendices 12 & 13**.

TERM SHEET NEGOTIATION

The best approach to negotiating a term sheet is to pick the few key terms that are important to you, develop a clear rationale for the changes you seek, and negotiate those. The critical terms most worth negotiating are:

- Valuation (but you need to take into account the whole deal structure in order to evaluate it accurately).
- Liquidation preference.
- Dilution protection.
- Board and veto provisions.

That said, these deal terms can be negotiated effectively only in the context of a complete investment proposal. For instance a 2x liquidation preference is more bearable if the company retains control over exit timing and method, and maintains a majority Board position. A 2x liquidation preference combined with a redemption provision, veto control over a trade sale and mandatory dividends is much less attractive. Negotiation requires trade-offs, give and take, and an ongoing sense of the 'forest' as well as of the 'trees'. Without the 'big picture' of the full investment proposal, you are unlikely to negotiate effectively even the most critical terms.

How successful you will be at your negotiations also is highly dependent on your specific situation. Companies that have generated interest from more than one investor, or that have other financing alternatives available, will have the most negotiating leverage and are likely to have the most negotiating success. If you are raising capital early, before you need it, that also provides you with negotiating leverage. You have the advantage of being able to walk away from a mediocre deal and the time to create alternatives. A successful serial entrepreneur or a company in a hot market segment will have more leverage than a first-time entrepreneur in a less attractive market space.

In all cases, it is critical to work with an experienced solicitor to review the terms offered, to understand how valuation and potential exits are affected, and to evaluate the specific controls the investors have secured. Walk through the term sheet carefully and understand the control provisions. It is only by understanding each term and how it works, and then stepping back to see the 'big picture' and how they interact as a whole, that you will be able to accurately understand the actual investment deal offered to you.

VENTURE CAPITAL TERMS EXPLAINED

VCs structure their investments with competing objectives in mind. First and foremost, they want to maximise their financial returns. That means putting together a deal that allows investors to capture a significant portion of any upside performance. VCs also want to protect their investment and mitigate their downside risk. To do so, they negotiate for control rights that give them the ability to make certain business, strategic and financial decisions for their portfolio companies, particularly in cases where the company is not performing well.

FIGURE 7: VENTURE CAPITAL TERMS

	Economic Protection	Control Rights
Type of Security	√	√
Price per Share	√	
Dividend Rights	√	
Conversion Rights	√	
Liquidation Preference	√	
Redemption	√	
Anti-dilution Protection	√	
Pay to Play	√	
Voting Rights		√
Right of First Refusal & Co-sale		√
Drag Along Rights		√
Pre-emption Rights	√	
Board of Directors		√
Protective Provisions		√
Information Rights		√
Representations & Warranties	√	
Exclusivity		√
Conditions to Close		√
Closing		√

The terms are presented here in the general order in which they occur on a term sheet. For other examples of term sheets and a discussion of venture capital investment terms, see **Appendix 14**.

Type of Security

Preference Shares

Professional investors always purchase preference shares. Preference shares give them a variety of rights and controls and rank ahead of ordinary shares in the event of a payout or exit.

If your company raises several rounds of capital, you will need to issue different classes of preference shares for each subsequent round of financing. By convention, these are referred to by increasing letters in the alphabet. So the first preference shares will be Series A class, then Series B, Series C and so on. There are two common types of preference shares: convertible preference and participating preference shares.

Convertible preference shares

By far the most common shares purchased are convertible preference shares. These are the standard security used by US VCs. Convertible preference shares, as the name implies, convert to ordinary shares in certain circumstances. They most commonly convert at the option of the investor, or automatically upon the occurrence of a pre-defined event (these details are further discussed below under the **Conversion** term).

To illustrate how convertible preference shares work, assume Moneybags VC invests €5 million into a company with a €5 million pre-money valuation. The deal is structured with convertible preference shares and a modest 1x liquidation preference (1x means '1 times', which means investors get their original investment amount back). From this transaction, Moneybags owns 50% of the €10 million company (post-money valuation). If the company is then sold for €20 million, Moneybags would have a choice of *either* taking their 1x liquidation preference of €5 million *or* converting to common and taking €10 million (50% of the €20 million). In this case, Moneybags would clearly choose to convert their preference shares to ordinary shares and receive the €10 million.

Participating preference shares

Participating preference shares are less common, but more favourable to investors. As such, they are more negotiable. The key characteristic of participating preference shares is that they 'double dip' into the proceeds from a sale or liquidation. The first dip is the liquidation preference they receive. The second dip is that they are then entitled to a portion of any remaining proceeds on an 'as converted' basis, based on their percentage ownership of ordinary shares. Unlike regular convertible preference shares, they don't have to choose between their liquidation preference and their ordinary share ownership – they get proceeds based on both. As a result of the double dip, the participating preference structure is quite investor-friendly. In the case of a moderate exit or liquidation, participating preference shares can leave ordinary shareholders with very little proceeds.

For example, assume the same situation just described above – that Moneybags VC invests €5 million and owns 50% of the €10 million company post-money. A year or so later, the company is sold for €20 million. **Figure 8** illustrates the difference in proceeds if Moneybags owns convertible *versus* participating securities with a 1x or 2x liquidation preference.

FIGURE 8: DIFFERENCE IN PROCEEDS BETWEEN CONVERTIBLE & PARTICIPATING PREFERENCE SHARES

Liquidation Preference	Proceeds to Moneybags VC	Proceeds to ordinary shareholders
1x convertible	€ 10m	€ 10m
2x convertible	€ 10m	€ 10m
1x participating	€ 12.5m	€ 7.5m
2x participating	€ 15m	€ 5m

Note that in the first case, when Moneybags holds convertible shares with a 1x liquidation preference of €5 million, they forgo the liquidation preference and instead convert their preference shares to ordinary shares. That way, they receive 50% of the proceeds, or €10 million, based on their 50% ordinary share ownership. In the 1x participating case, Moneybags receives the €5 million liquidation preference *and* the €7.5 million (half of the remaining €15 million) from their as-converted ordinary share ownership.

This example illustrates that the type of security matters most in middling to poor exits. In a moderate outcome, the ordinary shareholders are worse off as the liquidation preference gets higher and if the securities held by investors are participating rather than convertible. In the case of a 'home run' outcome (for example, if the company was sold for €100 million), the distinctions are much less meaningful, since both the investors and the ordinary shareholders make excellent returns.

Price per Share

This is the valuation section of the term sheet. It states the number of shares being purchased and the price per share. It also states the pre-money valuation that the investor is placing on the deal and attaches the most recent company capitalisation table to describe the number and type of shares upon which the pre-money valuation is based. If the capitalisation table is later determined to be incorrect, any adjustments in the capital structure will be borne through the dilution of the ordinary shareholders, not the investors.

Share price vs. valuation

It is worth emphasising that the true valuation of a financing depends on both the share price and the terms of the deal. There are several ways to adjust the valuation of a financing round without changing the actual share price.

For example, is the pre-money valuation based on the fully-diluted number of shares outstanding? A fully-diluted valuation includes the full employee option pool, even if only a portion has been issued to employees, as well as any other options, warrants or convertible debt. Including all the issued shares and share equivalents in the pre-money valuation effectively lowers the price to the new investor, since existing shareholders take the full dilution of all share and share equivalents outstanding. The same price per share based on non-fully-diluted shares outstanding represents a different effective valuation.

Other common ways to impact valuation through deal terms include:

- **Participating preference shares** which, as just illustrated, allow the investor to 'double dip' into the proceeds at exit. For a given price per share, the investor holding participating preference shares will receive a greater portion of the exit proceeds than the investor holding convertible shares.
- **The use of warrants:** Warrants are options that give the investor the right, but not the obligation, to purchase company shares at a pre-determined (and usually low) price in the future.
- **A dividend that converts to equity:** In that way, the preference shareholder obtains additional equity ownership without an additional cash investment.

Because these and other less common terms can affect valuation, it is essential to understand all the terms of an investment proposal and how they fit together. It is advisable to work closely with an experienced solicitor to understand and review the complete term sheet to assess accurately the valuation offered.

Dividend Rights

The dividend rights clause is a standard feature of most term sheets, because it provides a way for the investors to receive additional proceeds in the case of a mediocre or poor outcome, such as liquidation or redemption. The existence of a dividend clause is not negotiable, but the structure is. There are two parts to the dividend term, since all dividends must first be declared, and then paid.

Declaring dividends

Dividends are most commonly declared at the discretion of the Board. If this term is in effect, most start-up companies will simply not declare any dividends. A more investor-friendly term stipulates that the dividend is automatically declared quarterly or annually. It also specifies the dividend rate in terms of a fixed per share amount (for example, €0.10 per share) or as a percentage rate (for example, 8-15% per annum).

A dividend is declared as cumulative or non-cumulative. Cumulative dividends benefit investors, because they accumulate over time and are paid out if the company is liquidated, purchased or if the investor's shares are redeemed. Watch for this term, since an automatic cumulative dividend can add up to a meaningful amount of cash over a few years.

For example, take the case of a €5 million investment, held for 5 years, with a 10% annual automatic cumulative dividend. The annual dividend is €500,000, and accumulates every year for five years, totalling €2.5 million. That amount is paid out to the investors, *in addition to, and in advance of,* any exit proceeds.

Non-cumulative dividends are structured so that the company's obligation is limited to the current time period. If the company does not pay out the dividend during one period, no obligation for that dividend carries over to the next time period. Therefore, the maximum dividend obligation a company could accrue would be one year for an annual dividend.

In the example above, if there was a 10% annual *non-cumulative* dividend, and the exit occurred in year 5, the company would only pay out the most recent annual dividend of €500,000, since it has no ongoing obligation to pay out dividends from Years 1 to 4.

Paying dividends

The term sheet will specify *when* dividends are paid. There are two times dividends are paid: upon exit, and if declared by the Board. Most commonly, the payment of dividends occurs upon exit. The liquidation and redemption terms typically will require payment of any declared, but unpaid, dividends along with any exit proceeds, which gives the investor an extra return in both those cases. Aside from exit events, dividends are paid out only when, and if, declared by the Board (which, as mentioned above, is hardly ever).

The term sheet will also specify *how* dividends are paid. Dividends can be paid in order of Series (for example, first to the holders of Series D preference shares, then Series C, etc.). In a poor or moderate exit, the payment order matters, because a sequential payout could include the risk that the company runs out of cash before it reaches your shareholder class. Dividends can also be paid out on an equal basis (called *pari passu*), in which all preference shareholders receive equal distributions regardless of Series. In that case, if there were four Series of preference shareholders (Series A to D) and €2 million of dividends to pay out, each series would receive €500,000 equally.

Conversion Rights

By definition, convertible preference shares convert into ordinary shares. The conversion term defines the circumstances in which a conversion can occur, and the conversion ratio. The conversion term addresses both optional and automatic conversions. The optional conversion term is standard and not really worth negotiating. The structure of the automatic conversion term is only worth negotiating if you think there is a strong probability that the company will go public.

Optional conversion

It is standard for convertible preference shares to be convertible, at any time, at the option of the investor. In practice, investors only find it attractive to convert upon an exit event in which they will receive more proceeds through their percentage ownership as an ordinary shareholder than through their liquidation preference. The conversion price is usually set to the price of the preference shares, so the convertible preference shares convert to ordinary shares on a 1:1 basis.

For example, if a VC invests €2 million in Series A convertible preference shares at €4 per share, with an initial conversion ratio of 1:1, their 500,000 preference shares (€2m / €4.00) would convert to 500,000 ordinary shares. If there are 1.5 million ordinary shares outstanding in the company, the investors would own 33% if they converted their preference shares to ordinary shares. Therefore, investors would say that the VCs owned 33% of the company on an 'as-converted' basis. The conversion price, and therefore the ratio, can be adjusted in the future based on anti-dilution provisions.

Automatic conversion

The terms of an automatic conversion are negotiable. The automatic conversion term requires that convertible preference shareholders automatically convert when a 'qualifying IPO' occurs.

A qualifying IPO is usually defined as:

- A 'firmly underwritten' IPO, which means that the underwriters have committed to sell / place all the shares.
- An IPO that raises a minimum amount of capital.
- An IPO with a minimum offering price per share. Usually this minimum is expressed in terms of a multiple of the original purchase price of the preference shares (for example, 'at a price per share not less than three times the original purchase price of the Series C preferred'). The average multiple is three times the original purchase price, but can range from two to four times.

Investors specifically define a qualifying IPO to protect themselves against a situation in which they convert to ordinary shares, thus relinquishing all their rights and controls, and then the company conducts a small IPO at a low value that fails to generate good liquidity or returns. The investor is then stuck with illiquid or low-priced shares and no control provisions with which to modify the situation.

From the company's perspective, you want to be careful to ensure that the definition of a qualifying IPO is reasonable and potentially achievable, in terms of the minimum to be raised and the price. Otherwise, if you decide to go public, and the offering does not meet the standards of a qualifying IPO, the investors essentially can block the offering by refusing to convert to ordinary shares.

The other automatic conversion occurs when a specific percentage of the preference shareholders vote to convert (for example, the majority, $^2/_3$rds or 75%), then all other preference shareholders must convert. This clause prevents a minority or renegade preference shareholder from having an effective veto over the conversion.

Liquidation Preference

The liquidation preference is one of the most significant terms in a term sheet. It is a standard term, but negotiable. The liquidation preference specifies how the proceeds of an exit are divided among preference and ordinary shareholders. The term applies during a liquidation or winding up of the company, as well as to defined 'liquidation events', which usually include mergers, acquisitions (trade sale), the sale of 'substantially all' of the company's assets, and a 'change in control' of the company. It does not generally apply in the case of an IPO.

Liquidation preferences are most important in the case of a 'liquidation event'. In a real liquidation or winding up of the company, there is rarely enough cash available to pay creditors, let alone satisfy the conditions of a liquidation preference.

The liquidation preference ensures that preference shareholders receive their capital first, before any proceeds are distributed to ordinary shareholders. The liquidation preference is stated as a multiple of the investor's capital committed. For example, a 2x liquidation preference (where 'x' means 'times') means that the investors have a right to receive twice their invested capital back, before any lower-ranked preference investors or any ordinary investors. Preferences of 1x to 2x have been standard historically in the majority of venture capital transactions but, following the dot com crash, investors desperate to lock-in a return sought much higher preferences of 3x or more (there were even rumours of term sheets with 5x and 6x). Preferences have since fallen back to the 1x to 2x range.

The proposed payout of the liquidation preference can be structured any number of ways. Most commonly, it is structured on a 'last in, first out' basis, where the newest investors are paid first, then any remaining capital is paid out in descending order to the other preference shareholders, and last to the ordinary shareholders. So, the liquidation preference payout would go first to the holders of Series B, then Series A, then to the ordinary shareholders.

Sometimes, the participating feature discussed earlier will be included in the liquidation term. While a standard liquidation term would be written to pay out:

1. First to the holders of the Series B preferred ...
2. Then to the holders of the Series A preferred ...
3. Then to the holders of ordinary shares ...

it can also be written so that 3. includes preferred shareholders in the final pay-out:

3. Then *pro rata* to the preferred and ordinary shareholders on an as-converted basis.

Yet another reason to review and understand all terms in an investment proposal.

The liquidation preference can make an enormous difference in the case of a mediocre outcome. If investors have large liquidation preferences, the management team and other ordinary shareholders are at risk of receiving very little unless the company is sold at a very high valuation.

For example, if an investor invests €5 million with a 3x liquidation preference, and the company is later sold for €15 million, the investors will get the entire €15 million to fulfil their liquidation preference, which leaves ordinary shareholders (including the entire management team) with nothing.

Redemption

While the conversion term outlines what happens to the preference shareholders in the event of an IPO, and the liquidation preference describes what happens in a trade sale, merger or winding up, the redemption provision specifies what happens when there is no exit in sight. In some cases, several years could have passed since the investment was made and the company could be profitable and doing well but, for any number of reasons, including management's preference to remain private, general market conditions, or trade sale valuations, there is no short or medium term exit. Redemption protects investors against such 'living dead' companies that operate profitably but are expected to remain private for the foreseeable future. This is an investor-friendly term and it is negotiable.

Rather than forcing a sale or an IPO, the redemption clause offers the investor a way to achieve liquidity and to exit the investment over a specified period of time for a pre-defined price. The term usually requires the company to buy back the investment at a predetermined value. The value is generally the purchase price plus a fixed return (for example, the initial investment plus returns of 10% per year).

A standard redemption clause requires the company to buy out the investor's position in equal amounts over time – say, one-third in each of years 5 to 7. The clause is exercised at the option of the investor. If the company does not have enough cash to buy out the investment, the investors could force the sale of the company or its assets to raise the cash, or they could exercise control rights at the Board level, or change company management. Therefore, redemption clauses are often contentious when exercised. They can create significant tension between investors who want to exit a company that they perceive has little potential, and management who feel more positively about the future of the business but will face a cash crunch if the investor exercises the redemption clause. In addition, in both Europe and the US, there can be statutory restrictions and other legal obstacles about requiring a redemption, if the company has insufficient cash to pay.

In practice, redemption clauses are rarely exercised. Instead, they are usually used as leverage for investors to negotiate financial terms that are less onerous than the redemption clause, but which still give the investors an exit.

The redemption feature can sometimes be found in the **Type of Security** term, where some investors will characterise it as a Redeemable Preference security.

Anti-dilution Protection

The anti-dilution term protects investors against having overpaid for their shares. It also protects them in case the company underperforms and has to raise a down round of financing at a lower valuation than the existing investor paid. Every term sheet will have some sort of anti-dilution protection, but the extent of the protection, and how it is calculated, are both negotiable.

To avoid a significant reduction in their ownership percentage, investors protect themselves by adjusting the conversion price of their shares downwards to reflect the new price. That way, on an as-converted basis, they maintain their percentage ownership in the company. Anti-dilution protection comes in two different forms: full ratchet and weighted average.

Full ratchet anti-dilution

Full ratchet anti-dilution protection is a very investor-friendly term, in that it provides full dilution protection to existing investors, regardless of the size of the subsequent down round. Under this type of protection, if even one share is issued at a lower price, all of the prior investors' holdings are adjusted and re-priced as if they had invested at the new, lower price. Therefore, existing investors with full ratchet protection retain their percentage ownerships in down rounds, while ordinary shareholders or other investors without full ratchet protection suffer disproportionate dilution.

For example, let's look at a company that has completed one prior round of VC financing and has 3 million shares outstanding. The VC round was an investment of €1 million at a price per preference share of €1.00. The initial conversion ratio is 1:1 so the initial conversion price is €1.00.

	Shares	Percentage Ownership	Conversion Price
Ordinary Shares	2,000,000	67%	
Preference Shares	1,000,000	33%	€ 1.00
TOTAL Shares O/S	3,000,000	100%	

The company then raises a small down round of €200,000 at €0.50 per share, a 50% decline from the €1.00 share price from the previous round. Under full ratchet dilution, you can see that the VCs, who purchased the preference shares, do not suffer any dilution in their percentage ownership position. In fact, they gain additional ownership as a result of the reduction in price per share.

	Shares	Percentage Ownership	Conversion Price
Ordinary Shares	2,000,000	49%	
Preference Shares	2,000,000	49%	€ 0.50
Down Round shares	100,000	2%	€ 0.50
TOTAL Shares O/S	4,100,000	100%	

Under full ratchet anti-dilution, the ordinary shareholders absorb all of the dilution of the down round. In this example, their ownership position declines from 67% to 49%, as the result of the very small round of financing.

In practice, full ratchet dilution is rarely used, since it is a very divisive term. The impact of the full ratchet can be so severe, as this example illustrates, that it pits current investors and management against each other, and can divide current and new investors. Any new investor considering a down round investment in a company where existing investors have full ratchet anti-dilution will likely require that the full ratchet be waived, particularly in cases where the management team thereby is diluted to the point where their ownership is insufficient to keep them motivated.

Weighted average anti-dilution

Weighted average dilution is considered the standard anti-dilution term in the industry (for example, 80-90% of term sheets in the US contain this type of protection). It is deemed to be fair both to investors and to the company, because it takes into account the size of the down round relative to previous rounds. A down round that is small relative to prior rounds of financing will only have a moderate impact on the conversion ratio. It is therefore not as punishingly dilutive to ordinary shareholders as full ratchet protection.

A weighted average anti-dilution protection can be calculated as follows, based on as-converted shares outstanding:

$$\text{New conversion price} = \text{Old conversion price} \times \frac{(A+B)}{(A+C)}$$

where:
A = the number of company shares before the financing round.
B = for the current investment amount, the number of shares that would have been issued at the old conversion price.
C = the number of shares actually issued as part of the down round.

Looking again at the example above, if the same company raised the same €200,000 down round but its investors have weighted-average anti-dilution protection, the result is much different. Using the formula, we can calculate that:

$$\text{New conversion price} = €1.00 \times \frac{(3m + 50,000)}{(3m + 100,000)}$$
$$= €0.98$$

While the ordinary shareholders still take the most dilution – their ownership percentage falls from 67% to 64% – they are much better off than they were, holding 49% of the company under the full-ratchet scenario.

	Shares	Percentage Ownership	Conversion Price
Ordinary Shares	2,000,000	64%	
Preference Shares	1,016,393	33%	€ 0.98
Down Round shares	100,000	3%	€ 0.50
TOTAL Shares O/S	**3,116,393**	**100%**	

The VC investors take a very slight dilution, from 33.33% ownership to 32.61% (because of rounding, this change is imperceptible in the table). As you can imagine, such a financing would be much less contentious in this scenario, for both new and old investors, and the management team, than under full ratchet.

The weighted average protection can be either narrow-based or broad-based:

- **Narrow-based weighted average** is more investor-friendly. It calculates the anti-dilution protection based only ordinary and preference shares outstanding, but excludes any shares, options or warrants. Therefore, the preference shareholder owns a relatively larger percentage of the company and the protection is more dilutive to ordinary and founding shareholders.

- **Broad-based weighted average** is more company-friendly. It is based on the fully diluted number of shares outstanding (which is A in the formula above). This means that all outstanding shares and share equivalents, including the option pool's outstanding shares, and any warrants are included. Under a broad-based calculation, the preference shareholder will be identified as owning a smaller percentage of the company than in a narrow-based calculation, because the denominator will be larger. Therefore, the anti-dilution protection to preference investors is less than in the narrow-based scenario, and not as dilutive to ordinary shareholders and founders.

Anti-dilution carve-outs

Certain issues of new shares are excluded, or 'carved out', from triggering the anti-dilution clause. Usually, shares issued from the existing employee option pool are exempt. So, for instance, the term sheet might indicate that the company is allowed to issue an additional 100,000 shares as part of the employee pool to be awarded to management, and that the issue of these shares will not trigger the anti-dilution provision.

Pay to Play

Also called a *'play or pay'* or *'put up or shut up'* clause, the intent of this term is to provide investors with an incentive to participate in future rounds of financing or else to suffer a penalty. This term is considered both investor- and company-friendly. It is designed to prevent situations in which there is a down round and the investor who does not participate receives anti-dilution protection. It also discourages investors from 'cherry-picking', by only participating in certain rounds of financing while passing on others.

Investors are usually required to invest at least their *pro rata* amount to avoid incurring a penalty. Some common ways that investors suffer a penalty are:

- They lose their anti-dilution rights for the current and all future rounds of financing.
- All their preference shares convert to ordinary shares.
- They lose their right to participate in any future rounds of financing.

This term benefits both the entrepreneur and existing investors, since it helps encourage the participation of all existing investors in future rounds of financing.

Voting Rights

The standard voting term is that preference shareholders receive one vote per share and vote along with the ordinary shareholders on an as-converted basis.

However, many terms in a preference share investment proposal are subject to voting approvals. When you are combing through the term sheet to review each of the rights and controls the investor is proposing, it is critical to read very carefully and to understand such terms. You are looking for who controls each vote in each case and, depending on how the term is structured and worded, the control can vary tremendously. For example, if the conversion term states '… the stock shall convert upon approval of a majority of the preference holders, voting as a class', you want to understand who constitutes a majority of the preference shareholders, and therefore who has the control over that decision. Does one investor control a majority? If not, who does the largest investor have to get on their side to get a majority? Can several of the smaller preference investors band together and dominate the vote? Understand which investors control which decisions, and what their incentives are based on their deal price and structure. It will help you to anticipate and manage their behaviour.

Determining voting control

To determine who has control, first look to see who is voting. Is it all shareholders on an as-converted basis, all preference holders as a class, or just an individual preference Series (for example, 'subject to the approval of the Series C preference holders'). The number of shares in each of those cases will give you the denominator. For ease of calculation, let's assume we are looking at a company in which there are 100,000 ordinary shares, 10,000 preference shares, and 1,000 Series C shares. Then look at each investor and determine:

- How many shares of each Series they own.
- How many preference shares (of all Series) they own.
- How many ordinary shares on an as-converted basis they own.

This is your numerator. From this, you can determine what percentage each investor owns in each case. So, if Moneybags VC owns 6,000 preference shares, they own 6,000/10,000 or 60% of all preference shares, and would therefore carry 60% of a vote in which preference shares voted as a class. Assume that only 300 of those shares are Series C shares. Moneybags VC would only carry 30% (300/1000 shares) of a vote of the Series C preference shareholders.

Now you can look at each term and dissect what voting approval is required and determine who controls the vote. For example, if converting from preference to ordinary shares requires a majority approval of the preference shareholders voting as a class, then Moneybags VC controls that vote. An acquisition of the company requires the approval of $^2/_{3}$rds (66%) of the Series C preference holders? Then you know that Moneybags VC, who only owns 30% of the Series C shares, doesn't even have a say, since the other Series C holders can carry the vote without them.

Look too at investors that invest frequently, or syndicate, together, since they may have structured the voting controls to account for their voting together. So, if Moneybags VC and Deep Pockets VC invest together, look at how the voting controls play out if you add their votes together.

Right of First Refusal & Co-sale

The right of first refusal term helps investors and the company to manage ownership of the company, and is considered friendly to both. It is a standard term and not worth negotiating. The right of first refusal generally applies to shares that company founders and investors own. In some cases, it can be structured to apply to employee shares as well.

The term requires that a founder or investor shareholder, who wishes to sell their shares to a third party, must first offer to sell the shares to the company. If the company does not purchase the shares, the shares are then offered to the preference investor that negotiated this right. This term protects against the sale of shares to competitors or other undesirable third parties.

If an investor or shareholder waives their right of first refusal, the co-sale right (also known as a 'tag along' right) gives them the right to join in the sale on a *pro rata* basis. Shareholders with a co-sale right participate in the sale at the same price and on the same terms as the selling shareholder. This term makes it more difficult for any one shareholder to sell their shares because, if co-sale rights are exercised, the purchaser must be willing and able to purchase the additional shares in order to complete the transaction, or the original selling shareholder must reduce the amount of their sale to accommodate the shareholders who are tagging along.

Drag Along Rights

Drag along rights require preference shareholders to vote for and sell their shares in an acquisition or sale of the company's assets that has been approved by a specified percentage of the preferred shareholders. Therefore, this term prevents small preference shareholders from blocking or obstructing a trade sale exit. Investors obtain this right through an irrevocable proxy signed by other preference shareholders.

The drag along right can be limited only to transactions approved by the Board, or to transactions at or above a specified price. This term is attractive if you think you may achieve an exit through a trade sale, since it prevents a minority shareholder from vetoing the transaction.

Pre-emption Rights

Pre-emption rights apply when the company is issuing new shares, such as in a new round of financing. This term gives shareholders the right, but not the obligation, to invest up to the amount of their current percentage ownership (known as a *pro rata* basis) in future rounds of financing. This allows investors to maintain their percentage ownership in the company through subsequent rounds of financing.

This term is attractive to both investors and entrepreneurs. Investors seek it as a way to protect themselves against future dilution. If they participate in every future round of financing on a *pro rata* basis, their ownership percentage in the company will remain constant. Entrepreneurs like it because, in general, they want to maximise participation in each round of financing. However, the company may find it beneficial to limit this right to shareholders greater than a certain size in order to avoid having to offer the right and wait for a response from multiple small shareholders.

As discussed earlier, pre-emption rights are awarded statutorily in Ireland, and must be 'dis-applied' in the company's Articles of Association if the company does not want to award them automatically to all investors. Even if investors are not granted a pre-emption right, the company can still offer them the opportunity to participate in a financing on a *pro rata* basis.

Similar to anti-dilution carve-outs, certain share issues, such as issues from the employee pool, are exempt from triggering pre-emption rights.

Board of Directors

With the rare exception, VCs always secure a seat on the Board of Directors. As a minority shareholder (which VCs usually are), the Board provides an alternative forum for exercising influence and control over the company's development.

In the term sheet, the term related to the Board of Directors will usually specify:

- The size of the Board.
- The Directors by name.
- The election process for any remaining members (for example, what shareholder class will elect the Director, and what percent vote – majority, ²/₃rds, 75% – will be required to approve the choice).
- The number of Directors the investor can elect.
- Any Committees the investors require to be formed (for example, Audit, Remuneration, etc.) and on which Committees (if any) the investor Directors will sit.
- Sometimes the investors also specify how frequently (for example, every month, once per quarter) the Board will meet.

Investors who sit on the Board are not compensated with any Directors' fees or cash, since ultimately their Board participation is rewarded through the increased value of their investment. If you see a fee term (and they do exist in Ireland), push hard to eliminate it, as there is little justification for the company to use its scarce cash to pay existing investors to fill a Director position that the investors themselves insisted upon.

It is more usual to compensate outside Directors, usually through share options rather than cash. In that way, their interests are aligned with management and other ordinary shareholders, and the company does not have to dip into its cash reserves.

The Board is generally limited to three to five members for an early-stage company, one of whom is the CEO, with one or two representatives from the investors, and one or two outside Directors, elected by the investors or jointly with the CEO.

VCs place great importance on the Board and will not be shy about restructuring a Board that is made up of company insiders, friends and family, or angels who add little value.

Protective Provisions

Protective provisions give preference shareholders a veto right over certain decisions. The term gives investors control over corporate actions and decisions that could affect the value of their investment. Protective provisions are also called 'consent rights' or 'negative covenants'. They identify certain corporate actions that cannot be undertaken without the consent of a defined percentage (for example, majority, ^{2}/₃rds, 75% or unanimous) of the holders of preference shares. The preference shareholders can be required to vote together as a class, or sometimes different series of preference shareholders will carve out their own protective provisions. From the company's perspective, it is more attractive and less cumbersome to keep the protective provisions subject to the vote of the preference shareholders as a class, and to avoid awarding rights to individual series. The existence of this term is non-negotiable, but the specific provisions of it are negotiable.

Some corporate actions that are commonly included in the protective provisions clause give investors the ability to approve or veto:

- Issuing or authorising a class of shares that is *pari passu* (equal) or senior to the current preference share class. (This is effectively a veto right over future rounds of financing.)
- Amending the Articles of Association.
- Creating subsidiaries or acquiring shares of any other company.
- Approving an acquisition or merger of the company, or a sale of substantially all the assets.
- Winding up of the company.
- Mortgaging or pledging assets of the company.
- Declaring dividends.
- Undertaking any material change in the business of the company.
- Changing the number of directors.
- Issuing any options or warrants.
- Authorising a management or employee share option plan.
- Changing the corporation's fiscal year end or changing auditors.
- Incurring debt in excess of a specified amount.

- Loaning any money to officers, directors or employees of the company

Other protective provisions might be proposed to take into account the specific circumstances of your company.

Information Rights

Investors want to receive a regular flow of financial information as a way to monitor their investment. The **Information Rights** term specifies the information investors want to receive, and when. Information rights appear to be a reasonable and benign term, but can become burdensome if you do not pay attention to the details. In particular, you need to assess how many investors you are promising to inform, and how much information you will need to send them. You also want to make sure that you can send the information electronically (to reduce paperwork and mailing costs) and that the investors receiving it will sign a confidentiality agreement regarding the information.

Usual provisions of the term include the investors' right to receive audited financial statements annually, unaudited financial statements monthly and an annual budget. Less common terms include the right to receive notice of any defaults, violation of loan covenants, or 'key events' such as offers of purchase, threatened lawsuits or notice of regulatory breaches. This term also usually includes a provision that allows the investor to obtain greater access to the company's financial records such as a right of inspection by the investor or someone they delegate (for example, an accountant).

Information rights can be limited to certain shareholders (for example, preference shareholders or holders of at least 5% of the outstanding ordinary shares). This is administratively helpful to the company, as it allows you to avoid sending out monthly financials to a large number of relatively small shareholders who, practically speaking, may have little use for such detailed information.

Representations & Warranties

The representations and warranties term (known as 'reps and warranties') is a standard term, in which the company provides factual assurances to investors about the current state of the business. The objective is to provide investors with a full set of facts and information about the entity in which they are investing.

Typical reps and warranties include:

- The company is a corporation duly organised to conduct business under relevant laws, is in good standing and has the appropriate power and authority to conduct its business.
- The current capitalisation of the company.
- Disclosure of any litigation pending or threatened.
- The company owns its intellectual property.
- Financial statements are true, complete and accurate.
- All tax returns have been filed and taxes paid up-to-date.

If the company cannot represent a material fact (for example, all tax returns have been filed), it must disclose the exception (for example, except for the most recent year). These disclosures are typically contained in a separate Schedule of Exceptions to the reps and warranties.

The point of the reps and warranties is to protect the investor from discovering damaging information post-investment that lowers the valuation of the company. Therefore, if any of the representations or warranties the company made turn out to be untrue, the investors will seek to be compensated for the breach of warranty. Usually the company issues the reps and warranties, so compensation for any breach would be sought from company assets. Compensation can be made by issuing additional shares or reducing the conversion price to reflect the reduction in valuation of the company attributable to the breach. In some cases (particularly very early-stage companies), the founders may assume some limited liability (up to a fixed Euro amount) for breaches. This amount is negotiable and is generally based on the stage of the company, the size of the investment and the resources of the founders.

Exclusivity

An exclusivity or 'no shop' term limits the company's ability to continue to seek interest from other investors and to generate a competitive bidding situation. Since interest from other investors gives the company choices and negotiating leverage, this term is unattractive from the company's perspective. Any entrepreneur would prefer a financing round in which he can generate interest from several potential investors and then select the best financing deal based on careful consideration of all the alternatives offered. Many investors are happy to compete in a merit-based 'free market' for the right to invest. Other investors prefer to eliminate competition and to secure a contractual monopoly on the investment opportunity through the use of an exclusivity clause. This term clearly favours the investor, as it reduces the competitive pressure of the deal and buys them time to complete due diligence.

Exclusivity clauses vary in their intensity. Some require that the company refrain from *all* discussions with other investors. Other more reasonable clauses simply prevent the company from actively seeking out and initiating discussions with new potential investors, but allows them to continue discussions already in progress.

Exclusivity clauses also vary in their duration. Investors who issue term sheets early in the due diligence process may request six to eight weeks of exclusivity, which can be very damaging to the company if the deal falls through. More reasonably, others will request two to three weeks near the end of the process, in order to conduct or finish particularly sensitive or expensive due diligence.

If you have been fortunate enough to generate interest from several potential investors, there is a strong argument to refusing the exclusivity and allowing the competitive process to proceed.

If you have received limited interest, or the investor is insistent on an exclusivity clause, it is likely that you will have to sign it, but attempt to limit it as much you can – for example, by the length of time it applies for and by applying it only to the initiation of new discussions.

Conditions to Close

This term outlines the conditions that must be met prior to close. From the investor's perspective, conditions to close serve two purposes. First, they focus the company on meeting specific milestones that are important, or even deal-breakers, to the investor. If a condition to close is that the company must obtain signed share option agreements with all employees participating in the share option plan, then it is likely to become a top priority for the entrepreneur and will be completed. Second, the conditions to close give the investor legitimate ways to withdraw from the deal, since the conditions must be met for the deal to close.

Common conditions to close include:

- Satisfactory completion by the investors of all due diligence they deem necessary.
- Agreement upon final documentation.
- No material adverse changes in the company.

There may be other customised terms that investors require to be met prior to closing, such as initiation or completion of a key hire or submission of a detailed operating plan for the next six months.

Closing

This closing term sets an estimated date and time for the closing of the investment. Some deals may be structured in stages or 'tranches' that involve more than one closing.

Tranched investment closings are generally based on the achievement of certain milestones. For example, a €4 million investment could be tranched into two closings of €2 million each. The first €2 million would be invested, with the second being subject to the company meeting defined objectives.

Tranched financing can be an effective way for VCs to mitigate the risk of a deal, since it ties a portion of the investment to the company's achievement of key value-enhancing milestones. If the company fails to achieve the milestones, investors are technically released from their obligation to invest but, in practice, it will generally result in a renegotiation of the terms of the tranche. Therefore, if the company fails to perform, the investor has the opportunity to negotiate a better deal on the remaining investment. Tranching can also help the investor to ensure that the company's management team is focused on high priority goals.

It is less advantageous to companies to accept tranche terms instead of a full up-front investment. Companies that accept a tranched investment do so because it may be the only way to attract investors to their company, or they feel that the milestones are easily achievable so there is little risk to accepting them as a term. The risk is that failure to meet the specified milestones can put the company in a cash-strapped position with little negotiating leverage to do anything but accept whatever terms the investor dictates.

Legal Counsel

This term mandates that the company retain legal counsel acceptable to investors to complete the deal. This prevents investors from having to work with inexperienced or small solicitor firms, which have no prior expertise or inadequate capacity to complete the transaction expertly and quickly.

This term also usually specifies which documents company counsel will draft and which agreements the investor counsel will draft.

Expenses

It is standard for the company to pay the investor's legal, due diligence and other transaction expenses incurred to close the transaction. The expenses are usually capped in the €20,000 to €40,000 range. Anything over the capped amount would be borne by the investor. This clause also usually states that, in cases where the VC withdraws and the transaction does not close, the VC will pay their own expenses incurred to that date.

Companies should not be required (nor should they be asked) to pay any other expenses to investors. It is an unattractive exception that an investor would seek additional fees from the company such as Board of Director compensation, 'investment fees', or 'monitoring fees'. Remember, VCs are already paid a management fee to cover their overhead expenses, and they are compensated for their investment-related activities through 'carry' from the returns on those investments. There is no rationale for you to take capital from your financing round to pay them more.

THE CLOSE

Once the due diligence and term sheet negotiations are complete, the term sheet serves as the template for drafting the legal documents required to close the investment. Among these documents are:

- **The Subscription Agreement:** This document contains details of the investment, including the number and class of shares purchased, payment terms and representations and warranties and their exceptions.

- **A Shareholders' or Investors' Rights Agreement:** This agreement details the investor rights and protections such as protective provisions, Board representation rights, etc.

- **The amended Articles of Association**, which includes the rights attaching to the various share classes, the procedures for the issue and transfer of shares and the holding of shareholder and Board meetings.

Your objective, when entering the document drafting phase of the deal, is to have a complete and clear term sheet that can largely be translated into legalese, with minimal recourse to further business discussion and decision-making. You want the business and deal structure negotiations to be generally complete, prior to the involvement of each side's solicitors.

Again, the term sheet will usually specify whose legal counsel drafts which documents. In general, it makes most sense for the company's counsel to take the lead on the Articles and any other company-specific documents, while the investor's counsel will usually draft the Subscription and Shareholder's Agreements. If you are working with an investor syndicate, make sure there is a lead counsel, who is acting as the final arbiter of investor issues and who can coordinate sign-off from each party.

The closing can take anywhere from two to six weeks, depending on how responsive your solicitors are and how many negotiable issues must be resolved during this part of the process. The closing is rarely a physical process anymore, but is rather a matter of circulating documents for signature and wiring the cash. If an investor syndicate is investing, the investor's lead counsel will set up an escrow account into which each investor can wire their portion of the capital. When all signed documents and capital from each investor is received, the full amount is then wired in a single amount to the company.

CONCLUSION

Receiving a term sheet is a major step towards finalising and closing a financing round with a VC. Term sheets are relatively standard in that VCs consistently seek the same economic protections and control provisions to maximise the value of their investment. Where they differ is in the structure of each term.

When you receive a term sheet, ensure that it contains sufficient detail to accurately understand the deal being proposed. Work closely with a sophisticated, specialised and experienced advisor to sort through the structure and nuances of each term and how they impact the valuation and affect the outcome of an exit. Each term is only one piece of the puzzle. They must each be understood individually, but then placed together to get an accurate big picture of the entire deal.

PART IV:
EXITS

10
PUBLIC OFFERINGS

Scaling the mountain is what makes the view from the top so exhilarating.
Denis Waitley

The IPO is considered the ultimate in entrepreneurial success. What young Managing Director doesn't dream of listing his or her company on a stock exchange and enjoying the credibility and reputation that running a public company confers? Who doesn't doodle possible ticker symbols when deciding what to name their young start-up? IPOs or 'flotations' are so appealing because they not only represent corporate success, but also the possibility of enormous increases in your own personal wealth. From an analysis of the data on exits of companies that have received equity financing from VCs, it is also clear that IPOs generate, on average, the highest returns for investors.

Yet so many entrepreneurs fail to view an IPO as a realistic choice for an exit. Many Irish companies labour under the false belief that they are too small or have too little revenues to go public. In fact, you don't have to be a €100 million, or even a €50 million, revenue company to conduct an IPO. Companies with as little as €10 or €20 million in revenues can go public, at a cost of around 10% of the total capital raised. The listing criteria for exchanges like the OFEX and AIM in London, or the NASDAQ Small Cap in the US, are quite lenient with regard to market capitalisation requirements, and can be an appropriate source of liquidity for a wide range of companies.

Irish companies are in the enviable position of having many choices available to them when it comes to the stock exchanges on which they can list. As Irish companies that reach the stage and scale to consider an IPO have successfully established their business in other markets, they generally have the credible choice of either listing on the domestic exchange, or on a foreign exchange in the country in which they operate.

WHY GO PUBLIC?

A public offering is not a final exit for the management team, nor does it mark the end of your company's development and growth. To the contrary, while an IPO provides you and your team an opportunity to realise gains on your personal equity positions, it also returns significant control to the management team, as discussed further below. Because it is an equity financing event – you are raising equity capital from the public – it provides additional resources to fuel continued company development and growth.

Companies have a range of objectives when they make the decision to go public, including:

- **To raise capital:** Companies go public to raise the large amounts of capital required to help them execute a specific corporate strategy – financing rapid expansion, launching into new markets, or creating the stock currency to begin executing acquisitions. Relative to raising it through a private financing, a public offering offers the advantage of a higher average valuation. Public shares attract higher valuations from investors because they are freely tradable, so there is no need for a 'liquidity discount' and because there is considerably more detailed financial and business information available about the company.

- **To achieve some liquidity for founders / employees:** After devoting the 'sweat equity' and time to build a young company, it is not unusual for the management team and employees to want to realise some financial gains and lock in returns from their company's increase in value. If this is your objective, assess the potential impact of timing constraints. Management and employees will almost always have to agree to a 'lock-up' period, during in which they are prohibited from selling their shares. This period can last from 180 days to a full year. Even after the lock-up expires, public investors can interpret significant insider selling as a bad sign, which can compel top management to hold the stock even longer. Finally, management is increasingly obliged to consider the perception, as well as the reality, of insider trading, which could limit how quickly or how much they can sell at any given time.

A liquidity objective will also require you to pay particular attention to organising post-IPO support for your stock in the form of public relations and analyst coverage. You want to ensure that the stock's trading volume and price is sustained until the lock-up expires and management and employees are able to sell their shares.

- **To give investors an exit:** As we saw during the Internet boom, there are many times when investors will push a company to execute a public offering, if the timing or market conditions are right. Investors are very aware that market windows can close quickly and may advocate listing sooner than anticipated, in order to lock in attractive returns. Investors are subject to the same lock-up as management, so similar issues to those described above in the previous point also apply in this instance.

PREPARING FOR AN IPO

Executing a successful public offering requires substantial planning. The timeline for beginning to plan actively for a listing is usually 12 to 24 months before the anticipated admission to an exchange. The groundwork, however, can and should be laid earlier than that, since the UK and US exchanges have a number of common expectations for companies applying for admission.

Most importantly, a company that is planning to go public should be experiencing good growth and profitability to make it attractive to investors. It will also need to have its corporate records in pristine order from the very beginning. Part of the process of going public requires extensive due diligence from solicitors, so all corporate documents should be complete, accurate and well-organised. Most exchanges will want to see three years of audited financials, if the company has been in business that long. The auditors should be one of the 'Big Four' international accounting firms of Deloitte, Ernst & Young, KPMG and PwC.

The objective to go public will also impact on some of your key hires, as you will need to ensure that you have an 'IPO-ready' team. If you plan to list your company, it makes sense to hire key management team members (particularly a CFO) with prior experience of taking a company public or of running a public company. Finally, public exchanges look carefully at the corporate governance policies and practices of the companies they admit. You will need to have a Board of Directors that includes independent Directors, an audit committee, and that follows governance best practices. If the company does not end up going public, these preparations represent good corporate management practices and will help the company, even in the event that it executes a trade sale exit (discussed further in **Chapter 11**).

Even the best planning can't control general market conditions. Public markets are volatile, and the best laid IPO plans can become unachievable if your sector falls out of favour or the broader IPO market closes. If market conditions become unfavourable, you can wait it out through the cycle, raise additional private funds, or seek a trade sale exit. The good news is that planning for an IPO can have the added benefit of providing the company with negotiating leverage in a potential trade sale. If you can present going public as a viable alternative for your company, and one for which you have been preparing, it puts pressure on the acquiring company to make an offer that matches or exceeds the returns you would obtain through a listing.

IS AN IPO THE RIGHT EXIT?

While an IPO may be a compelling idea to a young entrepreneur for all the benefits and status it confers, taking a company public is an enormously complex and rigorous process that will be time-consuming and expensive. It is also not really an exit so much as a long-term commitment to building a business future in the public eye.

IPO advantages

There are a number of reasons that companies choose to pursue an IPO as an exit opportunity. A public offering can give the company:

- **Capital proceeds**: IPOs offer companies a way to raise significant capital through a single transaction. Companies seeking to move to the next stage of growth and expansion find that they need such an influx of capital in order to invest in the necessary infrastructure and staff prior to anticipated growth, to increase R&D efforts, or to have sufficient amounts of working capital.

- **Access to future capital**: After the IPO has taken place, the company retains the potential to raise additional capital on an as-needed basis, through relatively quick and easy subsequent financings and secondary offerings.
- **A currency to conduct acquisitions**: It can be faster and cheaper to acquire market share, products, customers, channels or other resources by purchasing them than by building them internally. For example, a company that wants to expand to the US may find it easier to purchase an existing firm with established staff, customers and distributors rather than to build its operations from scratch. Companies that want to pursue a strategy of growth through acquisitions find that public shares offer an excellent source of currency for executing purchases. Because public shares are concretely valued, it makes it much easier to conduct purchases with share currency. Having a ready source of capital to conduct acquisitions can allow the company to grow quickly, expand into new markets, integrate vertically, or purchase and integrate emerging competitors.
- **Liquidity for investors and employees**: For founders, an IPO can represent the first time that they can sell any of their shares and release a portion of the value they have built over the preceding years. Similarly, employees who have been compensated through equity can realise a portion or all of their gains.
- **Increased visibility, recognition and reputation**: Public companies, in general, find that they benefit from the increased cachet and aura of success that going public confers. The company's name becomes linked with achievement. In terms of recognition, the required increase in public communications, such as quarterly conference calls, analyst meetings, investment road shows and industry conferences all serve to raise the company's profile.
- **Increased perception of size and stability**: Companies don't grow overnight just because they are public, yet being public carries with it a connotation of weight, size and a certain *gravitas*. Instead of being a young small start-up, you will suddenly be able to impress potential customers, partners and suppliers with

your stories of going public. Companies often find that going public can have a positive impact on their sales efforts as they suddenly appear to be a lower-risk vendor.

- **Management control**: Unlike trade sales, in which the management team of the acquiring company takes over operations and control of the new entity, an IPO allows the existing management to remain in place and to continue to run the company. Management will also gain back significant control from investors, since preference shareholders convert to ordinary shares as part of the IPO and, in so doing, relinquish their preferred rights, controls and vetoes over key corporate decisions.

IPO disadvantages

On the other hand, IPOs are difficult and complicated exits. Compared to a trade sale, there are some less appealing aspects of a public offering:

- **The IPO can go poorly**: One of the biggest risks of going public is that the IPO fails to raise the capital and valuation of the company by as much as expected. A public offering can result in the company raising too little capital, not achieving the liquidity it was seeking, and having thinly traded stock. Public shareholders are a demanding bunch and the company must maintain growth and profitability of sufficient speed and scale to maintain interest and demand for their shares.

    Another hazard is that the company exposes itself to the broader risks of the market. You could go public and then a downturn in your sector caused by an external event or a change in sentiment could impact your company's stock price negatively, even if your performance remains strong. A disappointing outcome is probably the most significant risk of a public offering.

- **Costs of conducting an IPO**: The successful completion of an IPO requires the services of a variety of expert advisors. Expect the costs of the solicitors, accountants, investment bankers, underwriters, brokers, printers, and public relations firms to total close to 10% of the total funds raised for small offerings of less than €10 million. These fees can fall to as low as 5% for very large offerings. After the IPO, the company must continue to incur the expense of ongoing reporting and compliance, the cost of which will vary depending on the market and exchange on which you are traded.

The costs in terms of management time are also high. A public offering consumes management time, focus and energy throughout the IPO process – before, during and after.

- **Public disclosure**: Few companies relish the idea that their financial performance, executive remuneration, key financing transactions, and product development will be subject to widespread public scrutiny, yet the public offering process will demand the presentation, filing and sharing of information that the company previously considered private. And after the IPO, there are ongoing public reporting and information requirements that are specific, demanding and time consuming to fulfil.

- **Need to focus on short-term quarterly results**: Public companies are evaluated every quarter against whether they met revenue, growth and earnings expectations (expectations which the company may, or may not, have set for itself). As a corollary to the advantage of achieving technical management control in an IPO, it is not uncommon for managers of a public company to feel like they are managing to everyone else's expectations (shareholders, analysts, regulators) and to feel like they actually have very little control over key strategic decisions. This can be compounded by the ongoing need to achieve short-term milestones, which must often be met at the expense of longer-term investments and plans.

- **Marketing requirements**: Before and after the public offering, the company must proactively generate market demand for its own shares in order to help sustain the price and maintain trading volumes. Your PR firm and analysts will work to create demand as well, but a successful effort ultimately requires a significant commitment from the company and management. Creating and maintaining demand involves managing the expectations, and attracting the attention, of the press, analysts, investment banks and institutional investors. Most public companies find it makes sense to create an internal Investor Relations department, with staff dedicated to dealing with the investment community and investors.

- **Employee distraction**: Employees can become very distracted during a public offering. This distraction can continue following the offering as they focus on the company's stock price, the impact of the changes in price on their personal net worth, and their options for optimising tax consequences. As discussed in **Chapter 5**, employees who are compensated with equity are particularly sensitive to volatility or changes in the stock price. It is a huge culture change to become a public company, and you will have to work with employees to help them understand the listing process, what it means for the company to be public, and how the different expectations of a public company will translate into the work process and performance objectives.

WHERE TO GO PUBLIC?

Successful Irish companies become international very early in their development. Because the size of the domestic market is so small, Irish companies must open offices, sell to customers and penetrate markets around the world. As a result, when it comes time to think about a public offering, many Irish companies have the market presence and local relationships to consider a listing on at least one foreign exchange.

How do you best decide where to go public? There are several key considerations to evaluate:

- Where is your company well-known? Where are most of your customers, revenues, business offices and partners?
- Are there indications of interest from local institutional investors?
- Is there a local retail base that would be interested in buying your stock?
- What are the admission criteria for the exchange?

- Is a dual listing easily accommodated?
- What are the estimated costs of reporting, compliance and maintaining the listing?

In the past several years, a large percentage of Irish companies that went public have done so successfully in the UK. In addition, during the late 1990s, Irish companies became well-known for their successes in listing in the US. In fact, going public abroad has become more common than listing at home. Since 2000, the Irish Stock Exchange has seen more than 40 de-listings and, in the past four years, from 2000 to 2004, there have been only six new domestic listings.

UK Exchanges

The UK remains the most promising venue for Irish companies to go public. So many Irish firms have significant business operations in the UK that it is only natural to consider the British exchanges a viable exit option. The UK's vibrant and successful stock exchanges, most notably London's Alternative Investment Market (AIM), have been a top choice for Irish IPOs.

Alternative Investment Market

The lone success story in a line of failures, the London Stock Exchange's Alternative Investment Market (AIM) has survived the demise of similar European small company markets, including the Neuer Markt, EASDAQ, Euro.NM and the ITEQ. AIM is one of the friendliest stock exchanges to young companies and, since it began operating in 1995, it has become one of the most successful exchanges for small and medium-sized companies. Since 2000, 20 Irish companies have listed on the exchange, and the rate of listings appears to be increasing. Seven of the 20 firms listed in the first half of 2005.

AIM is most appropriate for companies seeking to raise €3 million or more in a public offering. The largest number of companies trading on AIM have a market capitalisation in the €10 million to €40 million range, although there are many companies on either side of that range as well. Where AIM differs from most exchanges is the absence of specific listing criteria that companies must meet in order to list. In particular, companies listing on AIM do not have to meet minimum requirements for size, revenue or income, market capitalisation, trading history, price per share or the percentage of company shares that must be in public hands.

Instead, the key listing requirement on AIM is the retention by the company of a nominated advisor. The 'Nomad', as they are called (from *Nom*inated *Ad*viser), must be a corporate finance firm, an accountant or a broker. AIM maintains a list of approved Nomads from which companies can choose. The Nomad confirms to AIM that specific information in the company's admission document is correct, and that the company is appropriate and suitable for public listing. The Nomad provides advice and oversight to listed companies on an ongoing basis.

AIM also recommends (but does not require) that you hire other key advisors to help you go public. These include a(n):

- **Accountant:** To ensure that your financials are independently audited.
- **Broker:** Many brokers are listed as approved Nomads. The broker must be a member of the London Stock Exchange. Their job is to manage and to help create a market for your shares and advise on the initial pricing of the shares.
- **Lawyer:** There are many legal agreements that must be drafted as part of an IPO. The lawyer also conducts due diligence, and leads the drafting of the prospectus.
- **Public relations firm:** Some companies choose to build this capability in-house. PR staff assist with the road show, dealing with analysts and investors, and helping with investor relations.

The public listing process itself takes about 12 to 24 weeks. AIM fees consist of a flat admission fee of £4,180 (about €6,000), and a flat annual fee thereafter of £4,180. The cost of advisors and the preparation for going public is generally estimated to be about 8-12% of capital raised.

OFEX

OFEX is generally considered to be the first rung on the UK exchange ladder. A typical OFEX company would have a market cap of less than €30 million (£20 million) and be seeking to raise from €1 million to €7 million (£1 million to £5 million) through the flotation.

OFEX stands for 'Off Exchange' and, as its name suggests, OFEX was not really a stock exchange when it was founded in 1995, but rather a trading platform run by a single brokerage firm. Since 2004, the exchange has re-invented itself. OFEX is now a publicly-traded electronic stock exchange with a competing market-maker system and institutional investors. New management is in place, including the former head of AIM, and new market rules were adopted in April 2005. There are currently about 140 companies on OFEX.

The admission requirements are quite friendly for young companies. OFEX does not require a minimum market capitalisation, trading history, or percentage of shares to be distributed to the public.

However, OFEX does require that companies meet other specific criteria for admission, including:

- Retaining an OFEX Corporate Advisor at all times. Similar to the Nomad on the AIM, companies applying to list on OFEX must retain a corporate advisor, who helps prepare the admissions documents, conducts due diligence, confirms that the information provided to the exchange is true, and serves as an ongoing advisor to the company.
- Demonstrating 'appropriate levels of corporate governance', which, at minimum, means the participation of non-executive Directors on the company's Board.
- Publishing audited financial reports and accounts (for three years or the company's operating history, whichever is longer).
- Possessing adequate working capital for at least 12 months after admission to the exchange.
- No restrictions on transferability of shares.
- Confirmation that the company's shares can be settled electronically.

OFEX requires a flat admission fee of £5,000 (about €7,250), with ongoing annual fees based on the company's market capitalisation. The estimated advisor costs associated with a listing are about £125,000 to £150,000 (approx. €180,000 to €220,000).

Irish Stock Exchanges

The Irish Stock Exchange (ISE) markets have undergone several changes in the past decade. The Developing Companies Market (DCM) and the Exploration Securities Market (ESM) both ceased to exist when the companies listed on them were transferred to the new Irish Enterprise Exchange (IEX) in April 2005. The Technology Market of the Irish Stock Exchange (ITEQ) was a short-lived and failed experiment that launched in 2000 and closed in July 2005.

IEX is the new exchange designed to attract and facilitate the listing of small and medium sized Irish businesses.

Irish Enterprise Exchange

The Irish Enterprise Exchange was launched in April 2005 to facilitate the public listing of Irish small companies. The IEX was formed by transferring eight companies from the former Developing Companies Market and Exploration Securities Market. The total market cap of the exchange in mid-2005 was about €600 million. Up to July 2005, only one new company had listed on the IEX, a London-based platinum and nickel exploration firm. The company was previously listed on the OFEX and pursued a dual listing on AIM and IEX.

The structure and rules of IEX were designed to mirror those of AIM in London. There are no minimum requirements for trading history, shares to be held in public hands, nor is Irish Stock Exchange approval required. In contrast to AIM, however, IEX requires that companies applying for admission have a minimum market capitalisation of €5 million. An admission fee of €4,000 is payable by all companies seeking admission of securities to IEX.

US Exchanges

Irish companies have a strong record of public listing on US exchanges. For example, AIB Bank, Bank of Ireland, Diageo and Elan list on the New York Stock Exchange (NYSE), while Baltimore, CRH, Datalex, ICON, IONA, Riverdeep, Ryanair, Trintech and Waterford Wedgwood all trade as American Depository Receipts (ADRs) on the NASDAQ stock market. Companies choosing to list in the US have many choices, including the New York Stock Exchange (NYSE), the

NASDAQ National Market and SmallCap markets or the American Stock Exchange (AMEX).

An NYSE listing is most appropriate for companies that meet the minimum market cap listing requirement of $500 million, and the annual revenue of minimum of $100 million. Since most Irish companies that go public are much smaller than this, this review will focus on the smaller cap exchanges such as NASDAQ and the AMEX.

The benefits of a US listing can be considerable. Particularly for foreign companies, it sets them apart as having reached a level of success that few others have. The US also has a very active and significantly-sized institutional and retail base of investors, which can provide an attractive and liquid market for selling shares.

But the environment for public companies has changed tremendously in the US in the wake of Enron and WorldCom accounting scandals. The US has become a much more expensive place to be listed since the introduction of Sarbanes-Oxley regulations (SOX) in 2002. In mid-2005, *The Economist*[3] reported that firms with revenues of less than €100 million could expect to pay around 2.5% of revenues for SOX compliance costs, a large figure to add on top of the already considerable costs of a public listing.

Registration rights

US listings also have the additional administrative requirement to register company shares with the Securities & Exchange Commission (SEC) in order to go public. In the US, a privately held company's shares are considered restricted and can only be sold or traded under defined circumstances. When a company initiates a public offering, it must register with the SEC the shares it wishes to trade publicly. The company must submit a variety of information in its registration documents to the SEC, including a draft prospectus for the offering as well as additional financial information, disclosures, and a 'management discussion' about the state of the business. The share registration approval can take anywhere from several weeks to several months. These administrative burdens are unique to a US listing, as no similar requirements are found on European exchanges.

---

[3] Sarbanes-Oxley: A price worth paying?, *The Economist*, 19 May 2005.

If your company is anticipating the possibility of a public offering on a US exchange, registration rights should be a negotiated term in any financing with preference shareholders. While these are rights for investors, it is in the company's interest to deal with them proactively, since it is unlikely the preference shareholders will provide the necessary approvals and votes for an IPO in the US unless they are able to register and sell their shares. Once the shares are registered and the restrictions are removed, the shares are fully liquid and can be traded freely.

Registration rights are a standard term in US term sheets and include:

- **Demand rights**: Because only the company can file to register shares with the SEC, investors negotiate for the right to 'demand' that their shares be registered for sale. The company registers the shares by filing the S-1 Form with the SEC. Usually a specified percentage of investors are required to invoke a demand (for example, a majority or ⅔rds vote of the preference shareholders voting as a class).

- **Piggyback rights**: These rights apply when the company is registering its own shares or those of another investor. They give the investor the right to register their shares (or piggyback) along with any shares the company is registering. In the case of an IPO, when an underwriter may cut back the number of shares being registered for sale, this right is written to ensure that the investor will be able to register his *pro rata* shares.

- **Registration on Form S-3**: Form S-3 is a shorter form than the traditional S-1 form normally required in a registration, and can be used by companies that have been public for a minimum of one year and have a market value of their publicly held shares that is greater than $75 million. Similar to a demand right, this allows investors to require that the company register their shares for sale with the SEC, but this term is less onerous and cheaper for the company than a demand right.

- **Registration expenses**: This term usually requires that all the expenses of registering shares, including fees, expenses and printing, will be borne by the company. The exception is that underwriters' commissions typically are paid by the investor.

♦ **Lock-up**: Since it is usually required by underwriters, investors will normally agree to a standard lock-up period of 180 days, as long as other shareholders, including management and other shareholders who have 1% or more of the company, agree to a lock-up of the same timeframe.

Registration rights do not have to be part of the share purchase agreement, but can be defined in a separate Registration Rights Agreement between the company and its shareholders (which can be created and signed after the financing). This option is helpful if a listing on a US exchange becomes a possibility after you have completed one or more rounds of equity financing.

NASDAQ National Market

Over the past decade, the NASDAQ has become known for its many successful listings of cutting-edge technology companies. Microsoft, Dell, Intel and Cisco are just a few of the top US technology companies that originally listed on NASDAQ and have chosen to stay. As mentioned above, Irish companies from a variety of industries have successfully listed and continue to trade on NASDAQ. Established in 1971, NASDAQ is now the largest electronic stock market in the US. Unlike the NYSE, NASDAQ has no physical trading floor. NASDAQ consists of the National Market and the Small Cap market, and, since 1998, also owns the American Stock Exchange (AMEX).

Companies that wish to list on the NASDAQ must meet one of three initial listing standards (**Figure 9**).

The costs of listing on NASDAQ include a $5,000 non-refundable application fee, plus an entry fee based on the number of shares listed, or ADRs issued, and outstanding in the US. For foreign companies, these fees start at $100,000 for 30 million or fewer ADRs, $125,000 for 30 million to 50 million ADRs and $150,000 for more than 50 million ADRs. Ongoing annual fees are determined on a sliding scale based on the number of ADRs listed on the exchange. The annual fee for fewer than 10 million ADRs is $21,225. The maximum fee, levied if more than 100 million ADRs are listed, is $30,000 per annum.

Figure 9: NASDAQ National Market Initial Listing Criteria

	Standard 1	Standard 2	Standard 3
Stockholder's equity	$15m	$30m	NA
Market value of listed securities **OR** Total assets & Total revenue	NA	NA	$75m **OR** $75m & $75m
Income from continuing operations before income taxes (in latest FY or 2 of last 3 FYs)	$1m	NA	NA
Publicly held shares	1.1m	1.1m	1.1m
Market value of publicly held shares	$8m	$18m	$20m
Minimum bid price	$5	$5	$5
Shareholders (100+ shares each)	400	400	400
Market-makers	3	3	4
Operating history	NA	2yrs	NA
Corporate governance	Yes	Yes	Yes

Source: NASDAQ Listing Standards & Fees, March 2005 (www.nasdaq.com).

NASDAQ SmallCap Market

The NASDAQ SmallCap offers less demanding standards that allow for smaller-sized companies to list (**Figure 10**).

Figure 10: NASDAQ SmallCap Market Initial Listing Criteria

	Listing Standard
Stockholders' equity **OR** Market value of listed securities **OR** Net income from continuing operations (in latest FY or 2 of the last 3 FYs)	$5m **OR** $50m **OR** $750k
Publicly held shares	1m
Market value of publicly held shares	$5m
Minimum bid price	$4
Shareholders (100+ shares each)	300
Market-makers	3
Operating history **OR** Market value of listed securities	NA*
Corporate governance	Yes

Source: NASDAQ Listing Standards & Fees, March 2005 (www.nasdaq.com).

* Non-Canadian foreign companies do not have to meet this criteria, which is usually 1 year of operating history or $50 million market value of listed securities.

For non-US issuers, entry fees are levied only on those shares or ADRs issued and outstanding in the US. The fees range from $25,000 for 5 million or fewer shares, up to $50,000 for more than 15 million shares. A $5,000 non-refundable application fee is included in those amounts. Annual fees for ADRs listed on the NASDAQ SmallCap Market are based on the number of ADRs listed. For up to 10 million ADRs, the annual fee is $17,500; over 10 million, it is $21,000.

American Stock Exchange

The American Stock Exchange (AMEX) was initially created as an alternative to the NYSE. The AMEX is a floor-based exchange that was purchased by the NASDAQ in 1998, although it continues to operate distinctly. The AMEX primarily lists small and mid-cap stocks, and is one of the largest options exchanges in the world. Natural resources, technology and healthcare companies make up over one-third of the AMEX Composite Index. Foreign companies that wish to list on the exchange must meet one of four Standards (**Figure 11**).

AMEX explicitly evaluates the qualitative, as well as quantitative financial, characteristics of the companies applying to list with it. Such qualitative characteristics include management reputation, financial integrity, historical growth, earnings and profits, and future potential.

Non-US companies pay half of the initial listing fee for AMEX and, if they issue no more than 5 million shares, the initial listing fee is $17,500 plus an ongoing annual fee of $15,000. At the other end of the range, if more than 50 million shares are issued, this incurs an initial listing fee of $32,500 and an annual fee of $30,000.

Interestingly, AMEX launched an Emerging Company Marketplace (ECM) in 1992, in order to provide an exchange for small and medium companies that did not meet the listing criteria for regular listing on AMEX. Initially, there were 22 firms listed, many with market capitalisations of less than $20 million. The ECM fell victim to several high-profile scandals related to its insufficient screening of companies, and was unable over time to attract a critical mass of companies. It closed in May 1995.

Figure 11: American Stock Exchange Criteria for Listing Foreign Companies

	Standard 1	Standard 2	Standard 3	Standard 4
Shareholder's Equity	$4m	$4m	$4m	NA
Pre-tax income	$750,000 in last FY, or in 2 of last 3 FY	NA	NA	NA
Public distribution	Note 1	Note 1	Note 1	Note 1
Price per share	$3	$3	NA	$3
Market value of the public float	$3m	$15m	$15m	$20m
History of operations	NA	2 yrs	NA	NA
Total market capitalisation	NA	NA	$50m	$75m or total assets & rev of $75m each in the most recent FY or in 2 of the last 3 FY

Source: American Stock Exchange (www.amex.com).

FY – Fiscal year

Note 1: Companies must meet any one of the following three minimum criteria for public distribution:
1. 800 public shareholders and 500,000 shares publicly held, **OR**
2. 400 public shareholders and 1m shares publicly held, **OR**
3. 400 public shareholders, 500,000 shares publicly held, and average daily trading volume of 2,000 shares for the previous six months.

POST-IPO

An IPO is not always successful. A company that has a poor public offering could find itself with a thinly-traded stock that provides little liquidity over time to investors or employees. A small cap company with a depressed share price can find that it is difficult to grow or to attract employees, partners and even customers. Growing through acquisition is not possible with a depreciated share currency. Instead of lingering indefinitely in poorly performing purgatory, there are a few alternatives the company can consider.

PIPE Financing

Public companies whose stocks are languishing but need to raise additional capital can pursue a PIPE financing (Private Investment in Public Equity). In a PIPE deal, VCs, private equity funds or hedge funds buy a new issue of the company's common stock at a 10-15% discount to the current market trading price per share. The new investors generally agree to a lock-up period of at least 180 days, and often longer, which prevents them from buying the shares at a discount and quickly 'flipping' them for a quick profit.

A PIPE deal is significantly faster and cheaper than a secondary offering because the shares are sold privately, incurring minimal legal, accounting, and underwriting fees. PIPE deals can be an extremely effective way to efficiently provide the capital boost to get a company through a market downturn, or temporary sector slump, or through a bad quarter.

Going Private

A second option for poorly performing public companies is to 'go private' again. There are a number of firms that specialise in this sort of transaction and can help you execute a buyout – either from management or with the help of private financing or a buyout firm.

CONCLUSION

Going public is like winning the entrepreneurial Olympics. Because only a few companies in each industry sector are large enough and successful enough to go public, the ones that succeed attain tremendous credibility and respect. Having taken a company public is also an impressive testimony to the expertise and credentials of each of the members of your management team.

Irish companies are well-positioned to list on any number of exchanges. London's AIM is currently the most popular among Irish companies, as it is friendly to medium-sized firms and offers good liquidity for most companies, with a relatively simple listing process. Ireland has a relatively low rate of IPOs among venture-backed companies, in part because many firms mistakenly believe that they are too small to go public, and in part because trade sales are so popular and generally occur first, at an earlier point in the company's development than an IPO.

11
TRADE SALES

Take care to sell your horse before he dies.
Robert Frost

It happens. One day, you walk into your office and get a call from Big Company Ltd, the market leader in your space, who has identified your company and your products as essential to its future success. Your ordinary day has just turned into the day you received an unsolicited offer to buy your company. Unlike IPOs, which must be meticulously planned and organised, trade sales (or at least offers to buy) can just happen. Start-up companies frequently become the acquisition targets of larger corporations that have noticed their success in a related or competitive market and want to purchase them for strategic reasons. For instance, IONA's acquisitions of Netfish Technology, EJB Home and Watershed Technologies were reportedly made for product extension and strategic reasons.

Or, more traditionally, you could have been planning carefully for a trade sale for some time and your company is well-positioned to be acquired. Your products are trouncing the competition, your customers are happy, and your company is well-organised and ready for examination by potential buyers. You've hired your advisors, talked to your investors and management team, and have put the word out that you are seriously seeking a buyer. Like IPOs, trade sales can be organised and planned to take place according to your timeframe.

Trade sales are the most common exit among Irish firms, so either scenario is a possibility for your company. Whatever way it happens, the issues that arise in relation to the completion of a trade sale are the same regardless of whether the approach by the external buyer is solicited or a surprise.

Trade sales offer several advantages as an exit:

- Most buyers offer a premium price in excess of the company's current value to facilitate Board and management approval for the deal. A buyer may also be willing to offer a premium price to reflect the strategic benefits of the deal for them, such as an increased market share, new or broader distribution channels, a complementary product, or the reduction in competition.
- Trade sales can be much faster and cheaper than an IPO, and can be done in private, without the need for public disclosure about the price, structure and terms of the deal.
- Trade sales require much less PR, marketing and selling activities than an IPO. Companies going public must 'sell' their shares to regulators, the exchange, advisors, financial institutions and public retail investors, whereas companies interested in a trade sale need only find and attract one buyer. The trade-off is that the one 'right' buyer can be much more difficult to identify, contact and interest.

What are the disadvantages of a trade sale? First, trade sales do not normally provide a quick and full exit for entrepreneurs and the management team. Key management team members or technical employees typically must agree to work at the new combined company to ensure a smooth transition or to meet the conditions of earn-out payments. Both these conditions delay the final exit until some time after the deal has closed. Investors may also be 'locked-up' for a short period, if the deal is partially paid for with the buyer's company stock. Second, the main disadvantage of a trade sale is that, on average, trade sales generate a lower return to investors and management than public offerings, and are therefore seen as less desirable exits.

A trade sale is also not without risk. Like any financing deal, a potential acquisition can fall apart for any number of reasons, and at any stage during the process. As a selling company, you can mitigate this risk by working in parallel to attract other acquirers or assess the possibility of an IPO exit, and by ensuring that your business continues to be well-run and meets performance targets throughout the deal.

11: Trade Sales

This chapter does not set out to provide a comprehensive discussion of trade sale transactions – primarily because you can expect to be well-advised during such a transaction. However, it does highlight the key terms and issues to consider in a trade sale transaction that might not be obvious from the outset. These topics are good discussion points to review with your advisors in order to determine their relevance to your company's particular situation / circumstance and characteristics.

PREPARING FOR A TRADE SALE

There are a variety of steps you can take early on to be prepared and positioned for a possible solicited, or unsolicited, trade sale exit.

Hold a Beauty Contest

As always, with any significant transaction, hire good advisors and hire them early. If you are preparing your company to be acquired, the first step is to hold a so-called 'beauty contest' of potential advisors. Talk to several different advisors within each category (solicitors, accountants, bankers), obtain proposals and bids, conduct reference checks and then select your team.

To conduct a trade sale, you will also want to hire and work with a corporate finance expert with experience negotiating trade sale transactions. All major investment banks, as well as specialised corporate finance firms, offer such services. The good news is that because trade sales are so common among Irish companies, there is a wealth of experience among the top 10 legal, accounting and banking firms in executing trade sale transactions.

With acquisitions in particular, the tax impacts of how the deal is structured can be enormously varied and complex. There are different tax consequences, depending on whether the transaction is an acquisition or merger, an asset or stock sale, or paid for in cash or stock. By working with a tax advisor from the beginning, you can minimise the negative tax effects that may arise from the transaction. When it comes to reviewing the initial terms of the deal and negotiating the final structure, a good solicitor with trade sale expertise, as well as experienced bankers, can help ensure you end up with a fair and reasonable deal.

Do the Numbers

Before the process begins, it is helpful to understand what an attractive price range would be for your company, and what valuations you would consider. If you have raised prior rounds of financing, you know that the purchase price a buyer offers is only a partial view of the true value of the deal. To get an accurate sense of what would be an attractive purchase price, start with the deal documents from your previous financing and an Excel spreadsheet.

First, look carefully at any liquidation preferences awarded to investors in previous rounds, as these will dictate how the sale proceeds are allocated. Determine what type of liquidation preference your prior investors have (for example, none, 1x, 2x) and whether they are entitled to participate on a *pro rata* basis in any other proceeds with ordinary shareholders. A high liquidation preference and / or low purchase price can mean that the ordinary shareholders receive very little or no proceeds at all from the deal. For example, if the last round of VCs invested €10 million with a 2x liquidation preference and a buyer is offering €20 million, then the full €20 million goes first to the VCs, leaving nothing left for ordinary shareholders. For an entrepreneur who has spent several years building the company, walking away with nothing is a very disappointing outcome.

Such a situation can lead to conflict between the management and the investors. The investors, who are getting their money back (perhaps with a return), will favour the deal. The ordinary shareholders, who are positioned to get nothing, would rather pass on the deal and wait for a higher price. If the preference shareholders control the vote, the only leverage ordinary shareholders may have is to make it clear to the buyer that, on such terms, they will leave the company once it has been acquired. The threat that management will walk could be a deal-breaker for the buyer, which would put pressure on the investors to choose between keeping their liquidation preference or negotiating it away to facilitate the completion of the sale.

If the liquidation preference is too high to give ordinary shareholders any proceeds, preference investors can either negotiate the size of their liquidation preference downwards to a point where ordinary shareholders find the deal attractive, or agree to a management carve-out. A carve-out sets aside a fixed amount or percentage of sale proceeds for the management team, and possibly other key employees. These carved-out funds are distributed ahead of the liquidation preference, so they represent guaranteed proceeds to the ordinary shareholders covered under the carve-out.

Standard liquidation preferences specify that investors receive their preference amount along with any 'declared but unpaid dividends'. Therefore, you will need to review dividend terms from previous financings to determine if you are required to pay any dividend out of the sale proceeds.

Look at the Terms

If you have received previous financing from equity investors, understand how prior preference terms apply in the case of an acquisition. Who really has control over the decision about whether to accept an acquisition offer from another company?

Consider:

- **Protective provisions**: Prior investors may have negotiated a protective provision in which a specified percentage of all the preference holders, or the holders of a certain series of preference stock, have veto rights over a trade sale of the company. Without the approval of this defined set of shareholders, the acquisition offer will be rejected.

- **Drag along rights**: Holders of drag along rights can force all shareholders to go along with a merger or other acquisition transaction approved by the Board of Directors or a majority of the investors. This term prevents one or a few minority shareholders from blocking an acquisition, but still requires the approval of the transaction by a specified percentage of preference shareholders.

- **Automatic conversion**: Most venture capital term sheets include a provision in which a specified percentage (for example, majority, $2/3$rds, 75%) of preference shareholders can vote to convert all preference shares into ordinary shares. This conversion has two consequences. First, a defined percentage of preference shareholders can force the rest to convert to ordinary shares, which eliminates the liquidation preference entirely. This alone can remove an obstacle to getting the deal done as it means that investors and ordinary shareholders are allocated proceeds from the sale on a *pro rata* basis. Second, if all the preference shareholders convert to ordinary, they may hold enough ordinary shares to carry a shareholder vote on whether to approve the acquisition offer.

You should also keep in mind that existing investor terms are negotiable in the face of a possible exit. If the investor is interested in the exit, the buyer has leverage to require a waiver or renegotiation of investor terms that are impeding the progress of the sale. In response, investors can either waive certain rights in the interest of facilitating the sale, or renegotiate them. For instance, if the liquidation preference was dividing the interests of management and the investors, the investors could do one or more of the following:

- Convert to ordinary shares, thus eliminating the preference.
- Waive their preference entirely, while still retaining their other preference rights.
- Renegotiate the preference down (from 2x to 1x, or 1x to 0.5x).
- Agree to a management carve-out.

Get Your House in Order

If you are preparing for a trade sale, it is important to review and understand the impact of existing agreements between your company and other parties. You must be able to clearly explain to a buyer the relevant provisions in an acquisition of key agreements, such as:

- **Customer, supplier and partner agreements**: You must be able to advise the buyer whether these agreements contain an assignment or transferability clause, allowing you to transfer the contract to the acquirer without any additional negotiation. Such a clause will allow the acquiring company to continue operations within your line of business with no interruptions, and no loss of contracted customers.
- **Employment agreements**: The buyer will prefer to have employment agreements that are transferable or assignable in

the case of a merger or acquisition. That way, the new employee can begin working at the combined entity on the same terms, and the buyer does not have to spend time re-negotiating employment contracts. This also enables the new company to easily keep key employees on board. If the agreement is not transferable or assignable, the employee is free to negotiate new employment terms with the acquiring company, or to resign if acceptable terms are not forthcoming. Demands from such employees can slow, stall or even kill an acquisition deal, if agreement cannot be reached with critical employees whom the buyer feels are necessary to the success of the acquisition.

- **Share option agreements**: A potential acquirer will want to understand what happens to the equity incentives of your employees. As discussed in more detail in **Chapter 5**, the share option agreement will indicate whether there is an accelerated vesting provision in the case of a merger or acquisition.

Even if you have many of these agreements in place, it is never too late to decide that a trade sale is a possibility for your company and to begin signing new agreements with relevant assignability and other 'acquisition-friendly' terms. New employment agreements can be modified when the old ones expire, and the share option plan can be amended. If you are a motivated seller, the more work you do ahead of the acquisition process, the easier and faster the sale will be.

Delegate

Even more so than an equity financing, acquisition negotiations are enormously time-consuming. To manage the acquisition offer effectively, you will need to retain some negotiating leverage by continuing to talk with other buyers, or evaluating the possibility of an IPO or another round of venture financing. In anticipation of the all-consuming nature of an acquisition transaction, delegate some of your duties to other staff members to free up your time. Select someone on your team to lead the due diligence process internally, so there is one consistent 'point person' for the buyer to work with. Ask your Board of Directors and Board of Advisors for short-term operational assistance in making sure the company continues to perform according to plan. Maintaining negotiating leverage, and also protecting yourself in the event the deal falls through, requires you to make sure your business continues to perform during the sale process and timeframe.

VALUING A TRADE SALE

There are many ways to think about value and to structure the price of a trade sale. As a seller, you should always watch the market for windows of enthusiasm that favour your industry or sector. A general trend of your sector being 'hot' will give you the leverage and opportunity to maximise your exit price, either through an IPO or acquisition. IPOs and acquisitions are related, in the sense that a strong IPO market will put upward pressure on acquisition prices. That is because, if an IPO is a realistic possibility for a company, an acquirer will have to compete against the proceeds that a public offering would generate, in order to interest the company in considering a trade sale.

There are several methodologies for valuing acquisitions, depending on the stage and sector of your company. Discounted cash flow and comparables analyses are frequently used in trade sales (see **Chapter 4** for a more detailed discussion of these methodologies). For later stage companies, a valuation based on current market price to earnings (P/E), discounted for various adjustments (for example, a liquidity discount), is appropriate. For an asset deal, the buyer will assess the total asset value of the company, excluding all liabilities such as bad debt, pensions, outstanding litigation, leases, or other obligations.

Acquisition prices will frequently include a premium above the calculated value of the company. While designed to secure the seller's approval of the deal, the premium also frequently reflects specific strategic value that the company offers the buyer. From a seller's perspective, it benefits you to understand as much as possible about your company's strategic importance to the buyer, in terms of extending or complementing the buyer's existing product line, providing a competitive advantage, opening a new distribution channel, or reducing a competitive threat. Are you the 'buy' in a 'buy *versus* build' decision? If so, estimate how much you are saving the company in development time and expense. Does the buyer require key management team members or technical employees to make the acquisition successful? If so, how many, who and for how long? The more you can understand the buyer's motivations, decision-making and objectives, the better poised you are to negotiate the price of the deal effectively.

Even at this relatively late stage in the company's development, valuation and price-setting is not entirely an objective or quantitative exercise. There is still investor judgment and a sense of the 'art' involved in the science of setting an acquisition price. Intangibles such as the urgency around acquiring the company's project, the existence of competitive buyers, or a hot public market in your sector can drive the price beyond what calculations alone would indicate.

STRUCTURING THE DEAL

Like private equity financings, the price per share or purchase price is only the first step in understanding the true value of the deal. The structure matters tremendously. To begin assessing the structure of the deal, it is important to obtain a detailed term sheet from the buyer. Similar to a venture capital term sheet, seek the most complete set of terms from the buyer as early as possible to enable you to assess accurately the attractiveness of the deal. Only a comprehensive term sheet will give you enough information to determine whether you and the buyer are within negotiating distance from each other's positions.

Important deal structuring terms include the following topics:

- Purchase price.
- Payment structure.
- Asset *versus* stock deal.
- Earn-outs.
- Representations and warranties.
- Fire sales.

Purchase Price

First and foremost, it is critical to understand very specifically what is included in the purchase price. What exactly is the buyer offering to purchase? You want to be able to determine what assets and liabilities will remain yours after the deal closes. For instance, does the purchase price include all your accounts receivable? Are they taking your employees, and if so, with or without assuming their accrued vacation time and other liabilities (*pro rata* bonus for the year, unused sick time, etc.)? Are they taking all your office equipment and computers, or will those remain for you to sell on eBay or at the local auction house? What about your office space? Are they taking over the lease or do you have to pay the penalty to exit it? Depending on the size and complexity of the deal, you and the buyer can approach the task of defining the purchase price either by specifying the assets that are included in the purchase, or, viewed the other way, by indicating that all assets except a defined list of 'excluded assets' are included in the purchase price. Whatever method you choose, the key is to be very clear and specific to avoid disputes and disagreements at the closing.

The allocation of the purchase price is also an important technicality, both for deal term enforcement and for tax purposes. For example, employee non-compete covenants can be deemed unenforceable unless 'consideration' has been paid to the employee in exchange for the non-compete. Therefore if non-competition agreements are an important aspect of the deal, part of the purchase price may need to be explicitly designated as payments for these employees. There are also tax consequences that arise depending on how the purchase price is allocated among asset classes (for example, capital equipment, goodwill, customer contracts, and accounts receivable). Optimising the allocation of the purchase price to minimise negative tax consequences is an extremely important task that requires the assistance of an experienced accountant and solicitor.

Payment Structure

The amount, timing and form (cash or shares) of payment should be clearly identified, as well as any conditions under which the payments can be delayed or withheld. If the payment is partially composed of the buyer's shares, undertake detailed research on the company in order to understand its volume, volatility, analyst coverage and past performance. What are the company's future prospects? This last question is particularly important if any of the employees of your company will be joining the new company, because their financial and career futures are now dependent on the new company. What are its growth rates, profitability, and revenues? Has the company experienced steady growth? What is its sales pipeline and how likely is it to meet future projections? What is the past history of its stock price? What is the trading volume? How many analysts provide research on the stock?

Finally, many purchase agreements will include an acceptable range in which the buyer's share price can trade. If the share price moves outside the range on either side before the deal closes, there is usually a specific term to identify how the payment will be modified.

Asset *versus* Stock Deal

An asset deal, as the name indicates, is when the buyer purchases only specified assets of the company. This type of deal is attractive to buyers because it allows them to select only the assets they want, while avoiding assuming the company's liabilities, which remain with the old corporate entity.

A stock deal is one in which the buyer purchases the whole company, by purchasing its outstanding shares. In a stock deal, the buyer purchases the company's full assets, liabilities, and any future claims against the company. Because of the risks involved in assuming liabilities in a stock deal, many buyers prefer an asset deal.

Earn-outs

An earn-out term requires the seller to be paid in tranches or stages. The seller receives a portion of the sale price upon the deal closing, and the remaining amount is paid out once certain specified performance objectives are achieved. Effectively, the seller has to 'earn' the remainder of the purchase price through specified performance or results. An earn-out term removes some of the risk of the deal from the buyer since, if the acquisition does not perform as planned, the earn-out is not paid, thus lowering the purchase price.

There are many issues with earn-outs and, if they are not structured properly, they can result in disputes later. Therefore, if you are contemplating accepting a earn-out as part of your trade sale, you should pay careful attention to the following issues:

- ♦ What exactly are the performance metrics and how will they be measured? Quantitative and objective measurements should be incorporated as much as possible.

- Similarly, the earn-out should describe what happens if you can't achieve results because of conditions outside of your control?
- What if the earn-outs are achieved, but on a delayed timeframe?

Sellers should always ensure that they have full control over the resources (financial, management, staffing, sales, marketing, IT, etc.) needed to achieve the earn-out results. If the seller is dependent on the buyer for specific resources, the buyer should guarantee to provide these as part of the deal.

Representations & Warranties

As part of the trade sale negotiation, the buyer will seek representations from the seller that the business is what he says it is. Similar to the reps and warranties in a venture capital investment agreement, the intent here is to limit the risk of the buyer by requiring the seller to disclose pro-actively and voluntarily any issues that affect the business.

Common seller warranties include:

- That the business is duly authorised, organised and in good standing under local laws.
- That it has proper corporate authority to operate the business.
- That the financial statements presented to the buyer present a complete, accurate and true view of the company's financial condition, and that there are no undisclosed liabilities.
- The seller has full and exclusive title to all its assets and intellectual property.
- The business has no undisclosed litigation outstanding, including from former or current employees.
- All contracts and agreements to which the company is a party have been disclosed.

Warranties are an important term in a trade sale because the seller is exposed to ongoing financial risk if the warranties are later 'breached' or deemed to be untrue. If the seller makes a warranty that is later 'breached', the buyer will seek to be 'indemnified' or protected against any losses related to the breach.

Trade sale indemnity terms are typically structured one of two ways. The first is most favourable to the buyer and requires the seller to indemnify the buyer completely against *all* losses that may arise in the event of a breach. The second, more common, approach for venture-backed companies caps the indemnity amount. A typical approach is to agree that a percentage of the purchase price (typically around 10-20%) is placed in escrow for a pre-defined period of time (usually 12 months from the date the transaction closes) as the full amount of capital available to pay any indemnification. This means that the company's shareholders will receive the sale proceeds in two tranches: the majority upon the closing of the sale, and the remainder 12 months later when the escrow expires. It also ensures that the buyer is financially protected to a certain degree against any breach on the seller's part.

Fire Sales

Some trade sales are essentially a company liquidation and are informally called a 'fire sale'. In this case, the investors and management are seeking a buyer because there are no alternative financing sources available and the company cannot sustain itself without additional capital. The proceeds from fire sales are usually minimal, and tend to be largely consumed by the payment of the company's employees and creditors. Investors receive little or nothing. If they get anything, it is usually in the order of cents on the Euro of their original investment.

A fire sale without a buyer becomes a liquidation. A liquidation is always a disappointment but does not have to be a disaster. The key to managing a wind-up of your business is to do it early and well. By accepting the fact that a liquidation is probable, you can take early action to contact creditors, suppliers and customers to negotiate some payment or settlement of your outstanding obligations (even if it is only cents on the Euro) and ensure a smooth transition. You can work with your Board, investors and advisors to orchestrate an orderly shutdown of the company, ensure that employees have a dignified departure, and complete any dissolution filings and notifications.

CONCLUSION

Trade sales are the most common exit in Ireland. Therefore, always regard key players in your industry segment as potential acquirers. If you are interested in being acquired, raise your profile and awareness among possible buyers early and maximise your visibility. Prepare for a trade sale in much the same way as you would for a round of venture financing or an IPO. Ensure your company's financials and corporate records are in order, review your key agreements and investor terms, and research market valuations in your industry. Because trade sales rarely represent a clean exit for management and key employees, conduct due diligence on your potential acquirers and pay close attention to post-closing issues such as earn-outs. Trade sales tend to occur earlier in a company's development than an IPO, but can still generate attractive returns.

12
CONCLUSION

Our greatest lack is not money for any undertaking, but rather ideas. If the ideas are good, cash will somehow flow where it is needed.
Robert Schuller

Investors frequently complain that they have plenty of capital available, but a shortage of 'investor-ready' companies in which to invest it. In Ireland, there is currently more than €150 million of capital raised and available to invest from Irish VCs alone. The challenge for entrepreneurs, then, is how to present their company as 'investor-ready' and as an attractive investment opportunity.

This book has presented a detailed discussion and advice about how to do just that. It has advocated:

- Creating a corporate structure and maintaining corporate records that will be clean and well-structured and can stand up to detailed due diligence.
- Working with experienced and sophisticated advisors, with expertise in conducting equity financings.
- Developing a compelling financing strategy to convince investors that you have an executable plan to raise the capital your business needs at increasing valuations.
- Building the most credible, experienced and ambitious management team that you can find.
- Raising each round of capital well before you need it, and generating interest from as many potential investors as you can.
- Ensuring that each round of financing is conducted with the next one in mind – with reasonable valuations and standard terms.

- Doing your valuation homework, so you can negotiate the best deal and also understand what a realistic price range is for your company.
- Taking a considered approach to selecting and reference-checking investors who have strong track records of being constructive and value-added partners.
- Understanding the importance of planning for a timely and profitable exit to provide the returns that investors require.

Raising equity capital is a rigorous and time-consuming process. The best entrepreneurs understand this and approach the process of raising capital for their company as seriously as the process of growing revenues. By taking this approach, you have the best chance of positioning your company as attractive to investors, and raising the capital you need to grow.

VENTURING FORWARD: THE FUTURE OF EQUITY FINANCING IN IRELAND

If equity financing is a young industry in Europe, then it is in its infancy in Ireland. It is only in the past decade that Ireland's venture capital industry has been formed and grown, and its long-term sustainability is still being tested. Ireland's largest venture capital firms will be fundraising from institutional investors during 2006 / 2007 and it remains to be seen whether their first decade of returns will attract the scale of institutional investor capital at home and abroad that is needed to ensure the future growth of the industry. Irish pension funds have essentially opted out of investing in venture capital, and this alone is a significant obstacle for Irish venture capital firms to overcome, as the most vibrant and strongest international venture capital industries are capitalised by pension funds.

The Irish government is an active and strong supporter of the Irish venture capital industry and deserves credit for its role in seeding and nurturing this new industry. Yet its enthusiastic support has resulted in the creation of too many funds that are likely to prove too small to survive and succeed on their own, without continued Government support. It is inevitable that, over time, some consolidation in the

12: Conclusion

venture capital industry will need to occur before a smaller group of large and sustainable funds emerges.

Looking ahead to the development of Ireland's equity financing environment, the real challenge is to successfully increase the supply of equity capital from informal investors. As this book highlights, the two most common sources of seed- and early-stage funding for start-up companies are friends and family and business angels. Capital raised from informal investors, although small in amount, is often critical to the growth and development of young companies and is an important bridge to professional investors, such as VCs.

To date, however, despite the well-documented evidence on the importance of informal investors to small company development, the Irish Government's fiscal policies focus almost exclusively on rewarding individual investments in property and hardly at all on encouraging equity investments in start-up companies. Property investments are promoted, encouraged and supported through a variety of Government incentives, tax breaks, schemes, programmes and subsidies. The result is that individual investors respond to these fiscal incentives and allocate their investible capital to tax-incentivised property investments rather than to indigenous enterprises. Irish investors thus by-pass equity investments in young companies in favour of property investments, both at home and abroad. The Government's biased fiscal policies contribute to the disproportionate investments by high net worth individuals in property over equity, and are at odds with Ireland's enterprise policy objectives of fostering the growth of small firms. Building companies, not buildings, is what creates sustainable jobs in a vibrant economy. Until the playing field is levelled by eliminating Government incentives to invest in property, it is hard to imagine how that will change.

This book also highlights the essential nature of returns and performance in driving and sustaining a vibrant equity financing cycle. Irish companies and investors can do more to concentrate their attention on planning and preparing for profitable exits, particularly public offerings. The Irish Stock Exchange (ISE) has taken second place to UK exchanges as a public equity-raising venue for Irish venture-backed companies. This is unlikely to change in the near future, unless the ISE pursues fundamental structural change such as demutualisation or strategic alliances that could improve the size, liquidity and competitive position of the exchange and increase its attractiveness to indigenous firms. Absent that, Irish companies are fortunate to have the credibility and critical mass in markets abroad that gives them the option to achieve successful listings on other exchanges.

While there is much work to be done to improve the domestic environment for equity financing, the future for Irish entrepreneurs looks very bright. At home, a real culture of entrepreneurship has taken hold, and Ireland's early class of serial entrepreneurs is slowly but surely expanding. The potential for the growth of a large and stable investor class has never been greater, given the recent increases in domestic wealth. Abroad, Ireland has an excellent reputation around the world for innovation, business growth and success. The road is well-worn to receptive markets overseas that offer a bigger stage on which Irish companies can play. An increasingly pan-European investing culture means that Irish firms can raise capital from international angels, venture capitalists and stock exchanges more easily than ever. At no time have the opportunities been more attractive and more compelling for creating new visions, building young companies, and venturing forward.

Go n-éirí an bothar libh.

APPENDIX 1
FORMING A COMPANY IN IRELAND

When you first create your business, you must declare its legal structure. The initial structure of your business is, strictly speaking, a legal decision, but one that also impacts upon your ability to raise equity finance. Most fundamentally, once you determine you are going to raise capital, you will need a corporate structure that allows for equity to be issued to multiple shareholders.

The best, and most conventional, initial structure for raising equity capital in Ireland is a private company limited by shares. This structure allows up to 50 shareholders, generally sufficient to raise several rounds of finance (current and former employees who own shares are not counted in calculating the 50 shareholder limit). It also offers 'limited liability' to shareholders, which means that they are not held personally responsible for the debts and other obligations of the company. However, in the event of an IPO, the company will need to convert to public limited company status. This involves changes to the company's Articles of Association, best dealt with by the company's solicitor.

Registering with the CRO

After deciding on the corporate structure, you will need to formalise it by registering with the Companies Registration Office (CRO). To register as a private company limited by shares, you will need to submit three specific documents to the CRO, outlining key characteristics of your company, including its capital structure and governance rules:

- Memorandum of Association.
- Articles of Association.
- Form A1.

Memorandum of Association

The Memorandum of Association identifies in one document the key defining characteristics of your company. It indicates the company name, its liability status (for example, limited liability or not), the purpose for which the company was formed and the types of business activities it is authorised to pursue.

The Memorandum is an important defining document and worth getting right the first time, as it is difficult to change later. Any changes to the Memorandum require a special resolution that must be approved by 75% of shareholders present and voting at a general meeting of shareholders. The changes must also be filed with the CRO.

The Memorandum also defines the initial capital structure of the company, as it is here that you are required to indicate the number and value of shares that you are authorising and issuing. Businesses that register as a limited company must issue shares not only as a corporate formality, but also to preserve the limited liability of the shareholders. More detail about how to think about the capital structure of your company is given in **Chapter 2**.

Articles of Association

The Articles of Association outline the rules governing the internal management of the company, such as issuing and transferring shares, voting rights, and the duties and powers of Board members. As the founder of the company, this is your opportunity to think carefully about how you wish to govern the company, and to codify those preferences in the Articles.

The CRO offers the option of accepting standard articles from the Companies Act or from company formation agents. However, standard articles obtained from such sources are often not structured appropriately for companies with multiple shareholders that plan to raise equity finance, and so they should be modified based on your preferences and the characteristics of your company.

Irish company law (specifically, Section 23 of the Companies Act, 1983) provides for statutory pre-emption rights to be awarded to ordinary shareholders. Pre-emption rights give the shareholder the right to invest in later rounds of financing up to the amount necessary to preserve their percentage ownership in the company. Many companies 'dis-apply' this statutory provision in the original Articles and either eliminate the right entirely, or re-draft it to reflect customised pre-emption rights.

Companies are required to name a minimum of two Directors in the Articles, one of whom must be resident in Ireland. If the company cannot provide a resident Director, it must post a bond with the CRO to the value of approximately €25,900. The bond can be obtained from insurance companies at a cost of about €1,600, which covers a two-year period.

Every limited liability company must also designate a Company Secretary (who can be one of the required two Directors, although they cannot act as Director and Secretary simultaneously). The responsibilities of the Company Secretary are to maintain current and accurate corporate records, including the share register and Board minutes, and to ensure the corporate obligations, such as annual report filings and the holding of an annual meeting, are met. This is a critical function for your company and the Secretary designation should be carefully awarded.

The Articles are often amended and restated in later rounds of financing. In VC rounds of finance, they are always replaced with Articles that contain terms to protect investor interests. If the amendments affect the structure of the company's share capital (which most financings do), the change requires a special resolution approved by 75% of the shareholders present and voting at a general meeting of shareholders.

Form A1

The CRO also requires Form A1, which is a signed declaration of the company name, primary business, and details of the presenter, the required two directors, company secretary and subscribers, and other details.

More information on the steps involved in forming a private company limited by shares is available in *How to Form a Limited Company*, 5th edition 2005, an eBook by Brian O'Kane, available from Oak Tree Press (www.oaktreepress.com).

US Incorporation

Many high-technology companies in Ireland seek to raise capital from US investors, or may consider a public offering on a US exchange. In those cases, Irish incorporation can be a barrier to attracting equity in the US. Companies seeking equity capital in the US may need to consider what Irish solicitors call a 'Delaware Flip', in which the company incorporates and domiciles in Delaware (the most popular state in the US for business incorporation). The State of Delaware Division of Corporations (www.state.de.us/corp) is a good source of information about the requirements and processes for registering a company in Delaware.

Conclusion

The initial documents that you submit to the CRO define the key operating rules of your company and the initial capital structure. They are crucial decisions that are time-consuming and administratively cumbersome to change later, so should be undertaken with thoughtful consideration of your future plans and with expert input with a view towards getting it right the first time. It is at this very early stage that you should begin seeking advice from a law firm that has experience with equity capital financing of young companies.

APPENDIX 2
NEWCO LTD FACT SHEET

Founded: Founded last May.

Headquartered in Dublin; sales office in London.

Ownership: Private.

€1.5m of angel capital raised in two rounds of financing to date.

Mission: NewCo has developed a proprietary, patent-pending technology that objectively measures and reports stock portfolio performance and makes trading recommendations based on quantitative analysis. Our technology outperforms the FTSE by 20% per year in back-testing.

Team: We are a staff of 15 with a core management team including: CEO, CTO, VP Sales and Controller. Our CEO is a former equity fund portfolio manager at London's BigAssets Bank. Our CTO worked previously at the IFSC, developing trading software for a major international stockbroking firm. We are seeking to hire a VP of Marketing and a Human Resources manager.

Products: For hedge fund managers, we offer *BigMoney*, a Web-based investment decision support tool that provides detailed quantitative analysis, optional criteria sorting, and idea generation.

Market: NewCo's products are targeted at investment management firms, including brokerage and mutual funds. The *BigMoney* product is targeted at hedge fund managers with pan-European stock portfolios.

Distribution: Distribution has been direct through our sales force, but we are just beginning to sign distribution agreements with indirect channels.

Competition:	Our primary competitor is OldCo, as well as existing analytic tools such as *StockPicker*. Neither has achieved the performance, nor have the patent protection, that NewCo's products offer.
Revenue Model:	Annual up-front subscription fees from €5k to €25k per investment professional.
Exit Strategy:	Management's goal is to build a profitable, scalable business and to prepare for an IPO or trade sale exit in Year 4 or 5.
Company Highlights:	◆ Currently have 3 investment management firm clients and two hedge fund beta testers. ◆ Signed our first agreement with an international broker providing access to 100 hedge funds. ◆ Several patents pending in the EU and US. ◆ Anticipate break-even by Q3 of next year. ◆ Presenting at the Annual Wall Street Financial Technology Products conference in May. The conference draws hundreds of international money managers, investment banks and hedge funds.
Contact:	Patrick Murphy, CEO E: patrick@newcoltd.ie T: (01) 555-5555 W: www.newcoltd.ie

APPENDIX 3
SAMPLE CONVERTIBLE LOAN TERMS[4]

15 September 20xx (the 'Issue Date')

The undersigned, NewCo Ltd, an Irish private company limited by shares (the 'Company'), for value received, hereby promises to pay to the order of Seamus Murphy (the 'Lender'), the principal amount of One Hundred Thousand Euro (€100,000), together with interest on such principal amount. This Note is subject to the following terms and conditions:

1. **Interest.**

    Commencing on the date of this Note and continuing until all principal and interest due under this Note are paid in full, the outstanding principal balance of this Note shall bear interest at the rate of six percent (6%) per annum.

2. **Payment.**

    The unpaid principal balance of this Note, together with any and all accrued but unpaid interest, shall be due and payable in full by 17:00 on 15 September 20yy. Such payment shall be made by wire transfer to the bank account or by bank draft to the address of Lender. Any prepayment permitted to be made under this Note shall be applied first to interest due, then any remaining balance shall be applied to the principal amount due.

3. **Right of Conversion.**

    3.1 Conversion into Company Securities. If, after the Issue Date but prior to the time this Note is paid in full, the Company raises €500,000 or more in a future round of financing (the 'Subsequent Financing'), all of the unpaid principal amount and all accrued but unpaid interest of this Note shall automatically convert on the date of such closing into fully paid shares (the 'Conversion Shares') at a price per share and on terms that are equal to the price per share and terms of the Subsequent Financing, discounted by 20% (the 'Conversion Price').

---

[4] See **Disclaimer**, page x.

3.2 *Mechanics of Conversion.* The conversion shall be deemed to have been effected on the date of the closing of the Subsequent Financing. Within five (5) business days thereafter, the Company shall cancel this Note and issue and deliver to Lender a certificate for the Conversion Shares (the 'Conversion Certificates'), registered in the name of the Lender, for the number of full shares of the Conversion Shares issuable at the Conversion Price.

3.3 *Effects of Conversion.* Upon conversion of this Note, the rights of the Lender under this Note shall cease. Upon issue of the Conversion Shares, the Lender shall be deemed to have become the holder of record of the Conversion Shares.

3.4 *No Fractional Shares.* No fractional share of the Conversion Shares will be issued in connection with any conversion hereunder. The Company shall pay a cash adjustment in respect of such fractional interest as determined by reference to the Conversion Price.

3.5 *Taxes on Conversion.* Any taxes required upon the issue of Conversion Certificates on conversion of this Note shall be paid by the Lender.

4. **Events of Default; Remedies.**

    4.1 *Default.* This Note will be in default if any payment of principal or interest due against the principal is not made when it becomes due and payable.

    4.2 *Remedies.* The Lender will have the right and sole discretion to declare the entire unpaid principal amount and all accrued interest under this Note immediately due and payable upon default, by giving written notice to the Company.

5. **Prepayment.**

    The Company may prepay the Principal Amount (and interest that has accrued against it) to the Lender at any time without penalty.

6. **Miscellaneous Provisions**

    6.1 *Governing Law.* This Note is made and executed under, and shall be governed by, the laws of the Republic of Ireland.

    6.2 *Enforceability.* This Note is binding upon the Company and its successors and inures to the benefit of the Lender, his heirs, transferees and assigns.

APPENDIX 4
SAMPLE REVOCABLE PROXY[5]

The undersigned (the 'Shareholder'), being the owner of 50,000 Ordinary Shares of NewCo Ltd (the 'Company'), of which each share is entitled to one vote, does hereby grant to Patrick Murphy, CEO (the 'Voter'), a proxy to vote on behalf of the Shareholder 50,000 shares at any future annual, ordinary or extraordinary meeting of the shareholders of the Company. The Voter, as proxy holder, is entitled to attend any said meetings on behalf of the Shareholder, or to vote the said shares through mail proxy, or by other means acceptable to the Company.

During the duration of this proxy, all rights to vote the said shares shall be held by the Voter, and shall not be voted by the Shareholder, provided that the Shareholder may revoke this proxy at any time.

Dated this 15th day of October, 20xx.

Signed:

_____

Name:

In the presence of:

_____

Name:
WITNESS

---

[5] See **Disclaimer**, page x.

APPENDIX 5
ORDINARY SHARE PURCHASE AGREEMENT TERMS[6]

Issue & Sale of Ordinary Shares

This term sets out the description of the shares being transacted (for example, 'Subject to the terms and conditions below, the Company agrees to authorise, issue and sell to the Purchaser, and the Purchaser agrees purchase from the Company at the Closing, a total of 50,000 shares of the Company's Ordinary Shares.').

Share Price

The share price is usually represented as both the price per share (for example, 'The Purchaser will purchase the shares at a price per share of €1.50.'), and in terms of company valuation (for example, 'The Share Price represents a pre-money valuation for the Company of €1.5 million and is based on the capitalisation table attached.').

Voting Rights

Each Ordinary Share is generally entitled to one vote.

Proxy Voting Rights

The investor and company can agree to implement a revocable or irrevocable proxy voting agreement, which is usually drawn up as a separate agreement (see **Appendix 4**).

Pre-emption Rights

Many friends and family rounds do not include these rights, but they can easily be specified if they are not already awarded through the Articles of Association (for example, 'The Ordinary Shareholders will have the right to maintain their percentage ownership in the company by purchasing on a *pro rata* basis any new securities issued by the company, other than

---

[6] See **Disclaimer**, page x.

options and shares issued under the company's employee share option plan.').

Board of Directors

Ordinary shareholders, voting as a class, have the right to nominate and elect one Director to the company's Board of Directors.

Transfer of Shares

This term limits the transfer of shares to those required by law (for example, 'No transfer of shares by any shareholder shall be permitted unless required by law …'). Some companies prefer to preserve some flexibility to allow transfers on a case by case basis (for example, '… or unless approved in writing by the Company's Board of Directors.').

Information Rights

Ordinary shareholders are entitled to receive the company's annual financial accounts for each accounting year. This term will usually specify when the shareholder is entitled to receive the information (for example, 'The Company's audited accounts shall be delivered to Ordinary Shareholders not later than four months from the end of the said accounting year, along with any management letters produced by the auditors in connection with the annual audit.'). It may also specify that the company can deliver the information electronically, by fax or by post to the shareholder's address on record.

Representations & Warranties

The company generally makes a series of representations and warranties to the Purchaser about the current state of the business. Examples of standard reps and warranties include:

- ♦ The Company is duly organised, validly existing and in good standing and has the necessary corporate power and authority to enter into this Agreement.
- ♦ The Company's capitalisation structure is accurately represented in the capitalisation table.
- ♦ The Company's financial information and accounts are accurately presented and up-to-date.
- ♦ The Company is in compliance with local employment, corporate, environmental, health, tax and competition laws.

- There are no debt, legal, pension, tax, employee or other obligations of the company that are material other than those disclosed.

Closing

This term is important to specify the payment of the investment capital. Several entrepreneurs described their experiences closing an early round of financing and then waiting for weeks or months for the cash. This term specifies that the closing must include receipt of the capital in order for the investment transaction to be finalised (for example, 'The Closing is expected to occur on 15 September 20xx and will take place at the Company's office, or at any other location the parties may mutually agree. At the Closing, the Purchaser shall deliver to the Company a certified bank cheque or wire transfer payable to the Company for the full purchase price of the Shares. The Company will prepare a share certificate representing the Shares purchased and promptly transmit such share certificate to the Purchaser.').

Standard or 'Boilerplate' Clauses

These terms are generally part of a standard shareholder agreement.

Disputes

For very early-stage financings, it can be helpful to specify that disputes will be resolved through mediation or arbitration, which is a less contentious and less expensive method than going to court (for example, 'Any dispute arising from this agreement that cannot be settled by consultation among the parties to this agreement shall, on the request of either party, be mediated in Dublin by a Practitioner member of the Mediators Institute of Ireland.'). Mediators can be named in this clause, chosen by mutual agreement, or selected by some other specified method agreed in advance.

Assignment

This clause ensures that the agreement remains between the original parties (for example, 'None of the parties may assign all or any of their rights under this Agreement without the prior written consent of each of the other parties.').

Entire Agreement

To avoid the issue of 'he said, she said' and the ambiguity of verbal 'promises', this term specifies that only agreements in writing, or changes to this agreement that are approved by the majority of shareholders and put in writing, are valid and binding (for example, 'This Agreement, together with all agreements and documents executed contemporaneously with it or referred to in it, constitutes the entire and only agreement between the parties in relation to its subject matter and replaces and extinguishes all prior agreements, undertakings, arrangements, understandings or statements of any nature made by the parties or any of them whether oral or written. No changes to or modification of this agreement will be effective unless agreed in writing by the company and holders of 51% or more of the shares then sold under this agreement.').

Notices

This section provides the official mechanism by which your shareholders and the company can be reached (for example, 'Any notices, claims, consents or other communications that must be served under or in relation to this agreement must be in writing and will be deemed to have been duly given when delivered by hand (with confirmation of receipt), sent by facsimile or sent by recognised overnight delivery service to the addresses below for the Company and Shareholder …').

Governing law

Particularly if you have investors in many geographic locations, it is important to specify the jurisdiction for the agreement (for example, 'This Agreement shall be governed by the laws of the Republic of Ireland.').

APPENDIX 6
NEWCO LTD SHAREHOLDER UPDATE

15 December 20xx

Dear Fellow Shareholders

I'm pleased to report that NewCo continues to show promising revenue and sales growth, and continues to generate interest from potential financial services customers. As general market conditions improve, we believe that NewCo is well-positioned to benefit from increases in stock trading. Some of our specific accomplishments this quarter include:

General Update

Most significant to our progress is an increased focus on our indirect distribution channel opportunities, which has the potential to increase our revenues significantly in the next several quarters. We are also focusing on the use of *BigMoney* for hedge fund strategy creation and trading, including derivatives. In this way, NewCo's products offer a full solution set to the largest financial services firms.

We continue to increase our sales and marketing efforts, leading to a shortened sales cycle for our *MakeMoney* product, as well as the development of solid customer relationships. Our new marketing hire, Emer Malloy, will be a key leader of some of our new initiatives.

Customers

NewCo set a new record these past two quarters, breaking the €100,000 revenue mark. We continue to manage a robust pipeline of opportunities, and are beginning to see customer referrals based on word of mouth. Our two most notable new customers were:

- Big City Firm in London has been on our list for several quarters. Big City signed a one year full-site contract for our full suite of *MakeMoney* products.

- Big Wall Street Firm in NYC is a key customer win as we begin our market entrée to the US. We were pleased to beat out *StockPicker* as the product of choice for Big Wall Street.

Product Development

NewCo continues to make excellent progress in product development. We have now successfully released a beta version of *MakeMoney* 2.0, on which we have filed a patent in the US. This release adds very significant strategic and business value to NewCo, providing us today with a complete product in quantitative stock selection and trading. This product has now been beta-tested at HighStakes Hedge Fund, and demonstrates superior performance and scalability.

Most notably, our *MakeMoney* 1.0 was also shipped to some major customers, including Cash Cow Bank (UK-based) and Euro Financial (Frankfurt-based).

People

Recently, we strengthened our management team and added the experience of a strategic advisor. This quarter, we hired Emer Malloy as our VP of Marketing. Emer's career includes marketing and financial services. Most recently, Emer was Director of Marketing at High Stakes Hedge Fund in Dublin where she drove the company's marketing strategy and helped to launch its US business operations. Prior to High Stakes, Emer traded futures at Low Stakes Investment Bank.

Additionally, NewCo invited Seamus Smith onto our Board of Advisors. Seamus is the former Head of Trading at BigBank in London, and is assisting us with customer leads, referrals, and a review of our products in *Trading Magazine*. Seamus also brings a wealth of experience with start-up companies, having co-founded DayTraders Ltd, which was acquired last year by BigBank.

Financing Plan

We continue to make excellent progress toward our goal of becoming cash-flow positive and profitable by next year. We have now closed the entire €1.5 million Series A financing. Management and the Board are considering future options for additional working capital, including:

- **VC Series B:** We anticipate needing to raise additional capital during the next fiscal year. To that end, we have initiated discussions with several VC firms, and have begun due diligence with one attractive candidate. We are hopeful that we can find the right VC partner with strong expertise in the financial services industry.

♦ **Inside investors:** In addition to VC financing, we are evaluating the option of an internal financing of up to €1 million. While this is lower than the total amount we need to raise, it could provide an important interim financing while we continue to negotiate VC capital.

Conclusion

We are close to cash-flow breakeven and the company is generally meeting its business plan projections. Our new product releases, growing base of customers and recent financing signal a promising future. We want to thank all of our shareholders for continued support and encouragement. Please feel free to contact me at the telephone number or email below if you have any questions about this report.

Sincerely,

Patrick Murphy, Managing Director
T: 01-677-5555
E: patrick@newcoltd.ie

ATTACHMENTS:

♦ NewCo Ltd Balance Sheet (Unaudited) as of 31 September 20xx.

♦ NewCo Ltd Profit and Loss Account (Unaudited) as of 31 September 20xx.

APPENDIX 7
SAMPLE BUSINESS PLAN CONTENTS

    Executive Summary

1. **Business overview**
2. **Management**
   Management team
   Organisation chart
   Board of Directors / Board of Advisors
3. **Target Markets**
   Market analysis
   Market growth potential
   Target market segments
   Competition analysis
4. **Sales & Marketing**
   Sales strategy & forecast
   Sales team & incentives
   Sales channels
   Customers (current and projected)
   Marketing & PR
5. **Products & Technology**
   Product description
   Features & benefits
   Development & launch schedule
   Pricing strategy
6. **Financial Overview**
   Summary financials
   Capitalisation & structure
   Prior financings & valuation
   Exit strategy

APPENDICES

1. **Financial Projections**
   Key assumptions
   Balance sheet
   Profit & loss account
   Cash-flow by month

2. **Management Team**
   Full CVs

APPENDIX 8
SAMPLE DUE DILIGENCE REQUEST

Financial Information

- Complete financial statements since company's inception (audited if available).
- Aging analysis for the company's accounts receivable.
- Financial or operating budgets since company's inception.
- The business plans, offering memorandums, private placement documents and term sheets associated with any prior financings.
- Copies of all material insurance policies of the company, including product liability, property or other liability.
- Schedule of any other insurance policies in force, such as key man insurance or Director & Officer indemnification policies.
- List of banks or other lenders with whom the company has a financial relationship.
- Past annual tax returns.
- A description of any changes in accounting methods in the past three years.

Agreements

- Documents and agreements relating to all sales, purchases, offers and grants of company shares or share equivalent securities (for example, warrants, options).
- All share option, share purchase and other employee benefit agreements.
- All agreements between the company and its customers, suppliers, partners or subsidiaries.
- All agreements and documents relating to company borrowings including loan or mortgage documents, lines of credit, debt instruments, or guarantees.

- Any debt arrangements, guarantees and indemnification between officers, directors, key employees, shareholders or related parties and the Company.
- Any employment, non-compete, confidentiality, loan or consulting agreements between the company and its employees.
- All lease, mortgage, deeds of trust or other agreements related to property transactions.
- All agreements among shareholders of the company.
- Any other material agreements, such as partnership, joint venture, alliances or acquisitions.

Corporate Documents

- The corporate minute book.
- A complete capitalisation table.
- Agendas and minutes of all Board of Directors meetings; copies of the last two quarter Board materials distributed to Directors in advance of the Board meeting.
- Charters of all Board committees; Minutes of all committee meetings.
- Copies of regularly produced reports, memos or information used by the management team or Board of directors to manage company operations.
- Schedule and description of all filed, awarded or owned intellectual property of the company including trademarks, copyrights and patents.
- Descriptions of any threatened, expected or actual claims, litigation or judgments against the company or any of its directors or management.
- A copy of company brochures, sales literature, and marketing materials.
- Copies of all company press releases for the past two years.

People

- A management organisation chart.
- Full CVs of the entire management team; description of the entire compensation package for each member; list of at least five

professional references with contact information for each member of the team.
- Full CVs of each member of the company's Board of Directors and / or Board of Advisors.
- List of the company's employees, with name, title, salary, bonus, share options, benefits and start date.
- Description of the incentive and commission programme implemented for each sales person; the current sales pipeline and any historical sales reports.
- List of all the company's customers; list of the company's top 10 customers with contact information; a list of the three largest customers who have quit / cancelled the company's services.
- List of the company's top suppliers, with contact information.
- Names and contact information of any consultants with whom the company has worked.
- Names and contact information of the company's advisors (including accountants, solicitors, patent attorney, executive search, etc.).
- Copies of any prior year staff annual performance evaluation reports.

Technology

- All product documents including user manuals, reference manuals, product fact sheets, white papers and industry articles.
- Description of source code protection, access and maintenance processes.
- Product release schedules and documents for prior and upcoming releases.
- Product development process documentation: quality assurance and testing.
- Manufacturing process description, including costs, quality assurance, capacity, packaging and distribution.
- Help desk or customer service records for number of problem calls, problem descriptions, and resolution in last six months.

APPENDIX 9
SAMPLE NOTICE OF BOARD OF DIRECTORS MEETING

Notice of the Regular Meeting of the Board of Directors of NewCo Ltd.

To: Patrick Murphy
         Seamus Malone
         Kevin Malloy

From: David O'Shea, Secretary

Date: 15 September 20xx

RE: **Regular meeting of the Board of Directors of NewCo Ltd on 15 October 20xx**

A regular meeting of the Board of Directors of NewCo Ltd is scheduled to be held on Tuesday, 15 October 20xx at 9:30 a.m. The meeting will take place at NewCo's offices in Dublin, located at One Main Street, Dublin 2.

Materials for the board meeting will be distributed separately by email. If you have any questions, please contact David O'Shea at T: (01) 555-5555 or E: secretary@newcoltd.ie.

Thank you.

APPENDIX 10
SAMPLE AGENDA FOR BOARD OF DIRECTORS MEETING

Agenda for the Regular Meeting of the Board of Directors of NewCo Ltd, 15 October 20xx, 9:30 - 14:00

Directors:
  Patrick Murphy
  Seamus Malone
  Kevin Malloy
  David O'Shea, Board Secretary

9:30 – 10:00 Administrative
- Recognition of Quorum
- Resolution (Vote to Approve)
- Minutes of the 15 August 20xx Regular Meeting

10:00 – 10:30 Technology Update
- Release 2.0 Development, Testing and Planned Launch Schedule

10:30 – 12:30 Business & Financial Update
- YTD Key Metrics review
- Q4 & Preliminary Year-End outlook
- Next Fiscal Year Objectives and Budget

12:30 – 2:00 Financing and Strategy Discussion (& Working Lunch)
- Financing plans and contingencies for next year
- Business development and sales priorities

2:00 Motion to Adjourn Meeting

APPENDIX 11
SAMPLE MINUTES OF BOARD OF DIRECTORS MEETING

Minutes of the Regular Meeting of the Board of Directors of NewCo Ltd, 15 August 20xx, 9:30 – 14:00

A regularly scheduled meeting of the Board of Directors of NewCo Ltd, an Irish private company limited by shares (the 'Company'), was held on the above date at the Company's offices beginning at 9:30 a.m. Present at the meeting were Directors Patrick Murphy, Seamus Malone and Kevin Malloy. No directors were absent.

The Board appointed David O'Shea to act as secretary of the meeting to record the minutes thereof.

Welcome & Agenda Review
Mr. Murphy began the meeting by welcoming the Board members and reviewing the Agenda for the meeting.

Approval of Minutes
Mr. Murphy then presented the draft of the Minutes of the meeting of the Board of Directors held 15 June 20xx. After discussion, upon motion duly made, seconded and unanimously approved, the Board of Directors adopted the following resolution:

> **RESOLVED:** That the Board of Directors hereby approves the minutes of the meeting of the Board of Directors held on 15 June 20xx.

Key Metric Reports
Mr. Murphy reviewed the Company's revenues, sales, costs and cash-flows for the second quarter of the year, as compared to the prior quarter and the second quarter of the prior year. Mr. Murphy then reviewed the Company's projected revenues, costs and cash flows for the next fiscal year. During this review, the Board asked questions of management and there was discussion.

Technology Update

Mr. Murphy then presented the document 'Release 2.0', a copy of which was filed with the minutes. The Board was presented with an update on the launch of the Company's product Release 2.0, which is proceeding according to schedule. Mr. Murphy reviewed the historical and projected sales cycles of Release 1.0.

The Board also asked Mr. Murphy for a detailed launch schedule to be presented at the next Regular Board Meeting. Mr. Murphy committed to that request.

Financial Results & Projections

Next, Mr. Murphy outlined the Company's results year-to-date and financial projections for Q4 and year-end. The Board was given a 13-page presentation (with additional supporting documents) entitled 'Financial Results & Projections', a copy of which was filed with the minutes.

Next Equity Financing

Mr. Murphy then indicated that the Company will require additional funding during the next fiscal year. Mr. Malone suggested that the Company should begin the funding process by seeking indications of interest from existing investors, and by creating a short list of preferred investors to approach. Mr. Malloy concurred with Mr. Malone's suggestion and Mr. Murphy agreed to begin the fundraising process.

Business Development

Next, Mr. Murphy reviewed the Company's business development priorities and outlined the Company's relationships with financial institutions, hedge funds, and traders and there was discussion about sales targets for Release 2.0.

Adjournment

There being no further business to come before the meeting, the Board unanimously decided to adjourn the meeting at 13:45.

David O'Shea, Secretary of the Meeting

APPENDIX 12
NEWCO LTD ABBREVIATED TERM SHEET

NOT LEGALLY BINDING

Investment Amount:	Moneybags VC proposes investing €2m in Participating Preferred Shares ('Series A Shares') in NewCo Ltd.
Price per Share:	The investment will be made at a price per share of €2.50 per share.
Valuation:	The fully-diluted pre-money equity valuation is €5m, giving a fully-diluted post-money equity valuation of €7m. This proposed valuation is based on the capitalisation table attached to this term sheet.
Liquidation Preference:	The Series A Shares will rank ahead of all other shares on exit and will have the additional right to receive as a preference to the other shareholders an amount equal to 1.5 times the subscription price per share.
	The remainder of the proceeds, if any, will be split among the Preference and Ordinary shareholders on a *pro rata* basis.
Anti-Dilution:	The Series A Shares shall benefit from full ratchet anti-dilution rights. If, after the closing of this Series A round of financing, NewCo issues any new shares at a price less than the price per share of the Series A Shares (the 'Reduced Price'), then the price of the Series A Shares shall be adjusted to equate to the Reduced Price.
	This clause will not apply in the case of issue of ordinary shares pursuant to the employee option pool.
Board of Directors:	Moneybags VC will have the right to appoint one Director to the Board of NewCo. At the option of Moneybags VC, the Director will have the right to sit on the Remuneration and Audit Committees.

Appendix 12

Conditions to Closing: Closing is subject to the following conditions:

- Completion of a technology review by an independent consultant.
- Completion of a financial review that concentrates on the adequacy of the company's cash flow and gross margin protections.
- Completion of a satisfactory Shareholder Agreement. This will include minority shareholder protection clauses.
- Final approval of the partnership of Moneybags VC.

Fees: The third party transaction costs will be borne by NewCo. If the investment is not completed because of a decision by Moneybags VC to withdraw, the costs will be borne by Moneybags VC.

Exclusivity: NewCo agrees to work with Moneybags VC to complete the investment as outlined above on an exclusive basis for a period of four weeks from the signing of this term sheet.

_____

For and on behalf of Moneybags VC

_____

Managing Director, NewCo Ltd

APPENDIX 13
BVCA MODEL TERM SHEET[7]

Strictly private and confidential
Not to be disclosed or distributed to third parties

Draft

Indicative Term Sheet

[For use on Series A round]

We are pleased to present our proposal for an investment in● (the 'Company').

1. Investment

1.1 You have told us that the proposed business plan calls for an equity injection of £●. Of this amount, funds managed by us (the 'Funds') will provide £● alongside investment by other venture capital funds or financial institutions (together the 'Investors'). We will act as lead equity investor.

1.2 The investment will be at a fully diluted pre-money valuation of £●, including employee share options (both granted or committed) equal to ●% of the fully diluted equity. This represents a ●% shareholding for the Investors on a fully diluted basis, following an expansion of the share option pool as detailed in paragraph 2.4. The current capitalisation of the Company is set out in Part I of Appendix 1 and the capitalisation of the Company after this proposed funding is set out in Part 2 of Appendix 1.

---

[7] See **Disclaimer**, page x. This term sheet was created by the British Venture Capital Association to illustrate common terms found in UK and European venture capital term sheets. It is reproduced from the BVCA's *A Guide to Venture Capital Term Sheets*, by kind permission. The entire *Guide* can be found at www.bvca.co.uk. A sample venture capital term sheet that illustrates standard US terms can be found at www.nvca.org.

1.3 The investment will be made in the form of convertible participating [redeemable] preferred shares ('Preferred Shares') at a price of £• per Preferred Share (the 'Original Issue Price') the terms of which are set out in Appendix 2.

1.4 [The investment will be made in full at completion.] / [The investment will be staged with •% being invested at completion (the 'First Tranche') and •% being invested subsequently ('Subsequent Tranches'). [The Investors will have the right, but not the obligation, to subscribe for Subsequent Tranches at the same price per share as the First Tranche at any time.] In addition, provided that the performance milestones referred to in paragraph 2.6 have been met, the Board of Directors of the Company (the 'Board') will have the right to call Subsequent Tranches within • months of a performance milestone being satisfied.]

1.5 The proceeds from the investment must be used for the Company's working capital requirements [in particular •].

2. Conditions of investment

2.1 The investment is conditional on negotiation of definitive legal documents, satisfactory completion of due diligence and approval by our Investment Committee.

2.2 Satisfactory completion of due diligence will include:

(a) Conclusion of our commercial due diligence [including •].

(b) References from customers and partners.

(c) Market and technology review by an independent third party.

(d) Management references.

(e) Review of current trading and forecasts for the next • – • months.

(f) Review of existing and / or proposed management service contracts.

(g) Review of the Company's financial history and current financial situation by our advisors including, a review of the last set of audited accounts and the latest set of monthly management accounts prior to completion of our investment.

(h) Full legal review of the Company by our lawyers, focusing particularly on ownership of all necessary intellectual property and benefit of all key commercial contracts.

(i) [VCT tax clearance from the Inland Revenue].

2.3 The Company must secure institutional co-investment of at least £• on identical terms from other venture capital funds or similar organisations acceptable to us. We will not underwrite the total funding sought nor guarantee the securing of co-investors.

2.4 The expansion of the share option pool prior to the investment to represent •% of the equity on a fully diluted basis. These extra share options will be reserved for new employees and will have an exercise price equal to the Original Issue Price (see paragraph 1.3) [or may be exercised at a discount to that price subject to consent from the relevant tax authority and the Investor Director (see paragraph 4.3)]. Following grant, these options will vest quarterly over a • year period, [subject to a minimum employment of • year].

2.5 The investment must comply with the money laundering regulations and rules of the Financial Services Authority.

2.6 [Appendix 7 sets out the performance milestones which must be satisfied within the periods stated before Subsequent Tranches can be called.]

3. Founder Shares

3.1 The Founders (being [INSERT NAME OF FOUNDERS], will hold A Ordinary Shares ('Founder Shares') which will be purchased for £• per share. [The Founder Shares will be subject to [vesting rights] [and good leaver/bad leaver provisions] as summarised in Appendix 3.]

4. Terms of investment

4.1 The Company and the Founders will provide the Investors with customary representations and warranties examples of which are set out in Appendix 4 and the Founders will provide the Investors with customary non-competition, non-solicitation and confidentiality undertakings.

4.2 The Board will have a maximum of • directors. [For so long as the Investors hold •% of the issued share capital of the Company on an as converted basis] the Investors will have the right to appoint [one] director (the 'Investor Director'). The composition of the Board on completion will be •. There will be a minimum of • board meetings each year.

Appendix 13

4.3 The Investor's or the Investor Director's consent will be required for certain key decisions, examples of which are set out in Appendix 5.

4.4 [The Investors will also have at all times the right to designate a non-voting observer to the Board.]

4.5 The Company will form a Remuneration Committee [and an Audit Committee] upon completion and the Investor Director will be the chairman [of both].

4.6 The Company will have an obligation to supply normal financial and operational information about the Company to the Investors.

4.7 The Investors and the Founders will have rights to acquire and sell shares as outlined in Appendix 6.

4.8 [If the Company were floated on a US market, registrable securities will include all Preferred Shares, or any shares issuable on their conversion and any other shares held by the Investors. The Investors will be given full registration rights customary in transactions of this type (including • demand rights, unlimited piggy-back rights and • S3 registration rights), with the expenses paid by the Company.]

4.9 The key members of the management team will be required to sign service agreements which include customary provisions for non-disclosure, non-competition, non-solicitation, confidentiality, assignment of intellectual property rights, and termination.

4.10 [Within [•] months of completion,] [Before completion,] the Company must obtain key man insurance, naming the Company as beneficiary on the lives of • and • for an amount of £• and director and officer liability insurance, both in a form acceptable to the Investors.

4.11 The Company will agree to pay to the investors an annual, index-linked monitoring fee of £• per annum plus VAT, charged quarterly in advance, plus reasonable out of pocket expenses in respect of each Investor Director.

4.12 [The Investors' investment appraisal and legal costs will be borne by the Company. In addition, on completion, the Company will pay to us a transaction fee of £• plus VAT.]/[The Company and the Investors will bear their own costs in relation to the investment, save that the Company will contribute an aggregate of £• to the expenses of the Investor.]

5. Confidentiality

5.1 This Term Sheet is written on the basis that its contents and existence are confidential and will not (except with our agreement in writing or in order to comply with any statutory or stock exchange or other regulatory requirements) be revealed by the Investors or the Founders to any third party or be the subject of any announcement.

5.2 The Investors and the Founders agree that they will enter into a non-disclosure agreement before the Investors begin their due diligence investigations.

6. Applicable law

This letter is governed by English law and on acceptance the parties submit to the non-exclusive jurisdiction of the courts of England and Wales.

7. Expiry date

The Founders and the Company are requested to confirm their acceptance of the terms of our proposal within 14 days of the date of this letter, failing which our proposal will lapse.

8. Exclusivity

In consideration of the Investors expending time and professional and other fees (the 'Costs') in progressing this offer the Founders and the Company agree and undertake that they will not directly or indirectly until the earlier of the expiry of • days from the date of acceptance of the terms of this proposal or the date that the Investors notify the Company of their intention not to proceed with this proposal (the 'Period') solicit, directly or indirectly, further offers for the purchase and / or subscription of shares in the Company (or any part thereof) or any material part of the business, assets or undertakings of the Company or enter into or continue to seek negotiations with any party other than the Investors in connection with such matters.

The Founders and the Company agree and undertake to inform the Investors immediately of the identity of any third party who contacts the Founders or the Company with a view to the sale of any interest in the shares of the Company or any part of the business of the Company.

[By accepting this offer the Founders and the Company confirm that if:

(a) they withdraw from negotiations with the Investors during the Period; or

Events (see paragraph 5)), plus all accrued but unpaid dividends. The Founders and Ordinary Shareholders will also be entitled to recover an amount per Ordinary Share equal to the amount paid up on those Ordinary Shares. To the extent that the Company has assets remaining after the distribution of that amount, the Preferred Shareholders will participate with the Founders and Ordinary Shareholders *pro rata* to the number of shares held on an as converted basis.

4. Sale of all or substantially all of the assets of the Company or a sale of shares involving a change in control (each, a 'Corporate Transaction') will be treated in the same way as a liquidation [if it is not a Qualified Sale (as defined below)] and the proceeds of sale will be distributed as set out in paragraph 3. [A Qualified Sale means a sale [where the consideration payable (including any deferred consideration) exceeds £•][pursuant to which Preferred Shareholders receive proceeds (in cash or marketable securities free of trading restrictions) per Preferred Share that are equal to or more than [the greater of: (i)] [• times] the Original Issue Price, [or (ii) a price which will result in the Preferred Shareholders earning a notional •% rate of return on the Original Issue Price calculated daily and compounded annually].]

5. Subject to any adjustment being made to the conversion rate following any recapitalisation, share split, consolidation or similar events (collectively 'Recapitalisation Events') and / or the operation of the anti-dilution provision in paragraph 10, the Preferred Shares will be convertible at any time at the option of an Investor into an equivalent number of Ordinary Shares.

6. The Preferred Shares will be converted automatically into Ordinary Shares, at the then applicable conversion rate:

    6.1 upon the completion of a firmly underwritten initial public offering ('IPO') of Ordinary Shares: (i) at a net offering price per share of at least [• times] the Original Issue Price (after adjusting for any Recapitalisation Events) and (ii) resulting in net aggregate proceeds to the Company of not less than £• (the 'Qualified IPO');

    6.2 when less than •% of the Preferred Shares issued in this financing remain outstanding;

    6.3 upon the affirmative vote of holders of more than •% of the outstanding Preferred Shares.

7. An IPO [that is not a Qualified IPO] will be treated in the same way as a liquidation. The Company will issue to each holder of Preferred Shares that number (if any) of Ordinary Shares so that the proportion which the Ordinary Shares held by that shareholder bears to the fully diluted share capital following completion of all such issues and the conversion of the Preferred Shares will be equal to the proportion which the proceeds that that shareholder would have been entitled to receive on a sale on that date would bear to the valuation of the Company at that date.

8. Immediately prior to an IPO all accrued but unpaid dividends on the Preferred Shares must be paid save to the extent that the Company decides to capitalise some or all of such amounts into Ordinary Shares. Any capitalisation will be at the price of the Ordinary Shares at IPO.

9. The Preferred Shares will vote with Ordinary Shares on an as converted basis as a single class on all matters, other than those referred to in Appendix 5.

10. The Preferred Shares will have a [full ratchet] / [weighted-average] anti-dilution protection in the case of any new issue of shares at a price below the Original Issue Price (after adjusting for any Recapitalisation Events) other than (i) shares issued pursuant to the share option pool approved by the Investors and (ii) shares issued to the Investors as a result of them electing to convert their Preferred Shares into Ordinary Shares. This anti-dilution protection will operate [so as to adjust the rate at which the Preferred Shares will convert into Ordinary Shares] [by the issue of Ordinary Shares at par [through a capitalisation of share premium account].]

11. If the Company makes a subsequent issue of shares in which the Investors are entitled to participate and an Investor elects not to do so (that is, does not wish to pay to play) for at least •% of its allocation [that Investor will lose its anti-dilution right in respect of any Preferred Shares it holds][that Investor's Preferred Shares will automatically convert into Ordinary Shares].

12. If no [Qualified] IPO or Corporate Transaction has occurred within • years from completion, each of the Preferred Shares will be redeemable at the option of the holder for an amount in cash equal to [the Original Purchase Price][the Liquidation Preference], plus all accrued but unpaid dividends.

13. If no [Qualified] IPO or Corporate Transaction has occurred within • years from completion or redemption of the Preferred Shares cannot be completed, the [majority of] Investors [holding •% of the Preferred Shares], will have the right to require the Company to engage in a liquidation process by way of IPO, Corporate Transaction or liquidation.

14. [REDEMPTION: The Company shall redeem the Preferred Shares [annually in one-third increments beginning on •] at a redemption price equal to the Original Issue Price per share plus all declared but unpaid dividends (if any). The Company shall also redeem the Preferred Shares (at the same redemption price) in the event of (i) a sale of substantially all the assets of the Company or (ii) the sale of Ordinary Shares carrying in excess of 50 per cent of the voting rights in the Company at a price per Ordinary Share which (on an as converted basis) values each Preferred Share at less than the Original Issue Price. Notwithstanding either of the above, the holders of the Preferred Shares shall receive advance notice of each redemption and shall have the option to convert any or all of the Preferred Shares otherwise due to be redeemed into Ordinary Shares prior to the mandatory redemption. In the event that the Company shall fail to make:

    (a) a mandatory redemption payment to the holders of the Preferred Shares while having funds and distributable reserves necessary to do so then the holders of the Preferred Shares shall have a majority of the votes on all matters submitted for the approval of the Company's shareholders until such defaults are rectified; or

    (b) two mandatory redemption payments to the holders of the Preferred Shares regardless of whether or not it has the funds or distributable reserves necessary to do so, then the holders of the Preferred Shares shall have the right to appoint a majority of the Board of the Directors of the Company until such default is rectified.]

Appendix 3: Rights Attaching to Founder Shares

1.* Subject to paragraph 3 below, the Founder Shares will vest equally on a [quarterly/monthly] basis over a • year period.

---

* Only to be used where Founders are to hold vested shares.

2.* If a Founder ceases to be an employee of the Company those Founder Shares which have not vested will convert into Deferred Shares. The Deferred Shares will have no right to receive a dividend, minimal rights to capital and will be non-voting. The Company will have the right to purchase back the Deferred Shares for an aggregate purchase price of £• at any time.

3.* If there is a Corporate Transaction at a time when any of the Founder Shares remain un-vested, the consideration may be structured in such a way that it defers realisation of the value attached to the un-vested shares until such time as they would have been vested.

4.* If a Founder is a Bad Leaver:

(a) within • months of the start of his employment all vested shares will convert into Deferred Shares;

(b) after • months from the commencement of his employment no shares will vest during the period of • months before the date of his departure.

5. In the event of an employee shareholder [(other than a Founder)] being a Bad Leaver all of his shares [(other than those held following the exercise of share options)] must be offered for sale at the lower of market value or the subscription price (as adjusted by any Recapitalisation) to the Company, [the employee benefit trust] and then the Investors. [If an employee shareholder [(other than a Founder)] is a Good Leaver he must similarly offer his shares for sale at the market price.]

6. [Unless otherwise determined by the Board,] 'Bad Leaver' means any employee shareholder [(other than a Founder)] who ceases to be employed within • years of completion or if later the start of his employment as a result of summary dismissal and whose dismissal is not found to have been wrongful or constructive, or who terminates his contract of employment within • years of completion or if later the start of his employment, other than as a result of constructive dismissal, death or permanent incapacity. 'Good Leaver' means any employee shareholder [(other than a Founder)] who ceases to be employed within • years of completion or if later start of his employment and who is not a Bad Leaver.

Appendix 4: Proposed Warranties

The Investors will require the following items to be warranted by the Founders and the Company:

- Status of the Company.
- Latest available audited accounts.
- Management accounts covering the period from latest audited accounts to completion of the proposed investment.
- Position since audited accounts date.
- Business plan.
- Ownership of assets and HP liabilities.
- Employment contracts.
- Intellectual property.
- No outstanding liabilities to executives.
- Pension plan.
- No litigation pending or threatened.
- No breaches of existing or recent contracts.
- Register of members correct / no other share issues committed.
- Insurance policies up to date.
- Loans/guarantees.
- Taxation.
- Property leasehold – terms / rights / obligations.

The above items are not comprehensive and are only intended to provide a guide to the warranties that are likely to be included in the Investment Agreement. In particular, additional items may require warranting following due diligence. The objective of these and other warranties will be to ensure that Founders and the Company have provided the Investors with accurate information on matters upon which the Investors have based their investment decision.

Appendix 5: Proposed Covenants

1. Investor consents

[So long as there are at least •% of the Preferred Shares outstanding] the prior written approval of the Investors [holding •% of the Preferred Shares] will be required to:

- Amend Memorandum and Articles of Association.
- Change share capital.
- Acquire any new business, shares or other securities.
- Sell or deal with assets other than in ordinary course of business.
- Wind up the Company.
- Appoint or remove directors to/from the Board of the Company and any subsidiary companies.

2. Board consent

The following issues to be discussed and approved by the Board including the Investor Directors:

- Make any change of trade / business plan [(including adherence to VCT 'qualifying' trade definition)].
- Declare ordinary dividends.
- Adoption of share option or other incentive plans and increase in share option pool.
- Approve annual budgets.
- Agree any borrowings, loans, advances or credit outside the annual budget.
- Create charges.
- Create any subsidiaries / joint ventures.
- Incur development or capital expenditure outside the annual budget.
- Agree or vary the remuneration / service terms of directors of the Company and any subsidiary companies.
- Acquire real estate and other real estate-related matters.
- Commence or settle litigation.
- Assign or license any of the intellectual property rights of the Company.
- Any guarantees / indemnities other than in ordinary course of business.
- Any material agreement other than in ordinary course of business.
- Any change of auditor / accounting reference date / accounting policies.
- Any including key man insurance.

- Any change of bank.
- Any appointment of an employee or variation of terms where emoluments exceed £•.

Materiality and other financial limits for the above to be discussed. The above items are not comprehensive and are only intended to provide a guide to the consent items that are likely to be included in the Investment Agreement.

Appendix 6: Conditions of Issue & Transfer of Shares

1. [Investors will have a right of first refusal on any new issue of shares of any class.] [Investors will have the right to participate with the holders of Founder Shares [and Ordinary Shares] in any new issue of shares of any class *pro rata* to their holding of shares (determined on an as converted basis).] [In addition, the Investors will have the right but not the obligation to subscribe for •% of the next £• raised by the Company in the following rounds of financing by the Company on no worse terms than offered to third party investors.]

2. [Investors] [All existing shareholders] will have a right of first refusal to acquire any shares which are proposed to be transferred or sold. Investors will be able to transfer Preferred Shares freely provided that the transferee agrees to be bound by the terms of the Investment Agreement.

3. For [•] years from completion no Founder Shares can be sold without the Investor's prior consent (the 'Prohibition Period') [and no Founder Shares can be sold until they have vested].

4. The Investors will have tag-along rights such that if any founder has an opportunity to sell [any of his shares] [shares exceeding •% of the issued share capital], the Investors must be given the opportunity to sell a *pro rata* number of their shareholding on the same terms and at the same price.

5. The Investors will have co-sale rights such that if any shareholder has an opportunity to sell any or all of its shares, the effect of which would result in a change of control of the Company, the Investors must be given the opportunity to sell all of their shares on the same terms and at the same price.

6. If holders of at least •% of the Preferred Shares[, Founder Shares and Ordinary Shares] agree to sell their shares, there will be drag along

rights so that all remaining shareholders and option holders will be required to sell on the same terms, provided that no Investor will be required to sell unless (i) the Investor will receive cash or marketable securities in return for its shares, and (ii) the Investor will not be required to provide to the purchaser representations or warranties concerning the Company (or indemnify those given by the Company or Founders) or covenants (for example, non-compete and non-solicitation of employees).

Appendix 7: Performance Milestones

[Insert as appropriate / agreed.]

APPENDIX 14
MODEL LEGAL AGREEMENTS

There are several industry websites that provide free model legal documents and templates for download. The legal agreements have been created by leading venture capital attorneys and investors and are specifically for use in equity financings. Some sites include explanations of terms, as well as discussion about how to structure the agreements.

These model documents are useful in that they will help you understand the general structure, length and complexity of the standard agreements used in raising equity finance. You can see what the standard clauses are for each agreement, and review the actual legal language used to draft one. These model agreements can also serve as a good starting point for negotiations, and can be a useful comparison when you evaluate an agreement or terms you receive from a potential Irish, UK or US investor.

As always, the documents are not meant to be used 'as is' in a commercial transaction, but rather should be modified and customised to reflect your own particular circumstances, the characteristics of your company, and local laws and customs. Below is the list of sample agreements you can find at each website.

British Venture Capital Association (www.bvca.co.uk)
- Confidentiality Letter
- Venture Capital Term Sheet (see **Appendix 13**)

Irish Venture Capital Association (www.ivca.ie)
- Non Disclosure Agreement

National Venture Capital Association (www.nvca.org)
- Venture Capital Term Sheet
- Stock Purchase Agreement
- Certificate of Incorporation
- Investor Rights Agreement

- Voting Agreement
- Right of First Refusal and Co-Sale Agreement
- Management Rights Letter
- Indemnification Agreement

European Business Angel Network (www.eban.org)
- Confidentiality Agreement
- Venture Capital Term Sheet
- Shareholder's Agreement
- Entrepreneur Contract
- Investor Contract
- Contract between an investor and an entrepreneur
- Investment Agreement
- Articles of association of a private company limited by shares

Onecle (www.onecle.com)
This site offers more than 50 different types of agreements, including share option, employment, share purchase and other agreements that have been filed by companies with the US Securities & Exchange Commission. Therefore, they are real agreements, reproduced in their entirety (although generally not with attachments), that are or have been used by actual companies.

APPENDIX 15
FURTHER RESOURCES

Part I: Preparing to Raise Equity Capital

Companies Act:	www.irishstatutebook.ie
Companies Registration Office:	www.cro.ie
Delaware (US) Registration:	www.state.de.us/corp
Irish Patent Office:	www.patentsoffice.ie
LK Shields:	www.lkshields.ie (Publications section, Business category)
National Center for Employee Ownership:	www.nceo.org
Office of the Director of Corporate Enforcement:	www.odce.ie

Part II: Informal Investors

Angel Capital Association:	www.angelcapitalassociation.org
British Business Angels Association:	www.bbaa.org.uk
Digital Hub:	www.thedigitalhub.ie
Dublin City Enterprise Board:	www.dceb.ie
Enterprise Boards:	www.enterpriseboards.ie
Enterprise Ireland:	www.enterprise-ireland.com
Entrepreneur.com:	www.entrepreneur.com
European Business Angel Network (EBAN):	www.eban.org
Garage Technology Ventures:	www.garage.com
Inc. magazine:	www.inc.com
Inter*Trade*Ireland:	www.intertradeireland.com
Kauffman Foundation:	www.kauffman.org
M50 Enterprise Programme:	www.m50-enterprise.ie
MIT Enterprise Forum:	http://enterpriseforum.mit.edu
Revenue Commissioners:	www.revenue.ie

Part III: Professional Investors

British Venture Capital Association:	www.bvca.co.uk
European Venture Capital Association:	www.evca.com
European Venture Capital Journal:	www.evcj.com
Irish Venture Capital Association:	www.ivca.ie
MIT Enterprise Forum term sheet:	www.mitef.org
National Venture Capital Association:	www.nvca.com
Private Equity Online:	www.privateequityonline.com
VC Experts:	www.vcexperts.com

There are a number of well-written books that provide anecdotal and informative views of the VC industry (mostly from a UK or US perspective):

- *BooHoo: A Dot.com Story from Concept to Catastrophe*, Ernst Malmsten, Erik Portanger & Charles Drazin, London: Random House Business Books.
- *Confessions of a Venture Capitalist: Inside the High-Stakes World of Start-Up Financing*, Ruthann Quindlen, New York: Warner Business Books.
- *Done Deals: Venture Capitalists Tell Their Stories*, Udayan Gupta (Editor), Boston: Harvard Business School Press.
- *eBoys: The First Inside Account of Venture Capitalists at Work*, Randall E. Stross, New York: Ballantine Books.
- *Making Bread: The Real Way to Start up and Stay in Business*, Brody Sweeney (the founder of O'Briens sandwich bars), Dublin: Liberties Press.
- *Starting Something: An Entrepreneur's Tale of Control, Confrontation & Corporate Culture*, Wayne McVicker, Los Altos, CA: Ravel Media LLC.
- *Startup: A Silicon Valley Adventure*, Jerry Kaplan, New York: Penguin.
- *Term Sheets & Valuations: A Line by Line Look at the Intricacies of Venture Capital Term Sheets & Valuations*, Alex Wilmerding, Boston: Aspatore Books.

Part IV: Exits

Alternative Investment Market (AIM):	www.londonstockexchange.com/aim
American Stock Exchange (AMEX):	www.amex.com
EDGAR online:	www.edgaronline.com
Federation of European Stock Exchanges:	www.fese.be
Ion Equity M&A Quarterly Tracker Update:	www.ionequity.com
Irish Stock Exchange:	www.ise.ie
London Stock Exchange (LSE):	www.londonstockexchange.com
NASDAQ:	www.nasdaq.com
Net Roadshow:	www.netroadshow.com
OFEX:	www.ofex.com
Securities & Exchange Commission:	www.sec.gov
WH Hambrecht:	www.openipo.com

APPENDIX 16
INVESTOR LINGO

Angels: High net worth individuals who invest their own money in early-stage companies. Angels usually invest amounts under €500,000.

Angel networks: Groups of angels who formally or informally band together to make investments of €500,000 and up.

As-converted: The characteristics of preference shares as if they had already been converted to ordinary shares (for example, 'The Series B preference shareholders own 30% of the company on an as-converted basis').

Bootstrapping: The art of financing the growth of a business without outside capital. Bootstrappers finance growth through customer revenues, keeping expenses low and other creative capital management techniques.

Bridge loan: A short-term loan, often provided by a company's existing investors, that can either be paid back or converted to equity. So-called because it is meant to provide the cash to 'bridge' the company to the next round of financing. Bridge loans are usually small, enough to get the company through a few months until the next financing closes. If a venture round of financing is slow to close, sometimes the investors will bridge the company to the close.

Burn rate: The amount of cash a company loses each month (for example, 'the company's burn rate is €100,000 a month for the next six months', which means the company has €600,000 of negative cash-flow over the next six months).

Capitalisation table (cap table):	The cap table lists all shareholders and holders of options and any other securities, the number of securities held, the amount invested by each investor, the price at which the securities were purchased, and the percentage ownership of each security holder. Companies use the cap table to keep track of their capital structure over time.
Carry (carried interest):	The portion of a venture fund's investment profits allocated to its General Partners (GPs). GPs typically receive 20% of the profits, and Limited Partners the other 80%.
Conversion ratio:	Most commonly, the relationship that specifies the number of ordinary shares into which one preference share is convertible.
Deal flow:	The number of investment opportunities an investor sees in a given period.
Dilution:	The decrease in an investor's (or any equity holder's) percentage ownership in a company due to the issue of new shares.
Disclosure letter:	A letter that lists or explains any exceptions to the representations and warranties the company or founder makes to the investor.
Down round:	A financing in which the price per share is lower than the previous round.
Due diligence:	Detailed research of a company's business, management and financials that an investor conducts prior making an investment decision. Legal due diligence is usually conducted by the investor's solicitor and involves a very detailed review of the company's corporate records, structure and governance.
Exercise price:	The fixed price, determined in advance, at which the underlying security of an option or warrant can be purchased. Also called the strike price. For example, if the exercise price of a share option is €2.00, the holder of the option pays the €2.00 to purchase the underlying ordinary share.

Exit:	The sale or liquidation of an investment. Typical exits include trade sales, Initial Public Offerings (IPOs), management buyouts, and write-offs. Investors realise the gains or losses of their investment through an exit.
Fiduciary duty:	The legal obligation to act in the best interests of another party or entity.
Fire sale:	A liquidation event in which the company is sold at a very low price relative to its prior valuations.
Flat round:	A round of financing in which the company's valuation is the same as the last round.
Flotation:	See **IPO**.
Follow-on round:	When an investor provides additional funding to a company after the initial investment.
Fully diluted shares outstanding:	The company's total shares outstanding are calculated by adding up all ordinary and preference shares, plus the number of ordinary shares that would be outstanding if all options, warrants and convertible securities were exercised or converted. All the company's securities are included on an as-converted basis.
General Partner (GP):	The partner in a limited partnership that is responsible for the day-to-day management and decision-making of the partnership. GPs have a fiduciary duty to their limited partners (LPs). Under a venture capital firm's limited partnership structure, the VCs are the General Partners.
Heads of Agreement:	See **Term sheet**.
Initial public offering (IPO):	The first time that a company sells shares to the public. Also know as a 'flotation'.
Institutional investor:	Organisations that professionally invest their own assets. Typical institutional investors are banks, pension funds, insurance companies, foundations and university endowments. Institutional investors are distinct from individual investors who invest their own personal assets.

Lead investor:	When a group of investors (angels, VC funds) band together to make an investment, one investor will 'lead' the group by investing the most capital and / or taking charge of negotiating the terms of the investment and managing due diligence.
Lifestyle company:	Private companies that provide a nice living for their founders, but do not exhibit high growth. These companies typically generate under €10 million in revenues, experience annual growth rates below 20 percent, and do not attract equity finance.
Limited Partner (LP):	The investor in a limited partnership who has no day-to-day management or decision-making control. Under the venture capital limited partnership structure, LPs are the institutional investors. LPs have limited liability, capped at the amount they invest, for the debts of the partnership.
Limited partnership:	The standard legal structure used by most venture funds.
Liquidation or winding up:	An exit in which the company is insolvent and goes out of business. A liquidation consists of the sale of a company's assets for distribution to creditors and shareholders.
Liquidity:	The ability to convert an asset (such as a security) to cash. An exit is a liquidity event for an investor.
Lock-up:	A specified time period after an IPO in which equity investors and company employees are prohibited from selling their shares. A typical lock-up period is 180 days.
Market capitalization:	The value of a public company, calculated by multiplying the number of outstanding shares by the price per share.
Pari passu:	A Latin term that roughly means 'equal basis.' It is generally used to describe securities or rights which are equal. For instance, 'The proceeds from liquidation will be distributed *pari passu* among all preference and ordinary shareholders' would mean that the proceeds were divided equally among all the preference and ordinary shareholders.

PIPE (Private Investment in Public Equity):	A type of investment in which a private investor, such as a VC, makes an investment in a public company. The investment is usually made at a discount to the current public price of the common shares.
Portfolio company:	One of the companies in which an investor has invested.
Post-money valuation:	The value of a company immediately after the most recent round of financing. The post-money valuation is calculated by multiplying the company's fully diluted shares outstanding by the share price of the latest round.
Pre-emptive right:	The right of an investor to participate in a financing to the extent necessary to ensure that, if exercised, their percentage ownership of the company's securities will remain the same after the financing as it was before.
Pre-money valuation:	The value of a privately held company prior to the most recent round of financing. The pre-money valuation is not a calculation but is determined by the investor.
Pro rata:	A Latin term meaning 'proportionally'. Used most often to refer to investor rights 'in proportion' to their ownership in the company (for example, each investor has the right to invest up to their *pro rata* amount ...).
Ratchet:	A mechanism that allows the terms of a deal to be modified based on future performance. Most commonly used as a protection against investor dilution during down rounds. So 'full ratchet anti-dilution' re-prices the investor's position based on a current down round of financing.
Redemption:	Refers to a company's repurchase of a security from an investor. A redemption can be mandatory, or optional at the option of either the investor or the company.

Returns:	The profits from an investment that are generated upon exit. Investors think about returns by calculating the Internal Rate of Return (IRR), which gives a percentage return. More informally, they talk about return multiples, such as a 10x return that indicates that the investment returned 10 times its initial cash value.
Round (of financing):	Each financing event or transaction is referred to as a round.
Serial entrepreneur:	Coveted among investors, a serial entrepreneur is one who has previously successfully built and exited one or more companies.
Series:	Series are used to designate sequential rounds of financing raised by the company. By convention, each round of preference share investments is referred to by letter, beginning with A (for example, the Series A investment is first; a later round is Series B, etc.).
Sweet spot:	The type of investment opportunity an investor seeks, usually defined by size, stage and industry (for example, Moneybags VC's sweet spot is €2-€10 million investments in early stage technology companies).
Syndicate:	A group of investors who come together to make an investment. A syndicate is commonly formed in order to raise sufficient capital, or to share the risk of the deal. A syndicate is usually organised and managed by a lead investor.
Term sheet:	An outline of the structure of the financing deal an investor is proposing. The term sheet is a written document usually 2-10 pages long, that the investor will present to the company. Also known as a 'Heads of Agreement'.

Tranche:	A French word meaning 'to slice'. Investments that are made in stages based on the achievement of certain milestones are referred to as 'tranched investments', since the investment amount is disbursed in parts, rather than in total when the deal closes.
Up round:	A round of financing in which the valuation is higher than the last round.
Vesting:	The process by which employees obtain ownership rights over shares, share options or other equity awards.
Write-off:	An exit in which the value of the investment is declared to be €0.

INDEX

acquisition(s)   12, 59, 137, 149
    premium   186
ADR(s) *see* American Depository Receipt(s)
advisor(s)   6, 21-24, 129-130, 134
    advantages of   21
    beauty contest(s)   181
    convertible loan   69, 72
    customer   184
    customer, and assignment / transferability clause   184
    employee   18
    employment   184-185
    employment, and assignment / transferability clause   184-185
    fees   22
    finding good   23
    importance of   21
    intellectual property   18, 20
    investors' rights   155
    irrevocable proxy   147
    model legal   239-240
    negotiating on fees   22
    non-disclosure   109
    overseas   23-24
    partner   184
    partner, and assignment / transferability clause   184
    registration right(s)   173
    revocable proxy   74, 101
    sample ordinary share purchase   206-209
    share option   18, 55-63, 185
    share purchase   69, 73-75, 118
    share purchase, terms   73-75
    shareholders'   155
    subscription   155
    supplier   184
    supplier, , and assignment / transferability clause   184
    technology transfer   18
AIB Bank   170
AIM *see* Alternative Investment Market
Alternative Investment Market   159, 167-168
    fees   168
    listing criteria   167-168
    Nomad   168
American Depository Receipt(s)   170, 173, 175
American Stock Exchange   171, 173, 175-176
    Emerging Company Marketplace   175
    fees   175
    listing criteria   175-176
AMEX *see* American Stock Exchange
Angel Capital Association (US)   94
angel financing   87-104, 111

angel investor(s) *see* business angel investor(s)
angel(s) *see* business angel(s)
anti-dilution
    business angel investor(s) 103
    carve-out(s) 143-144
    full ratchet 140-142
    protection 42
    term sheet(s) 128, 129, 140-144
    weighted average 103, 142-143
Articles of Association 18, 74, 101, 147, 149, 155, 197, 198-199
    as converted 132, 136, 140

---

bad leaver(s) *see* leaver(s), bad
Baltimore 170
Bank of Ireland 170
barriers to entry 92
beauty contest(s) 181
BES *see* Business Expansion Scheme
beta testing 91
Board of Advisors 79, 185
    compensation 79
Board of Directors 79, 100, 103, 120-126, 147-148, 162, 185
    agenda for meetings 125
    audit committee 162
    Board Book 124-125
    Chairman 125
    committees of 148
    compensation 123, 148, 154
    composition 122-123
    Directors & Officers liability insurance 123
    duties of 121
    election process 148
    fiduciary responsibility 117, 121
    governance best practice 162
    meetings 124-125, 148
    minutes of meetings 125, 199
    notices of meetings 125
    performance 125-126
    sample agenda 219
    sample minutes 220-221
    sample notice of meeting 218
    Secretary 125
    term of office 123-124
    term sheet(s) 128, 129, 147-148
bond
    in lieu of resident Director 198
bootstrapping 5, 46
bridge loan 120
British Venture Capital Association 239
    model term sheet(s) 224-238
business angel investor(s) 17, 194
    anti-dilution 103
    choosing 95-98
    criteria for investment 88-93
    dividends 102
    due diligence 98-99
    evaluating 97-98
    finding 93-94
    information rights 101
    liquidation preference 102-103
    ordinary share(s) 100-102
    post-investment 103-104
    pre-emption rights 101
    preference share(s) 102-103
    proxy voting 100-101
    reference-checking 97-98
    referrals to 93
    representative on Board of Directors 100, 103
    restrictions on share transfers 101
    structuring investment 99-103

Index

types of 95
valuing investment 99
veto rights 102
business angel network(s) 3, 102
   advantages of 94
   finding 94
business angel round
   structuring 99-103
   valuing 99
business angel(s) 3, 7, 24, 51, 87-104
Business Expansion Scheme 80-81
business pitch 68, 88, 110
business plan 4, 6, 69, 88, 115
   sample contents 110, 213-214
   venture capital investor(s)'
   requirements 110
buyback 61-63
BVCA *see* British Venture Capital Association

cap table *see* capitalisation table
capitalisation table 14-16, 42, 44-45, 51, 98, 133
   following narrative 15-16, 18
Caribou Coffee 36
Carnegie, Andrew 47
carried interest 108
carve-out(s) 183
   anti-dilution 143-144
change in control 59, 138
Cisco 173
clean deal 18
cliff vesting *see* vesting, cliff
close 155-156
closing
   term sheet(s) 153-154
Coffee Republic 36
collateral 2

common stock *see* share(s), ordinary
Companies Act 1963 198
Companies Capital Duty 13
Companies Registration Office 14, 74, 197-199
company
   forming limited liability 18, 197-200
   structure of 6, 11, 12-17
Company Secretary 14, 199
comparables analysis 35, 186
competitive analysis 92-93, 98
conditions to close
   term sheet(s) 128, 153
consent right(s) *see* veto, and term sheet(s)
control 16-17
   change in 59
   reduction in / loss of 5
conversion
   automatic 136-137, 183
   optional 136
   qualifying IPO 136-137
   term sheet(s) 128, 131, 136-137, 183
convertible loan agreement(s) *see* agreement(s), convertible loan
convertible loan(s) 71-72
   discount to later financing rounds 71-72
   repayment in event of liquidation? 72
   sample loan terms 203-204
convertible preference share(s) *see* share(s), convertible preference
corporate documents *see* documents, corporate
corporate finance 181

corporate recordkeeping *see*
    recordkeeping, corporate
corporate records
    see records, corporate
Costa Coffee   36
County & City Enterprise Boards
                                            80
CRH   170
CRO *see* Companies Registration
    Office
customer agreement(s) *see*
    agreement(s), customer

Datalex   170
DCF *see* discounted cash flow
DCU   83
deal(s)
    clean   18
    hairy   18-19
debt financing   2, 5, 12
    bridge loan   120
    convertible loan(s)   71-72
Dell   173
Deloitte   161
demand right(s)
    see right(s), demand
Diageo   170
Digital Hub   84
dilution   42-46, 51
Director(s)   17
    requirement for resident   198
    right to elect   17
Directors & Officers liability
    insurance   123
discounted cash flow   35, 36,
                                        38, 186
dividend(s)   12, 102
    converting to equity   134
    cumulative   135
    declaring   134, 149
    non-cumulative   135
    payment   135
    term sheet(s)   128, 134
documents
    company formation   18
    corporate   6, 16, 98, 115
double dip   132, 134
down round(s)   27, 34, 42,
                        103, 117, 120, 140
    managing   117-118
drag along right(s) *see* right(s),
    drag along
drip-feeding   25
    avoiding   25
due diligence   18, 98-99,
                                  114-115, 155
    binder   98, 115
    sample request   215-217

earn-out(s)   189-190
    trade sale(s)   189-190
EASDAQ   167
Economist   171
EI *see* Enterprise Ireland
Einstein Brothers Bagels   36
EJB Home   179
Elan   170
Emerging Company Marketplace
                                        175
employee agreement(s) *see*
    agreement(s), employee
employee departures
    share option(s)   60-63
employee equity   6, 47-64
employee non-compete covenants
                                         188
employee share option plan   16
employees

Index

issuing equity to 47-49
employment agreement(s) *see*
    agreement(s), employment
Enron 171
Enterprise Ireland 80, 81-82, 83
    network of offices 82
    Seed & Venture Capital
    Programme 81
Enterprise Platform Programmes
    83
entrepreneur(s)
    successful 24
entrepreneurship
    culture of 196
equity awards
    types of 49-54
equity capital *see* equity financing
equity financing 2, 194
    amount of 6, 29-31
    attractions of 5
    avoiding drip-feeding 25
    disadvantages of 5
    down round(s) 27, 34, 42
    drip-feeding 25
    flat round(s) 31, 42
    IPO(s) as 160
    Ireland 194-195
    negotiating leverage 28
    timing of 6, 28-29
    why raise? 4
equity financing cycle 2, 3
equity investor(s) 3, 4
    criteria for investment 4
Equity Network 80, 82-83
equity-like awards 53-54
    tax effects of 54
Ernst & Young 161
escrow 155, 191
Euro.NM 167

European Business Angel
    Network 94, 240
excluded asset(s) 188
    trade sale(s) 188
exclusivity
    term sheet(s) 128, 152
Executive Summary 110
exit(s) 3, 7, 88, 90, 139
    IPO(s) as 159
    trade sales as 179-180
exit scenario modelling 37
expenses
    term sheet(s) 154

F&F *see* friends & family
factsheet 68, 201-202
fiduciary responsibility of
    Directors 117, 121
filing(s)
    public 36
    regulatory 18
financial projections
    69, 98, 111, 115
financial statements (historical)
    69, 98, 111, 115, 150
financing strategy 6, 25-32, 46, 88
    example 27
    questions addressed 26
    role in increasing valuation 27
fire sale(s) 191
flat round(s) 31, 42
flotation(s) 3
    see IPO(s)
Form A1 (CRO) 197, 199
Form S-1 (SEC) 172
Form S-3 (SEC) 172
friends & family 3, 7, 67-85, 194
    finding investors 69-70

formal investment
    presentation   69
fundraising   67-85, 100
information rights   74
investment round, structuring
    71-75
investment round, valuing
    71-75
mixing business and pleasure
    75-77
post-investment   78
pre-emption right(s)   74
protecting   77-78
proxy voting   73
restriction on share transfers   74
voting right(s)   73
friends & family investor(s) *see*
    investor(s), friends & family
Frost, Robert   179
fully-diluted valuation *see*
    valuation, fully-diluted

---

go private   177
golden handcuff(s)   57, 59
Golden Rule   107
good leaver(s) *see* leaver(s), good
governance   18, 162, 169
Government
    biased fiscal policies   195
    support for venture capital
        industry   194-195
        programmes   80-84
growth   91-92

---

hairy deal   18
Halo NI   82
Havel, Vaclav   1
Heads of Agreement *see* term sheet
hedge funds   177
high potential start-ups   81
HPSUs *see* high potential start-ups

ICON   170
IEX *see* Irish Enterprise Exchange
indemnity(ies)   190-191
    trade sale(s)   190-191
information right(s)
    see right(s), information
insider trading   160
Institute of Technology
    Blanchardstown   83
Institute of Technology Tallaght   83
institutional investors   3, 194
Intel   173
intellectual property agreement(s)
    see agreement(s), intellectual property
intermediaries
    VC(s) as   3, 7
internal round(s)   120
    mitigating potential damage of   120
international sales   91
Internet boom   34, 161
Inter*Trade*Ireland   80, 82-83
investment bank(s)   181
investment fees   154
investor(s)
    angel   17, 71
    friends & family   67-85

Index

informal 7
professional 7
sophisticated 18
VC 71
investor-ready 82, 193
  how to prepare to be 193-194
investors' rights agreement(s) *see* agreement(s), investors' rights
IONA 170, 179
IPO(s) 3, 37, 90, 138, 159-178, 179, 186, 197
  advantages 162-164
  as equity financing 160
  costs 164-165
  disadvantages 164-166
  objectives 160
  planning for 161-162
  qualifying and conversion term 136-137
Irish Enterprise Exchange 170
  fees 170
Irish Stock Exchange 167, 170, 194
  Developing Companies Market 170
  Exploration Securities Market 170
  Irish Enterprise Exchange 170
  ITEQ 170
Irish Venture Capital Association 24, 239
Irish venture capital industry 111
irrevocable proxy agreement(s) *see* agreement(s), irrevocable proxy
ITEQ 167

Kennedy, John F. 127
KPMG 161

leaver(s)
  bad 60, 62
  buyback 61-63
  good 60, 61, 62
  unvested share(s) / share option(s) 60
  vested share(s) / share option(s) 60
legal agreement(s) *see* agreement(s), legal
legal counsel
  term sheet(s) 154
lifestyle business(es) 90
limited liability company
  forming in Ireland 197-200
  forming in US 199
liquidation 137, 191
liquidation event 138
liquidation preference 129, 131, 138-139
  business angel investor(s) 102-103
  difference between convertible and participating preference shares 132-133
  term sheet(s) 128, 129, 137-139
  trade sale(s) 182
liquidity discount 160
listing
  deciding where to list 166-167
  domestic exchange(s) 159, 170
  fees 168, 169, 170, 173, 175
  foreign exchange(s) 159, 167-169, 170-176

listing criteria 168, 169
living dead 139
lock-up(s) 160, 177, 180
   term sheet(s) 173
London Stock Exchange 167

M50 Enterprise Platform
   Programme 83
majority ownership *see*
   ownership, majority
management 89
management buy-out(s) 3
management team 110
market 90
   segmentation 90-91
   validation 91-92
market capitalisation 159, 167, 168
Memorandum of Association 18, 197-198
mergers 137
Microsoft 53, 173
minority ownership *see*
   ownership, minority
monitoring fees 154

NASDAQ 170, 173
NASDAQ National Market 171, 173-174
   fees 173
   initial listing standards 173-174
NASDAQ Small Cap market 159, 171, 173, 174-175
   fees 175
   initial listing criteria 174-175
National Venture Capital
   Association 239
NDAs *see* agreement(s), non-disclosure

negative covenants *see* veto, and term sheet(s)
negotiation 40
   term sheet(s) 129-130
   negotiation leverage 110, 152, 184, 185
Netfish Technology 179
Neuer Markt 167
New York Stock Exchange 170-171, 173, 175
no shop *see* exclusivity
Nomad 168
non-disclosure agreement(s) *see*
   agreement(s), non-disclosure
Nova/UCD 83
NYSE *see* New York Stock
   Exchange

O'Briens 36
OFEX 159, 168-169
   Corporate Advisor 169
   fees 169
   listing criteria 169
Onecle 240
ordinary share(s) *see* share(s), ordinary
ownership
   majority 17
   majority, and the illusion of control 16-17
   minority 17
   minority, and control of key decisions 17

Index

pain point 92
pari passu 135
participating preference share(s) *see* share(s), participating preference
partner agreement(s) *see* agreement(s), partner
pay to play
  term sheet(s) 144
Peets Coffee 36
performance indicator(s) 33
performance metrics 36
personal guarantee 2
phantom share(s) *see* share(s), phantom
piggyback right(s) *see* right(s), piggyback
PIPE *see* private investment in public equity
Plato 11
play or pay clause 101
post-IPO stock support 161
post-money valuation *see* valuation, post-money
pre-emption right(s) *see* right(s), pre-emption
preference share(s) *see* share(s), preference
pre-money valuation *see* valuation, pre-money
Pret à Manger 36
price per share / security
  term sheet(s) 128, 133-134
private investment in public equity 177
pro rata 101, 118, 138, 146, 147, 172, 184
protective provision(s) *see* veto, and term sheet(s)

proxy voting *see* voting, proxy
public capital
  pros and cons 84-85
public filing(s) *see* filing(s), public
public market(s) 14, 34, 36, 162
public offering(s) 3, 7, 37, 159-178
  objectives 160
PwC 161

---

rate of return 37
recordkeeping
  corporate 16, 17-20
records
  corporate 6, 161
redeemable preference share(s) *see* share(s), redeemable preference
redemption
  term sheet(s) 128, 139-140
registration expenses
  term sheet(s) 172
registration on Form S-3 172
  term sheet(s) 172
registration right(s) *see* right(s), registration
registration right(s) agreement(s) *see* agreement(s), registration right(s)
regulatory filing(s) *see* filing(s), regulatory
representations and warranties 75, 151
  compensation for breach of 151
  Schedule of Exceptions 151
  term sheet(s) 151
  trade sale(s) 190-191
restricted share(s) *see* share(s), restricted

revocable proxy
   sample   205
revocable proxy agreement(s)
   see agreement(s), revocable proxy
right of co-sale *see* right(s), co-sale
right of first refusal *see* right(s), first refusal
right(s)
   co-sale   146
   co-sale, and term sheet(s)   146
   consent *see* veto, and term sheet(s)
   demand   172
   demand, and term sheet(s)   72
   drag along   146-147, 183
   drag along, and term sheet(s)   146-147, 183
   first refusal   146
   first refusal, and term sheet(s)   146
   information   150
   information, and term sheet(s)   150
   piggyback   172
   piggyback, and term sheet(s)   172
   pre-emption   74, 78, 101, 147, 198
   pre-emption, and term sheet(s)   147
   registration   173
   registration, and term sheet(s)   172
   veto   17
   voting   17, 73, 100
Riverdeep   170
Roosevelt, Eleanor   67
Ryanair   170

SAR *see* stock appreciation rights
Sarbanes-Oxley   171
   compliance costs   171
scale   91-92
Schuller, Robert   193
SCS *see* Seed Capital Scheme
Seattle's Best Coffee   36
SEC *see* Securities & Exchange Commission (US)
Securities & Exchange Commission (US)   18, 171, 240
   Form S-1   172
   Form S-3   172
   requirement to register with   171
Seed & Venture Capital Programme   81
Seed Capital Scheme   80, 83
Seedcorn Competition   82
Sequoia Capital   110
serial entrepreneurs   89, 108
series   131
shadow director(s)   79
Shakespeare, William   87
share capital
   structure of   12-17
share option agreement(s) *see* agreement(s), share option
share option(s)   6, 14, 49-52
   awarding   51-52
   employee departures   60-63
   pool   50-51, 133
   Revenue approved / unapproved schemes   49
   tax effects of   49
   vesting   56-60
   volatility   50
share purchase agreement *see* agreement, share purchase
share register   16, 18, 199

Index

share transfer restriction(s)   63, 74, 101
share(s)
    as employee incentive   14
    authorised   13
    authorising and issuing   13-14, 149
    convertible preference   131
    issued   13
    market value of   13
    nominal value of   13
    number to authorise and issue   13-14
    ordinary   12, 73, 100-102
    par value of   13
    participating preference   132, 134
    phantom   53
    preference   12, 78, 102-103
    redeemable preference   81
    restricted   52-53
    uses of   12
shareholder update   78, 103
    sample   210-212
shareholder(s)
    privileges of   12
    rights of   12
shareholders' agreement(s) *see* agreement(s), shareholders'
Shaw, George Bernard   25
smart money   87
sophisticated investor(s) *see* investor(s), sophisticated
SOX *see* Sarbanes-Oxley
special resolution   14
Starbucks   36
stock appreciation rights   53, 54
stock split   14
subscription agreement(s) *see* agreement(s), subscription

supplier agreement(s) *see* agreement(s), supplier
sweat equity   160
syndicate(s)   146, 155
    venture capital investor(s)   113-114, 155-156

---

tag along right(s) *see* right(s), co-sale
tax return(s)   18
team
    recruiting and building, challenge of   47
technology transfer agreement(s) *see* agreement(s), technology transfer
term sheet(s)   7, 114, 118, 127-156
    anti-dilution term   128, 129, 140-144
    Board of Directors term   128, 129, 147-148
    BVCA model   224-238
    closing term   153-154
    conditions to close term   128, 153
    conversion term   128, 131, 136-137, 183
    co-sale right(s) term   146
    demand right(s) term   172
    dividends term   128, 134
    drag along right(s) term   146-147, 183
    exclusivity term   128, 152
    expenses term   154
    first refusal right(s) term   146
    information right(s) term   150
    legal counsel term   154
    liquidation preference term   128, 129, 137-139

lock-up term	173
negotiation	129-130, 155
pay to play term	144
piggyback right(s) term	172
pre-emption right(s) term	147
price per share / security term	128, 133-134
redemption term	128, 139-140
registration expenses term	172
registration on Form S-3 term	172
registration right(s) term	172
representations and warranties term	151
sample of abbreviated	128, 222-223
sample of complete	128
type of shares / security(ies) term	128, 131-133, 140
valuation term	129, 133-134
veto term	128, 129, 149-150, 183
voting term	144-146
Timothy's Coffee	36
trade sale(s)	3, 34, 59, 90, 103, 137-138, 162, 179-192
acquisition premium	186
advantages of	180
asset *versus* stock deal(s)	189
disadvantage(s) of	180
earn-out(s)	189-190
employee non-compete covenants	188
excluded asset(s)	188
fire sale(s)	191
indemnity(ies)	190-191
liquidation preference	182
payment structure	188-189
preparing for	181-186
purchase price	187-188
purchase price, allocation for tax purposes	188
representations and warranties	190-191
structuring deal	187-191
tax effect of	181
term sheet(s)	187
valuing	182, 186-187
tranched investment	153-154
tranches	153, 189, 191
Trintech	170
type of share(s) / security(ies) term sheet(s)	128, 131-133, 140

UK exchanges	167-169, 194
up round(s)	117
US exchanges	170-176
benefits of listing	171
US incorporation	199

valuation	1, 6, 27, 33-46, 69
financing strategy's role in increasing	27
fully-diluted	133
getting the best	38-40
lower in Europe than US	34
market	34-35
methodologies	35-38
post-money	40-41
pre-money	37, 40-41, 51, 133
term sheet(s)	129, 133-134
understanding how measured	33
VC(s) *see* venture capitalist(s)	
venture capital	7
Ireland	194-195
venture capital firm(s)	107-126
General Partners	107

Index

    Limited Partners   107
    operation   107-108
venture capital fund(s)   107-108
    vintage year   107-108
venture capital industry
    Irish Government support for   194-195
venture capital investment
    process   114-116
venture capital investor(s)
    as risk-takers   114
    business plan   115
    business plan requirements   110
    choosing   113
    compensation   108-109
    due diligence   114-115
    finding   111-112
    finding overseas   111
    investment decision   115-116
    investment presentation to   115-116
    lead investor   113-114
    non-disclosure agreements   109
    participation in subsequent rounds   118-119
    reference-checking   113
    referral to   111
    representation on Board of Directors   120-121, 147
    reputation   108, 118
venture capital investor(s)
    structuring investment   116
    subsequent financing   117

syndicate(s)   113-114, 155-156
term sheet terms explained   130-154
venture capitalist(s)   3, 7, 24, 51, 99, 107-126, 194
vesting   52, 56-60
    accelerated   58-59
    cliff   57
    schedule(s)   57-60
    time or performance?   58
veto
    and term sheet(s)   128, 129, 149-150, 183
    right(s)   17, 102, 183
virgin angel   95
voting
    irrevocable proxy   73
    proxy   73-74, 100-101
    revocable proxy   73, 101
    rights   17, 73, 100, 144-146
    term sheet(s)   144-146
vulture capitalist(s)   120

Waitley, Denis   158
warrant(s)   134
warranties   75, 151
Waterford Wedgwood   170
Watershed Technologies   179
weighted average cost of capital   38
winding-up   12, 103, 137, 149
    see also liquidation
WorldCom   171

OAK TREE PRESS
is Ireland's leading business book publisher.

It develops and delivers
information, advice and resources
to entrepreneurs and managers –
and those who educate and support them.

Its print, software and web materials
are in use in Ireland, the UK, Finland,
Greece, Norway and Slovenia.

❖

OAK TREE PRESS
19 Rutland Street
Cork, Ireland
T: + 353 21 4313855
F: + 353 21 4313496
E: info@oaktreepress.com
W: www.oaktreepress.com